The European Union's fight
against terrorism

MANCHESTER
1824

Manchester University Press

The European Union's fight against terrorism

Discourse, policies, identity

Christopher Baker-Beall

Manchester University Press

The right of Christopher Baker-Beall to be identified as the author of this work
has been asserted by him in accordance with the Copyright, Designs and Patents
Act 1988.

Published by Manchester University Press
Altrincham Street, Manchester M1 7JA
www.manchesteruniversitypress.co.uk

British Library Cataloguing-in-Publication Data
A catalogue record for this book is available from the British Library

Library of Congress Cataloging-in-Publication Data applied for

ISBN 978 0 7190 9106 3 hardback

First published 2016

The publisher has no responsibility for the persistence or accuracy of URLs
for any external or third-party internet websites referred to in this book,
and does not guarantee that any content on such websites is, or will remain,
accurate or appropriate.

Typeset by Out of House Publishing
Printed in Great Britain
by CPI Group (UK) Ltd, Croydon, CR0 4YY

Contents

Acknowledgements

I began my academic journey at Nottingham Trent University in late September 2001, only a few weeks after the attacks on 11 September. The first lecture I attended was given by Professor Stephen Chan. I remember sitting transfixed for an entire hour as Professor Chan proceeded to give a lecture, entirely from memory, on the history of Russian and American involvement in Afghanistan, the rise of the Taliban and the emergence of Al-Qaida. Throughout, the audience was so quiet that one might have heard a pin drop. At the end of the presentation the lecture theatre erupted with applause. I can remember thinking that I wanted to be able to do that, to be able to speak for an hour and captivate an audience. I think it was then that I subconsciously made the decision that I wanted to be an academic. My undergraduate studies were heavily influenced by the teachings of two academics. In particular, Chris Farrands, who inspired my interest in the subject of International Relations, and Roberta Guerrina, whose classes on the idea of Europe sparked my interest in European Studies and the European Union. I am grateful to both for introducing me to subjects that I have come to love and am now lucky enough to teach to a new generation of students. After completing my degrees at undergraduate and MA level at Nottingham Trent University in August 2006 I won a scholarship to study EU counter-terrorism policy at Loughborough University.

There is one person in particular that I must thank for the opportunity and that is the late Dave Allen, who was Head of Department at Loughborough at that time. I first met Dave at a conference in Nottingham in 2005 where we discussed potential opportunities for postgraduate study in the Department of Politics, International Relations and European Studies. Like many students who have come out of that department at Loughborough, I will forever be grateful to Dave for giving me my shot. After winning the award, I remember discussing with Dave who would be my supervisor and I clearly remember him telling me that he had the perfect supervisor for me. To Helen, I would like to thank you for your support throughout my PhD and for teaching me to think and write like an academic. I could not have done it without you and

I am forever grateful for your continuing support. You really were the perfect supervisor that Dave promised me. I would also like to thank Olly, who joined my supervisory team about two years into the project, for teaching me how to understand and 'see' discourse analysis as a method. I could not have written this book without the help and support that both have provided throughout my career to date. After completing my PhD I was given an opportunity to teach at Loughborough by Lee Miles on his MA Foreign Policy module. As well as this, in August 2012 I was given an opportunity by Ces Moore to teach modules at third-year and MA level on terrorism, Security Studies and Critical Security Studies at the University of Birmingham. I will forever be grateful to Lee and Ces for these opportunities in that not only did they help to improve my knowledge of International Relations, and therefore the book, but without them I would not have landed my first permanent job at Nottingham Trent University in the summer of 2013. I would like to thank Ces in particular for lending his time, support and guidance on all things academic, as well as our always interesting football-related discussions.

On to the book itself and there are many people who have supported me during the writing process to whom I owe a deep debt of gratitude. To all of my colleagues in the Division of Politics and International Relations at Nottingham Trent University, my thanks for providing such a supporting and collegial environment that is a pleasure to work in. I certainly feel as though I was granted the time and space to complete this project. To my colleagues in the Critical Terrorism Studies working group, my thanks for providing such a friendly and open outlet for early career academics to share their research. In particular, I want to say thanks to Charlotte Heath-Kelly and Lee Jarvis, with whom I worked as co-convenor of the working group, I learnt so much from you when editing the special issues of *Critical Studies on Terrorism* and working on our edited collection on *Counter-Radicalisation: Critical Perspectives*. My thanks to everyone who has provided comments on earlier drafts of the work produced in this book, including Oliver Daddow, Helen Drake, Chris Farrands, Charlotte Heath-Kelly, Richard Jackson, Lee Miles and Ces Moore – to Helen and Richard in particular for reading and commenting on the entire draft script. To all of my students and in particular those who have taken my second-year module on Understanding Foreign Policy, learning is a two-way process and I have learnt as much from you as I hope you have learnt from me. My thanks to all of you for being such willing, interested and engaged students – it really has been a pleasure to teach all of you. I would also like to thank two students in particular for their editorial help on the manuscript for this book: Alan Armstrong and Gareth Mott, who I am certain will both go on to be exceptional academics in the future.

Earlier versions of parts of this book have appeared in other publications. The discussion of EU actorness in the Introduction and the analysis of the figure of the 'terrorist' other in Chapter 3 were developed out of the article, 'The evolution of the European Union's "fight against terrorism" discourse: constructing the terrorist "other" ', *Cooperation and Conflict*, 49:2 (2014), 212–238 (DOI: 10.1177/0010836713483411; reproduced with the permission of SAGE Journals). Chapter 2 was developed out of parts of the book chapter, 'Writing the Threat of Terrorism in Western Europe and the European Union: An Interpretive Analysis', in Mark Bevir, Ian Hall and Oliver Daddow (eds), *Interpreting Global Security* (Routledge, 2013; reproduced with the permission of Taylor & Francis). Chapter 4 was developed out of the article, 'The discursive construction of EU counter-terrorism policy: writing the "migrant other", securitisation and control', *Journal of Contemporary European Research* (JCER), 'Special Issue: Security and Liberty in the European Union', 5:2 (2009), 188–206 (reproduced with the permission of UACES and the JCER). Thank you to the copyright holders for permission to draw on those publications.

Above all though, I want to say thank you to my friends and family. To my Mum and Dad, I really could not have got to where I am today without your love, help and considerable support. I want to thank you for everything you have done to support me over the years. It is to you that I dedicate this book. Finally to Tamara, who had to deal with periods where I was unable to give her the attention that she deserved, my thanks for being so loving, positive and supportive whilst I was writing the book. Your inspirational words always kept me going during the periods when I felt like I would never finish this project. I could not have written this book without you.

Introduction: the language of the European Union's 'fight against terrorism'

Perhaps even more insidious than the threat to our lives, is the threat that terrorism poses to the very nature of our societies. Terrorism can strike anywhere, anytime, anyone. It is frightening in its unpredictability and unsettling by its random nature ... For all of us, the fight against international terrorism is a growth area. And because terrorism is a global phenomenon, we need a global response. (Javier Solana, 2005)[1]

I would say that the threat has changed a lot not only since the Madrid bombings but since 9/11. At the time we were confronted with an organisation – Al Qaeda, which was very well-structured, like a multi-national company. It has morphed into something completely different. We now have franchises of al Qaeda everywhere in the world. We have seen some 'lone wolves' – people acting by themselves with no link to the al Qaeda core. And we have recently seen a rise of Europeans going to Syria – going there to fight. And that raises a specific security challenge. (Gilles de Kerchove, 2014)[2]

This book is about the language of the European Union's (EU) response to the threat of terrorism: the 'fight against terrorism'. Since the events of 11 September 2001, the threat of terrorism has come to occupy the minds of Western politicians and policy-makers as the pre-eminent security threat of the post-Cold War era. In Europe, a wave of successful terrorist attacks in Madrid, March 2004, London, July 2005 and Oslo, July 2011, have helped to confirm this perception and necessitated that the EU become ever more active in the field of counter-terrorism. The emergence of so-called 'Islamic State' in July 2014, including the supposed threat to Europe from 'returning foreign fighters', has further complicated the contemporary European security environment and strengthened the perception that terrorism is indeed the most pressing security concern of the post-Cold War era[3]. In response to the dilemma posed by terrorism, the EU has developed a complex and multidimensional institutional response that has sought to coordinate member states' policies, harmonise national legislation and provide operational support for national authorities, which it has labelled the 'fight against terrorism'.[4] However, the 'fight against terrorism' is more than just a set of institutional or public policy responses designed to tackle the threat of terrorism. The 'fight against terrorism' is also an influential political discourse that plays an important role not only in the formulation of EU counter-terrorism policy but also the justification for, and legitimisation of, the EU's ever-increasing role in the fields of internal and external security policy.

From this perspective the 'fight against terrorism' can be understood as both a set of actual counter-terrorism practices (new laws, agencies and institutions) designed for the purpose of responding to terrorism and an accompanying set of assumptions, beliefs, ideas and knowledge, constituted through a language or discourse of terrorism.[5] Importantly, the 'fight against terrorism' as a discourse structures the EU response to terrorism through the prism of identity. As Stuart Croft explains, discourses create and reflect particular identities:

> They construct those who are our allies and those who are our enemies. When not in flux, they settle who 'we' are, and who 'they' are; what 'we' stand for, and what 'they' mean to us. They construct the space for 'our' legitimate activity; and the space for the behaviour we will (and will not) tolerate from 'them'. At times 'we' and/or 'they' construct such hostility that violence results, and lives are lost.[6]

If we apply this insight to EU counter-terrorism policy, it becomes apparent that the 'fight against terrorism' discourse plays a central role in constructing an EU sense of 'self', what I shall refer to in the context of this research as 'EU identity', which is thought to be under threat from a radically different and dangerous 'other': the 'terrorist' other.[7]

The main argument put forward in this book is that the counter-terrorism policies of the EU are constituted through representations of identity, but it is also through the formulation of counter-terrorism policy that the identity of the EU is created and recreated. This is in essence an adaption of Lene Hansen's argument about foreign policy, namely that 'foreign policies rely upon representations of identity, but it is also through the formulation of foreign policy that identities are produced and reproduced'.[8] Building on this assertion it is claimed here that counter-terrorism policy represents another site, like foreign policy, through which identities are created and recreated. This is to suggest that material factors and ideas are intertwined to such an extent that they cannot be separated, or in other words, the practice of counter-terrorism is only *made possible* through the language of counter-terrorism (and vice versa). Together language and practice co-constitute social and political reality, providing the context within which action can be taken. To make this argument is to raise the important point that a fully informed understanding of the EU's counter-terrorism response would be impossible without a discussion of the language of the 'fight against terrorism'.

In drawing attention to the importance of identity in the formulation of counter-terrorism policy, I want to make three further points that necessitate an investigation of the language of the EU's 'fight against terrorism'. The first point relates to the relationship between the 'fight against terrorism' and the American 'war on terror'. Although the counter-terrorism response adopted by the EU diverges from the American approach in a number of important ways, the 'fight against terrorism' has to be understood within the context of the 'war on terror'. The main difference between the two approaches is that the United States (US) 'war on terror' has constructed the threat of terrorism as existential and predominantly an 'external' security concern, whereas the EU has interpreted the threat of terrorism as primarily an 'internal' security concern best dealt with through the criminal justice systems of its member states.[9] However, there are also a number of significant similarities between the 'fight against terrorism' and the 'war on terror' in terms of the language that constitutes each discourse. Both the 'fight against terrorism' and the 'war on terror' represents overlapping sites where a 'conventional wisdom' about terrorism has been created and reinforced.[10] This is reflected in the ways in which each discourse rearticulates 'accepted knowledge' about what terrorism is, who the terrorists are and what type of threat they represent in the post-September 11 era. Similarly, the 'fight against terrorism' and the 'war on terror' are comparable in that they are both influential political discourses that have been invoked by politicians and policy-makers to justify and legitimise not only practices of counter-terrorism but also their own political authority in the field of security.

The second point involves the discursive construction of the terrorism threat and the significant role that 'imagination', 'anticipation' and 'precaution' plays in this. It will be argued throughout this book that the 'fight against terrorism', like the 'war on terror', rests upon a particular vision of terrorism in the post-September 11 era as new, dispersed and unpredictable. As the quotation by Javier Solana would seem to confirm, terrorism remains such a concern for the EU because of its 'unpredictability' and 'random nature'.[11] However, the perception of the terrorism threat does not stop at this. For Solana, like many other Western politicians, terrorism is seen as a threat to 'the very nature of our societies'. Yet even a cursory glance at the evidence would seem to suggest that, in the West at least, this perception is overstated. The actual statistical risk of being involved in a terrorist incident, for any individual living in a Western democratic country, is extremely low. Indeed, a study of the location and nature of terrorist attacks confirms that the actual threat posed by terrorism to Americans or Europeans is negligible.[12] Regardless, the language of counter-terrorism continues to emphasise that terrorism is an extreme threat. As Bill Durodié explains: 'What we see is a fantasy that has been created … We have an exaggerated perception of the possibility of terrorism that is quite disabling. We only need to look at the evidence to understand that the figures simply don't bear out the way that we have responded as a society.'[13] What characterises the language of the 'fight against terrorism', like the 'war on terror', is that it has contributed to the transformation of the complex and disparate threat of terrorism into, at times, a unified and singular threat that, in the words of Solana, 'can strike anywhere, anytime, anyone'.[14] In the minds of politicians and policy-makers this perception of the terrorist threat is seemingly confirmed with every new attack, requiring them to respond pre-emptively through the anticipation and imagination of the potential terrorist threats of the future.[15] Yet, the suggestion that terrorism represents such an existential threat to Europe remains an exaggeration. As I will show in the study of the 'fight against terrorism' that is conducted in the following chapters, an analysis of the discourse is essential in that it can help to reveal the discursive techniques through which the threat of terrorism is exaggerated.[16]

The third point concerns the relationship between the construction of the terrorism threat and the justification for some type of counter-response. As the quotation from the EU Counter-Terrorism Co-ordinator (EU CTC), Gilles de Kerchove, indicates, the growth of 'al Qaeda franchises' across the globe, the emergence of so-called 'lone wolves' and the issue of European citizens 'going to Syria' are interpreted as problems that raise 'specific security challenge[s]' for the EU. Whilst it is clear that the terrorist threats identified by the EU are certainly real, they are viewed through the afore-mentioned lens of 'an exaggerated perception of risk', which 'lends itself to growing demands for greater regulation and social control'.[17] As de Goede explains, this language deploys 'imaginative visions of catastrophic futures in order to foster policy action and precautionary intervention in the pre-sent'.[18] The 'fight against terrorism' is therefore also about a particular way of governing society: namely, governance through precautionary responses to risk. This form of governance is not new in the EU experience. The pre-cautionary principle was first recognised in the 1992 Maastricht Treaty, and then by the European Commission in 2000, with respect to environmental policy.[19] What is new is its application in the field of security. The emergence of the precautionary principle, when applied to the contemporary Western counter-terrorism and security apparatus, has given birth to 'new rationali-ties of government that require that the catastrophic prospects of the future be tamed and managed'.[20] An analysis of the language of the 'fight against terrorism' is therefore crucial if we are to understand how the EU legitimises this developing role in the field of counter-terrorism governance and as a *provider of security* for its citizens.

With these points in mind, the research conducted in this book has three main aims. First, to develop a discourse theory of identity and counter-terrorism policy in order to explore the ways in which the EU's counter-terrorism discourse, the 'fight against terrorism', has been constructed and the ways in which it functions. Second, to bring a concern with identity into understanding and explaining the emergence and evolution of EU counter-terrorism policy specifically, as well as its developing role as a security actor more generally. Third, to provide an extensive analysis of the wider societal impact of the EU's counter-terrorism policy and to reveal the various ways in which the 'fight against terrorism' is contributing to the 'securitisation' of social and political life within Europe.[21] Before moving forward to consider these research aims, the remainder of this chapter will do several things. First, I will begin by discussing the relationship between terrorism, counter-terrorism and security before locating this analysis firmly within the 'critical' tradition of International Relations (IR). Second, having established the motivation for adopting a critical perspective, I will discuss what is meant by the notion of 'actorness' with specific reference to how the EU is conceptualised as a security actor for the purpose of this research. Third, I will consider both the 'traditional' and 'critical literature' on EU counter-terrorism policy, identifying the unique contribution that the research conducted in this book will make to debates in this field of study.

Terrorism and security: a critical approach

One of the core themes of this book is the relationship between terrorism, counter-terrorism and security. Security is most commonly associated with 'the alleviation of threats to cherished values'.[22] Traditionally, it is concerned with those issues that can potentially threaten the survival of a referent object of security.[23] Terrorism relates to security in the sense that acts of terrorism or the threat of acts of terrorism are conventionally portrayed by various actors as a threat to the security of the state or to an individual's own sense of security.[24] Counter-terrorism is intimately related to the concept of security in that it is generally understood to be a technical practice, most commonly formulated and implemented by the state, which is designed to reduce or eliminate the potential for a referent object of security to become the victim of terrorism. Terrorism and counter-terrorism are related in the sense that without a clear understanding of *what terrorism is* and *who the terrorists are* it is impossible for a counter-terrorism response to be formulated. In the EU the 'fight against terrorism' has come to represent the most common-sense counter-approach through which to respond to the threat of terrorism and provide security for the citizens of its member states. However, it is argued here that this 'fight' is a social construction, as is terrorism and 'that which we call security, the very meaning of which varies according to context, place and time'.[25]

Traditionally, in the academic discipline of IR and the sub-field of International Security Studies (ISS), security has been understood through an emphasis on the physical (or political) dimension of territorial entities, as 'the absence of existential threats to the state emerging from another state'.[26] Traditional perspectives on security have been characterised by their state-centric focus and their commitment to a rationalist approach to world politics. According to Laura Shepherd and Jutta Weldes, these approaches treat security as 'defined in relation to the state, as intimately related to power, understood primarily, if not exclusively, in military terms'.[27] Rationalist approaches to security are based upon two main assumptions, which also apply to traditional understandings of the concept of terrorism. First, they assume that social reality exists independently of our knowledge of it and that this reality can be accessed by state officials, policy-makers and analysts in a neutral manner, allowing for threats to the state to be objectively recognised. Second, they embrace a methodological position of naturalism, which assumes that the methods of the natural sciences can be transposed into analyses of human social and political life. From this position the characteristics of states are treated as given and fixed, with security or counter-terrorism involving the securing of states against either internal or external and objectively identifiable threats, rendering states and their security issues as natural and unproblematic facts. In essence, rationalist approaches ignore the importance of identity and can be criticised for attempting to fit the world into their pre-existing assumptions about it.

The research conducted in this book draws on an alternative approach to the study of security and terrorism from that which underpins the orthodox rationalist theories of IR, ISS and Terrorism Studies. This analysis of EU counter-terrorism policy embraces a critical approach to security and terrorism that is situated within the emerging fields of Critical Security Studies (CSS) and Critical Terrorism Studies (CTS). It should be stated at the outset that labels such as 'critical security studies' or 'critical terrorism studies' are not unproblematic. The use of the prefix 'critical' should not lead us to assume that this is a single, monolithic or homogeneous perspective from which the concepts of security or terrorism can be interrogated.[28] Instead any reference to 'critical' work should be recognised and understood primarily as a rhetorical device. There is no singular definition of what it means to be 'critical' in IR, CSS or CTS. Rather there is an array of different perspectives that have become associated with this term.[29] Steve Smith explains there are considerable variances between the different approaches that make up the field of CSS, with these approaches 'united more by perceived defects in the orthodoxy than by any particular alternative vision'.[30] Similarly, the field of CTS takes a broad view of what it means to be 'critical' in the sense that it encourages the application of a variety of diverse perspectives to terrorism research and entails disagreements and divergence amongst scholars over the key issues.[31]

What unites the fields of CSS and CTS is that they reject the application of what Robert Cox has termed 'problem-solving theory' to research on security and terrorism, embracing instead the idea of 'critical theory'.[32] In effect, problem-solving theory helps to maintain the status quo on security and terrorism by replicating or strengthening certain dominant beliefs about those concepts that already exist. As Cox explains: 'Problem-solving theory takes the world as it finds it, with the prevailing social and power relationships and the institutions into which they are organised, as the given framework for action. The general aim of problem solving is to make these relationships and institutions work smoothly by dealing effectively with particular sources of trouble.'[33] In contrast, critical theory allows us to challenge, to deconstruct and to pull apart those dominant beliefs about security and terrorism that have come to form the 'conventional wisdom' on these issues in the post-September 11 era. As Cox explains: 'It stands apart from the prevailing order of the world and asks how that order came about. Critical theory, unlike problem-solving theory, does not take institutions and social and power relations for granted but calls them into question by concerning itself with their origins and how and whether they might be in the process of changing.'[34]

For CSS this embrace of critical theory has provided the basis for a more theoretically inclusive approach that allows for 'many perspectives that have been considered outside of the mainstream of the discipline [of ISS] to be brought into the same forum'.[35] These 'critical approaches' are united on the basis that they share both a general dissatisfaction with orthodox approaches to the study of security and a disillusionment with the agenda of mainstream security studies in the post-Cold War era.[36] Similarly, theoretical pluralism with respect to critical approaches is a strong aspect of the CST research programme. As Richard Jackson *et al.* explain, the critical thrust of CTS can in part be explained by: a sense of unease over the way in which the 'war on terror', or the 'fight against terrorism' for that matter, has been prosecuted; a concern over the state-centric nature of terrorism research and the 'embedded' nature of many terrorism experts; a dissatisfaction with the perceived methodological and analytical weaknesses of traditional approaches to terrorism studies in the post-September 11 era; and the aforementioned issue with the dominant and ideal type of knowledge prioritised within the field being 'problem-solving' theory.[37]

The research conducted in this book can be firmly located within the broad approach to CSS and CTS outlined above in that I borrow ontological, epistemological and theoretical commitments from each research agenda to underpin my analysis of the EU's 'fight against terrorism'. First, epistemologically speaking, this research promotes the idea that concepts such as security or terrorism are 'essentially contested' and socially constructed. This is to imply that the meaning of security or terrorism generates such debate that no objective or neutral definition is possible.[38] This commitment is important in that it recognises that security and terrorism are social rather than objective facts and therefore truly objective or neutral knowledge about security or terrorism can never be realised. It views the study of both security and terrorism – and the knowledge about these concepts that is derived from those processes of study – as something that is rooted within the social-cultural context within which it emerges.[39] Second, following on from this, it adopts an ontological position that is broadly speaking constructivist and a theoretical perspective that others might label critical constructivist. It is critical constructivist in the sense that it accepts that meaning can only ever be generated through an intersubjective social process, which constitutes the world as we know it. This commitment is important in that it positions the identity of an actor and the discourse through which that identity is created as mutually constitutive. This is relevant for the study of the EU's 'fight against terrorism' in that it reinforces my earlier point, drawing our attention to the role identity has played in the formulation of the EU's counter-terrorism response.[40] Having offered a brief outline of the main commitments that underpin the research in this book I will now move on to consider in more detail what is meant by the notion of 'actorness' in the context of the EU.

The EU as an actor in the field of security

In the period since the events of 11 September 2001, the EU has identified responding to terrorism as a priority objective in all areas of security policy where it has developed a capacity to act. The emergence of security structures at the level of the EU provides a challenge to the traditional conceptualisation of security discussed above. Not only are some parts of security policy formulated at the supranational level (above the nation-state) but EU security policy contains elements that traverse the distinction between the domestic and the international. From this perspective the EU is viewed not as a unitary actor or as a traditional state-like system of government but rather as a system of governance, which as a result of its institutional, juridical and spatial complexities can be described as constituting 'the first truly postmodern international political form'.[41] I therefore consider the EU a 'transformational polity' in the sense that it raises questions about the appropriate mechanisms for political organisation beyond the state.[42] In particular, the EU raises questions that challenge the pre-eminence of the state as a provider of security for its citizens. This is because it is possible to identify various emerging structures and processes that are being developed beyond the state for the purpose of responding to security threats, such as terrorism. Specifically, it contributes to the practice of security through the production of common 'internal' and 'external' security policies.[43] The realms of 'internal' and 'external security' have traditionally been treated as separate; however, since the events of 11 September 2001, the boundaries that exist between these once-distinct policy domains have become (or are perceived to be) increasingly blurred. It can therefore be argued that while the EU is not a state, it certainly has a developing role as a provider of security. Yet as I have already indicated, the EU is not a unitary actor. Rather it is a complex system of governance that includes a heterogeneous array of institutional actors, agencies and organisations all simultaneously working together and competing with one another for political authority in multiple policy arenas, including the field of security.[44]

Conceptualising the EU in this way is not without consequence. It raises a particular question that must be answered before an analysis of the EU counter-terrorism discourse can proceed: to what extent does the problematic status of the EU as an actor influence or affect how it interprets terrorism? As I explained earlier, the research in this book is underpinned by a constructivist ontology that promotes the premise that 'social reality is produced through meaningful action'.[45] The social unit (in this case the EU) achieves actorness as a result of the meaning-based interaction of its members with their surroundings, thereby articulating the social unit as an actor in a particular social field. This research therefore draws from an extensive academic literature on the EU that endorses a constructivist understanding of actorness.[46] Henrik Larsen explains that understanding actorness in this way involves a focus on two main points: 'Whether and how a group of states, institutional actors or others construct themselves as an international actor; and ... [w]hether and how the surrounding world constructs this group as an actor.'[47]

However, I go beyond this conceptualisation of actorness in two ways. First, I view actorness as also being about how a group of states, institutional actors or others construct themselves as an internal domestic actor, which is itself interrelated with the way a group of states, institutional actors or others construct themselves as an international actor; and second, I suggest that meaning can be studied through language in the form of discourse. I will elaborate on this second point in greater detail in Chapter 1 where I outline a discourse theory of identity and counter-terrorism policy. Furthermore, I want to briefly emphasise that from this perspective the focus of a discourse approach is language, and in particular how discourses, like the 'fight against terrorism', construct identities and social subjects within a given context or situation. If we accept that the EU constitutes an actor in any of the various policy contexts in which it operates, and that we can access this notion of actorness through a discourse approach, the focus then turns to what kind of actor is constructed, including what types of identity are articulated as an inherent component of that actorness.[48]

Research in this area has focused primarily on the role of discourse in relation to the EU as a foreign policy and external security actor. A significant contribution to this literature has come from Ian Manners and Richard Whitman, whose analysis of EU foreign policy has led them to argue that the EU does indeed have a clearly discernible 'international identity', which in terms of its global role makes the EU 'greater than the sum of its parts'.[49] In particular, they draw attention to the 'international identity' of the EU in order to highlight the principles upon which the identity of the EU is based and the ways in which these principles influence how the EU asserts itself in its foreign affairs. Similarly, other studies have focused upon the important role that the concept of identity has played in terms of the EU's external role in world politics, including: the idea of 'Europe' in promoting integration through the construction of a 'security identity'; the role of EU expansion or enlargement in the formation of 'European identity'; the extent to which the EU can be considered a global military actor; the importance of practices of 'self' and 'other' in the construction of a normative dimension to EU identity; the transformation of the EU from a 'civilian power' to a 'global power'; and the emergence of the EU as a 'holistic' international security actor.[50] This body of research on EU foreign policy is characterised by a focus on three aspects of its 'international identity': first, how the EU perceives itself as an actor in foreign policy; second, how other actors in the international system perceive the EU as an actor in foreign policy; and third, the ways in which the 'international identity' of the EU is constituted through the construction of difference with other actors in the international system.

This research on European foreign policy has important implications for the research carried out in this book. It suggests that when considering the EU as an actor in the field of counter-terrorism it is essential to consider also the role of identity and the strategies through which representations of 'self' and 'other' are articulated. As Ben Rosamond explains, the EU's external activity is highly discursive in the sense that 'it is aspirational, declaratory and full of positioning statements', noting that this discursive dimension can be identified across a range of policy documents.[51] He asserts that this discourse, which characterises the way in which the EU projects itself externally, involves the articulation of the significance of the EU's external role as well as the claim that the EU is a purposeful and coherent actor. He notes that this assertion of coherence and purpose in all fields of external action does not necessarily preclude the projection of multiple or, at times, contradictory roles. This suggests two interrelated points: first, the EU is engaged in a continuous discursive struggle to define the substantive ways in which the EU should impact upon the world; second, there are numerous components to the EU's 'international identity', all of which relate what it is to how it acts.[52] This line of argument has resonance for the research carried out in this book on EU counter-terrorism policy in two ways. First, as will be demonstrated throughout the book, EU counter-terrorism policy, like EU foreign policy, is also highly discursive, aspirational, declaratory and full of positioning statements. Second, the EU's 'fight against terrorism' discourse has not operated in isolation from the EU's foreign policy discourse but has developed simultaneously in parallel and as part of the EU's attempts to carve out a role for itself in world politics.

The main issue with the research on EU foreign policy and identity is that whilst it has analysed the external projection of the EU's international identity, little research has focused on the internal projection of the EU's identity. The research in this book offers a novel contribution to this literature by moving beyond a sole focus on the external projection of the 'international identity' of the EU to also consider the internal projection of EU identity through its counter-terrorism and internal security policies. In this sense, I suggest replacing Manners and Whitman's notion of the 'international identity of the EU' with the concept of 'EU identity', which it is argued captures more completely the various ways in which identity impacts upon the EU as a security actor.[53] By conceptualising the identity of the EU in a broader sense it is possible to respond to Manners and Whitman's call for further research that can identify and analyse the various 'others' with which differentiation occurs.[54] In this way I intend to go beyond a narrow focus on the construction of external 'others' to consider also the role of those internal 'others', including 'others' who traverse the internal/external divide, through which the identity of the EU is constituted, differentiated and (re)produced. By doing this I aim to offer a reflection on the important role of EU identity in the formulation of counter-terrorism policy that is more holistic in orientation.

The final point to raise on the issue of EU actorness is the extent to which it can be considered a unitary actor on counter-terrorism and security issues. As I have already noted, the EU is not considered to be a unitary actor in the classic sense of the term. However, it can be viewed as a unitary actor in so far as it operates as an 'authoritative discursive site' where the collectively agreed view of the organisation on foreign policy or counter-terrorism issues are established. The various policy 'texts' or spoken language of EU officials taken together represent a common language on foreign policy and counter-terrorism and provide a framework for cooperative action in the field of security.[55] Yet it is also possible to recognise that, although we can identify the many ways that 'EU identity' is expressed both internally and externally, in other ways this identity is constantly in the process of evolving, with the EU remaining 'simultaneously a highly variegated and heterogeneous set of processes and actors'.[56] It must therefore always be remembered, as Manners and Whitman suggest, that the identity of the EU is 'fluid, consisting of ongoing contestations of complex, multiple, relational identities'.[57] This conceptualisation of EU actorness provides the background for the analysis conducted in this book, highlighting the relationship between the identity of the EU and the type of security actor the EU constructs itself as being. From this perspective, the EU is viewed as a place where multiple discourses on identity, security and terrorism are (re)articulated, (re)produced and refracted back into social and political life. Having established how EU actorness is viewed for the purpose of this research, I will now turn to consider the developing role of the EU in the field of counter-terrorism.

The EU as a counter-terrorism actor: traditional approaches to EU counter-terrorism policy

The events of 11 September 2001, provided a significant challenge to the EU and in particular to its developing role as a provider of 'internal' and 'external security'. After the signing of the Treaty on European Union (TEU) at Maastricht, in 1992, EU security policy was split between the second pillar, the Common Foreign and Security Policy (CFSP), which dealt with external security, and the third pillar, Justice and Home Affairs (JHA), which was concerned with internal security. Since the adoption of the Lisbon Treaty on the Function of the European Union (TFEU), in 2009, this institutional arrangement has changed, with the EU pillar structure replaced by areas of 'exclusive competence', 'shared competence' and 'supporting competence'. The CFSP can be described as the foreign policy of the union incorporating a number of important policy areas that include diplomacy, security and defence issues. Before the signing of the Lisbon Treaty it incorporated the European Security and Defence Policy (ESDP), which has since been renamed the Common Security and Defence Policy (CSDP). Similarly, JHA has swiftly developed into one of the largest and most important policy areas, encompassing the convergence of criminal law, judicial and police cooperation, asylum and immigration policy, as well as much of the EU counter-terrorism policy. After Lisbon many of the policy areas that constituted JHA were absorbed into the consolidated union structure under the guise of the Area of Freedom Security and Justice (AFSJ). The formulation of EU counter-terrorism policy has historically occurred across all areas of internal and external security policy.

Although external security concerns have featured strongly in the formulation of EU counter-terrorism policy, in terms of the 'fight against terrorism', the EU has framed its counter-terrorism effort as predominantly an 'internal security' concern best dealt with through criminal and judicial measures. The reason for this can be traced back to member states' past experiences with terrorism. European states such as France, Germany, Italy, Spain and the United Kingdom have historically had to deal with internal or domestic terrorist threats and have as such developed domestic responses based primarily upon policing and the application of criminal law.[58] As such, the EU's crime and justice centred approach to counter-terrorism can be explained by the dominant role interior ministries have played in the formulation of policy. This is true both historically and in the present context. Writing in 1986, Christopher Hill noted that European states would tend to eschew the use of force (on the grounds that it would create a cycle of reaction and counter-reaction) in order to focus on the 'root causes of terrorism'.[59] This type of framing remains remarkably similar in the present context. As Geoffrey Edwards and Christoph Meyer point out, in the period after the events of 11 September 2001, it was the pre-existing superior expertise, administrative capabilities and strategic interests of the JHA ministers that helped to explain why it was they, their related working groups and committees who led the EU counter-terrorism effort and not foreign ministers as originally envisaged.[60]

It is important to note, with regard to the dominant role played by the interior ministers in the formulation of counter-terrorism policy, that the EU's response is 'one of the most complicated areas in institutional terms and can encompass measures across all three pillars'.[61] Much of the research conducted on EU counter-terrorism policy demonstrates awareness of the pre-Lisbon cross-pillarisation of the EU counter-terrorism response and therefore defies simple explanation. Research in this area consists of various studies involving the historical and legal evolution of EU counter-terrorism policy, as well as public policy approaches that reflect on processes of EU governance in this area including issues involving implementation. In order to grasp the significant contribution this research makes to explanations of EU counter-terrorism, I divide my analysis of this literature into research that explores the internal dimension of EU counter-terrorism, research that explores the external dimension of EU counter-terrorism and research that explores EU counter-terrorism as a holistic field of study. I then reflect on what this literature contributes to our understanding of the EU's counter-terrorism response. Taken together I argue that this body of research can be understood as the traditional literature on EU counter-terrorism policy.

The first body of literature deals with the EU's internal response to the threat of terrorism. This research builds on the above premise that as a result of the prominent role played by interior ministers, JHA is an obvious place to explore EU counter-terrorism capacities. Mark Rhinard, Arjen Boin and Magnus Ekengren have provided an in-depth analysis of the institutional capacities of the EU in terms of its approach to 'managing the terrorist threat'.[62] They identify five areas of JHA activity that stand out in relation to the 'fight against terrorism', which have been analysed in detail by scholars working in this field of study. The first is improvements in cross-border police cooperation, including the strengthening of European police agencies (such as Europol) through the sharing of experience and best practice in response to cross-border crime. The second area of JHA activity is judicial cooperation, which relates to the creation of a European 'legal space' with regard to crime and terrorism that has witnessed the strengthening of European agencies like Eurojust. The third area relates to information exchange. This area is split between information used for law enforcement purposes, such as the Schengen Information System (SIS), and the more sensitive information used for intelligence and strategic analysis. Here they note a developing counter-terrorism role in intelligence cooperation for the Joint Situation Centre of the Council (SitCen), which provides leaders with analysis of threats such as terrorism. The fourth area is immigration and border control, including an emerging counter-terrorism capacity for the EU border agency Frontex. The final area they identify concerns the financing of terrorism, which includes measures and instruments that allow for the freezing of assets and the tracing of monetary transfers across borders. Within this body of research on the internal dimension of EU counter-terrorism policy there are studies that: consider the legitimacy of the formal and informal counter-terrorism networks that have been created at the European level; analyse the policy-making process with specific reference to key institutional actors; challenge the effectiveness of counter-terrorism implementation in the JHA arena; and evaluate the extent to which coordinated efforts in the field of JHA provide 'added value' to national counter-terrorism efforts.[63]

The second body of literature explores the EU's external response to terrorism, focusing on two significant aspects of the 'external' dimension of EU counter-terrorism policy: first, the framing of the counter-terrorism response through interaction with international organisations, such as the United Nations (UN); and second, the development of a transatlantic framework with the US through which to respond to the perceived threat of terrorism. Kim Eling has explored the relationship between the EU and the UN noting that the EU went to great lengths to implement policies designed in the UN framework.[64] She argues that in the period after 11 September 2001, the EU's foreign policy commitment to 'effective multilateralism' was underscored by two main achievements on counter-terrorism. First, the aim of tackling the financing of terrorism was driven almost entirely by the agenda set in this multilateral forum. Second, the aim of preventing terrorism came to effect the programming of EU development assistance. Eling contends that in both cases the existence of UN standards and policies enabled the EU to go beyond what it may have been able to achieve in terms of creating new policy tools to tackle terrorism. Similarly, Wyn Rees has offered a comprehensive analysis of the evolving relationship between the EU and the US in the field of counter-terrorism.[65] Rees' insightful analysis charts areas of success in terms of bilateral counter-terrorism arrangements between the EU and the US in the internal sphere of security (for example, intelligence sharing and the Passenger Name Record agreement), whilst simultaneously highlighting key areas of divergence between the EU and the US that have occurred in terms of external security cooperation.[66] Certainly, the second pillar has seen less progress in terms of more developed EU counter-terrorism capacities, which as David Spence suggests can partly be explained by the sensitive nature of foreign and defence policy.[67] EU states have tended towards bilateral arrangements rather than engage in initiatives that might compromise national sovereignty. Indeed, the limited progress highlighted above has led Daniel Keohane to argue that the EU's foreign policy response has been vague in aspiration, extremely cautious and starved of meaningful additional resources.[68]

The third body of literature has dealt with developments in EU counter-terrorism policy from a holistic perspective that has tried to account for the cross-pillar nature of the response. Monica den Boer and Jörg Monar have spoken of the events of 11 September 2001 as a challenge to the EU's role as a 'security actor in both external and internal matters', noting that the terrorist threat 'must be regarded as the first truly "cross-pillar" test of the Union's role as a security actor'.[69] Monar's analysis in particular suggests EU counter-terrorism policy consists of four characteristics that provide an excellent way of categorising all of the developments outlined above.[70] First, there has been the development of a mixture of 'internal' and 'external' security measures. Second, the creation of a combination of legislative and operational measures designed to advance the internal aspects of EU counter-terrorism policy. Third, the development of a mixture of repressive and preventative measures. Finally, a strong emphasis has been placed on strengthening the EU's institutional capacity to deal with the common threat of terrorism. To date, there have been three extended studies that have attempted to chart the cross-pillar, institutional and policy dynamics of the EU counter-terrorism response since 11 September 2001. Oldrich Bures provides an overview of the array of counter-terrorism measures developed by the EU since that date, arguing that they have been beset with problems over implementation that have led to questions regarding their effectiveness; Javier Argomaniz has charted the complex and multidimensional range of counter-terrorism policies developed by the EU to determine the extent to which the EU can be considered a coherent counter-terrorism actor; and Raphael Bossong has offered a comprehensive analysis of the historical emergence of EU counter-terrorism policy focusing specifically on the formative period between 2001 and 2005, arguing that the policies adopted during that period have significantly influenced the entire course of European security ever since.[71]

The traditional literature on EU counter-terrorism is significant for several reasons. First, it charts the historical development of EU counter-terrorism policy since its inception in the 1970s, providing analysis of the context within which policy action was taken. Second, it helps to identify the main institutional actors at EU level responsible for the formulation of EU counter-terrorism policy. Third, it outlines many of the various policy initiatives developed to combat terrorism, highlighting areas of success, areas of failure and offering recommendations for further action in the policy sphere. Fourth, it draws out the problems that have occurred in terms of the implementation of numerous counter-terrorism measures agreed upon at EU level, demonstrating the difficulty that the EU has had in terms of ratifying and implementing controversial measures from the top down. Finally, it raises important questions about the legitimacy of the EU's developing role as a counter-terrorism actor. However, traditional approaches to counter-terrorism also have significant weaknesses. Importantly, these type of approaches remain wedded to a 'problem-solving' approach to counter-terrorism that uncritically accepts the possibility that these policies and practices could happen, including an uncritical acceptance of claims about the threat that terrorism poses to European society.[72] As Doty points out, these approaches 'presuppose the identities of social actors and a background of social meanings', failing to take into account the role that discourse and language plays in constructing the world within which they operate.[73] In particular, what these approaches do not do is to investigate or analyse the language of EU counter-terrorism policy in any great detail, beyond a basic consideration of EU 'threat perception'.[74]

Traditional approaches to EU counter-terrorism are characterised by an inattentiveness to discourse and language that this book shall seek to address. As was noted earlier, the reason for this focus is to demonstrate how the practice of counter-terrorism policy is inextricably linked to the language of counter-terrorism policy. The purpose of this is to show how the 'fight against terrorism' discourse is constructed and how it provides a language for talking about terrorism, including how it constructs an accepted knowledge or 'conventional wisdom' about *what terrorism is* and *who the terrorists are*. Moreover, a discussion of the language of the 'fight against terrorism' is essential to understanding how the discourse conditions the type of policy responses that have been developed, structuring certain courses of action towards terrorism whilst precluding others. It is important to note that there is a small body of research on EU counter-terrorism, which can be described as 'critical' in orientation, that also shares some of these concerns. This research interrogates the language of EU counter-terrorism, considers the EU intra-institutional challenge to the dominant counter-terrorism logic and demonstrates the way in which the threat of terrorism has been invoked by politicians and policy-makers to help legitimise the creation of a broad EU security framework that goes far beyond a mere focus on counter-terrorism. I will now turn to consider this research before clarifying the unique contribution that I intend to make to the debate on EU counter-terrorism policy.

The EU as a counter-terrorism actor: critical approaches to the 'fight against terrorism'

The critical literature on EU counter-terrorism policy can be split into two bodies of research. First, a small number of studies focus on the important role that language and discourse play in the formulation of EU counter-terrorism policy. Second, a larger body of research explores EU counter-terrorism as a manifestation of new practices of security governance, reflecting a normative question over the extent to which the EU has preserved an appropriate balance between liberty and security.

With regard to the first body of research, there have been only three studies that have investigated the discursive construction of the EU's 'fight against terrorism'. Anastassia Tsoukala has conducted a thematic content analysis of debates in the European Parliament on combating terrorism that arose in the immediate aftermath of September 11.[75] Her analysis is significant in that it reveals a degree of intra-institutional conflict wherein the position of the European Parliament on responding to the threat of terrorism was markedly different to that of the dominant discourse articulated by the other key EU institutions, the European Council and the European Commission, responsible for counter-terrorism policy.[76] Richard Jackson has examined the main characteristics and evolution of the EU's 'fight against terrorism' discourse in comparison with the US 'war on terror'.[77] He highlights the significant differences between the EU's 'criminal justice' and the US 'war-based' narratives that constitute each discourse, whilst recognising that both approaches are similar in that they rest 'upon a series of highly contested assumptions and narratives about the nature and causes of the terrorist threat'.[78] Oz Hassan has offered a genealogical analysis of the EU's evolving role as a counter-terrorism actor wherein he argues that the EU has 'inflated' the threat of terrorism, securitising the EU's response 'in the pursuit of internal, external and normative objectives'.[79] Hassan's analysis is novel in that it traverses both aspects of the critical literature demonstrating how the discourse of EU counter-terrorism is making new practices of security governance possible, which he suggests 'may well be doing more harm than good, inside and outside of the Union'.[80]

The second body of literature takes this discussion forward by analysing the new forms of security governance that have arisen at the European level, and which have been made possible through the invocation of security threats like terrorism. Most notable here is the research of Didier Bigo, who has identified what he terms 'a field of professionals of the management of unease'.[81] This refers to a multiplicity of actors that include domestic and EU politicians, police and intelligence officials, army officers, security experts, journalists and parts of civil society, all of whom simultaneously work together and compete to establish their own political authority in the field of security. Bigo draws attention to this transnational field of security professionals in order to demonstrate 'the impact of its internal mechanisms on the everyday work of various security agents as well as on the definition of security threats in both the political and security realm'.[82] In this way, as Jef Huysmans and Anastassia Tsoukala explain, the definitional borders between key concepts such as war, terror, threat or freedom are being reframed.[83] This research traces the link between discourse and practice by showing how the framing of security threats makes possible the blurring of 'the operational borders of security agencies ... as police and military-related activities exceed their traditional field of action, and intermingle with one another', with 'sectoral borders ... discarded as security-related issues are increasingly handed over to private agencies, and security concerns are thought to be of interest even to ostensibly irrelevant sectors, such as business and finance'.[84] In essence, these transformations in the field of security at the European level reflect what Marieke de Goede has termed an emerging 'European security culture'.[85] This culture of security is based around the identification, prevention, anticipation and early intervention in response to security threats like terrorism. Yet, as de Goede suggests, the discursive invocation of terrorism as threat has given way to a practice of European counter-terrorism that 'far exceeds the focus on terrorism and fosters a set of wide-ranging security programmes that transcend the formal borders of the union'.[86]

This body of critical research is important for the analysis of the EU's 'fight against terrorism' conducted in this book for two main reasons. First, the research conducted by Tsoukala, Jackson and Hassan remain the only studies to have analysed the language of EU counter-terrorism policy through a discourse approach. This is a significant gap in the literature that this book will seek to address. Second, this book will also focus on the practices of security made possible by the language of counter-terrorism, and whilst I agree with Bigo and Tsoukala that 'speech acts are not decisive', it remains the case that an in-depth analysis of the language of EU counter-terrorism is essential if we are to gain a more comprehensive understanding of the processes through which these practices are legitimised.[87] It is shown throughout that a discursive analysis of the EU's 'fight against terrorism' can offer something distinctive to our understanding of the formulation of counter-terrorism and security policy at the EU level.

Chapter outline

Chapter 1 outlines the analytical techniques that I use to explore the EU's 'fight against terrorism' discourse. The chapter begins by arguing that in order to develop a comprehensive understanding of EU counter-terrorism policy it is necessary to consider the language of counter-terrorism. I argue that language and identity are significant in that they help to construct the 'fight against terrorism' discourse, which I argue makes the practice of EU counter-terrorism and security policy possible. I then move on to consider three theoretical concepts that underpin my investigation into EU counter-terrorism policy: discourse, representation and securitisation. For each concept I consider how it is understood for the purpose of this research; including its relationship with the concept of identity, which I argue holds significance for all three concepts. I finish by outlining the methodological approach I use to conduct this analysis of the 'fight against terrorism'. Drawing inspiration from the research techniques of Roxanne Lynn Doty, Jennifer Milliken, Richard Jackson, Lene Hansen and Laura Shepherd, I introduce my own three-step process of discourse analysis. I conclude with a discussion of how the analysis was itself completed and why various texts were selected for analysis.

Chapter 2 provides a genealogy of the threat of terrorism discourse, as it has been articulated in Western European, European Community (EC) and EU security discourses. The first section investigates the intellectual and practical origins of the threat of terrorism discourse in Western Europe between the 1970s and the events of 11 September 2001. It traces the emergence of terrorism as a transnational security problem for European governments, exploring the link between the discourse on terrorism and the creation of a transnational framework for cooperation on matters of cross-border law enforcement (Trevi); and later a holistic system of governance for the provision of internal security under the auspices of the EU's Area of Freedom, Security and Justice. The second section investigates the (re)emergence of the EU's 'fight against terrorism' discourse following the events of 11 September 2001 and its subsequent evolution across three periods: the post-September 11 period, the post-Madrid period and the post-Breivik period. I go on to identify the 'key texts' that will be analysed, drawing out the main strands of the 'fight against terrorism' discourse that make up the focus of the empirical analysis conducted in the rest of the book.

Chapter 3 builds on the overview of the EU's terrorism as threat discourse that was conducted in the previous chapter by analysing four of the discourse

strands in a detailed manner. In the first part of the chapter I begin by mapping each of the discourse strands, demonstrating how they help to construct
the figure of the 'terrorist' other. I show how the 'terrorist' other is constructed
within the discourse as an extreme and radical threat to the EU as simultaneously a 'criminal', a 'new' and 'evolving' threat, as well as potentially a
non-state actor, a member of a group or an individual, such as a 'lone actor'
or a 'returning foreign fighter', who seeks to inflict 'massive casualties' against
the EU and its member states. The second part of the chapter reflects on the
how the 'fight against terrorism' discourse functions. I argue that it structures
the EU approach as a criminal justice-based approach to counter-terrorism,
which can be differentiated from the US war-based discourse of the 'war on
terror'. I show how the EU understanding of terrorism is based upon and
constructs an 'accepted knowledge' about terrorism that is highly contested,
as well as considering the political and societal implications of the discourse.

Chapter 4 explores the strand of the 'fight against terrorism' discourse
that constructs the 'openness' of EU society as particularly 'vulnerable' to
the threat of terrorism. In this chapter I focus on how the discourse implicitly constructs the 'migrant' other as a potential terrorist threat through
the linking of counter-terrorism to migration and border control policies.
In the first part of the chapter I identify three intertwined strands of the
'fight against terrorism' discourse. First, the idea that the EU's 'globalised'
or 'open' society represents a potential source of terrorist threat. Second, a
discourse of 'surveillance' and 'control', which operates to justify and legitimise the counter-response to the threat. Third, in response to the phenomenon of EU citizens leaving to fight in conflicts in other parts of the world, the
construction of the figure of the 'returning foreign fighter'. The second half
of the chapter shows how the EU has invoked the terrorist threat in order
to legitimise ever-increasingly sophisticated policies, practices and measures
aimed at the 'control' of the 'migrant' other. It is argued that this is reflective
of – and helps to contribute to – wider securitisation processes within the
EU. The chapter concludes by analysing how the emergence of the figure of
the 'returning foreign fighter' has further strengthened the perception that
border control should form a central element of the EU's counter-terrorism
response.

Chapter 5 investigates the strand of the 'fight against terrorism' discourse
that connects the threat of terrorism to 'violent religious extremism', 'radicalisation' and the threat of the 'Muslim' other. The first part of the chapter
maps the emergence and evolution of this strand of the discourse. I show
how in its initial phase the language of 'radicalisation and recruitment'
to terrorism contained an assumption that 'radicalisation' was something
more likely to occur in Europe's 'Muslim communities'; the impact of this
was to implicitly construct the 'Muslim' other as a potential terrorist threat.

I then demonstrate how the EU discourse on 'radicalisation' moves away from the framing of 'radicalisation' as a problem inherently linked to Islam, arguing that by 2015 a broader conceptualisation of 'radicalisation' emerges centred on 'violent extremism', rather than solely religion, as the motivation for contemporary terrorist threats. The second part of the chapter critiques the concept of 'radicalisation', demonstrating how knowledge about 'radicalisation' is highly contested and retains an implicit racial bias against the 'Muslim' other, which it has been unable to shed. I conclude by considering how the logic of counter-radicalisation is making possible a new form of precautionary security governance, the impact of which is the further securitisation of social and political life within the EU.

Finally, in the Conclusion, I highlight the main contribution that this research makes to debates on EU counter-terrorism policy. The chapter is split into five parts. In the first part I argue that an exploration of language, identity and the study of 'others' is essential if we are to develop a comprehensive understanding of the EU's 'fight against terrorism'. In the second part I consider the relationship between the 'fight against terrorism' discourse and the EU's emerging role as a holistic security actor, arguing that the discourse is helping to make possible emerging security practices that are contributing to a blurring of the domains of internal and external security. In the third part I borrow Marieke de Goede's notion of 'European security culture', to show how the EU is developing a particular security identity that is committed to the creation of a system of precautionary security governance. I argue that an analysis of the language of the 'fight against terrorism' helps to reveal the logic that underpins this emerging system of governance. In the fourth part I reflect on the implications of the 'fight against terrorism' for 'human rights' in the EU area, as well as the extent to which the EU counter-terrorism response can be considered effective. The fifth part offers some discussion of future avenues for research, including some of the limitations of my interpretive approach. Finally, I offer some concluding remarks on the significance of the EU's 'fight against terrorism' discourse.

Notes

1 Javier Solana, 'Protecting People and Infrastructure: Achievements, Failures and Future Tasks', speech delivered at the EastWest Institute, Second Annual Worldwide Security Conference (Brussels), 7 February 2005, available online at: www.eu-un.europa.eu/articles/fr/article_4320_fr.htm (accessed January 2015).
2 Gilles de Kerchove, 'Terror Threat Still Present in Europe', *Deutsche Welle*, 11 March 2014, available online at: www.dw.de/de-kerchove-terror-threat-still-present-in-europe/a-17486669?maca=en-rss-en-all-1573-rdf (accessed January 2015).

3 I recognise that labeling the terrorist group 'Islamic State' as Islamic State is controversial. I refer to the group as Islamic State throughout the book not to make
   a political point but simply because this is the name the group uses to describe
   themselves. I recognise that Islamic State is not a state. I also recognise that it is
   not Islamic.
4 Javier Argomaniz, *The EU and Counter-Terrorism: Politics, Polity and Policies
   after 9/11* (London and New York: Routledge, 2011).
5 Richard Jackson, *Writing the War on Terrorism: Language, Politics and
   Counter-Terrorism* (Manchester: Manchester University Press, 2005), see p. 8.
6 Stuart Croft, *Culture, Crisis and America's War on Terror* (New York: Cambridge
   University Press, 2006), p. 1.
7 I will use the terms 'EU identity' and the 'identity of the EU' interchangeably
   throughout this book.
8 Lene Hansen, *Security as Practice: Discourse Analysis and the Bosnian War*
   (London and New York: Routledge, 2006), p. 1.
9 For excellent analyses of the 'writing' of the US 'war on terror' as a political
   discourse, see: Jackson, *Writing the War on Terrorism*; Lee Jarvis, *Times of
   Terror: Discourse, Temporality and the War on Terror* (Basingstoke: Palgrave
   Macmillan, 2009); for an excellent analysis of the cultural construction of the
   'war on terror', see Croft, *Culture, Crisis and America's War on Terror*.
10 Stuart Croft and Cerwyn Moore, 'The evolution of threat narratives in the age
   of terror: understanding terrorist threats in Britain', *International Affairs*, 8:4
   (2010), 821–835.
11 Solana, 'Protecting People and Infrastructure'.
12 See Jackson, *Writing the War on Terrorism*, p. 93. Rik Coolsaet has argued that
   citizens of 'Muslim countries' are the primary victims of terrorism, with some
   estimates stating that casualties are 40 times higher in those countries than in the
   West. See Rik Coolsaet (ed.), *Jihadi Terrorism and the Radicalisation Challenge
   in Europe* (Aldershot: Ashgate, 2008), p. 1.
13 Bill Durodié, *The Power of Nightmares: The Shadows in the Cave* (documen-
   tary), directed by Adam Curtis (BBC, 2005).
14 Solana, 'Protecting People and Infrastructure'.
15 For discussion of the relationship between counter-terrorism and the principles of
   pre-emptive and precautionary security, see Claudia Aradau and Rens van Munster,
   'Governing terrorism through risk: taking precautions (un)knowing the future',
   European Journal of International Relations, 13:1 (2007), 89–115; Louise Amoore
   and Marieke de Goede (eds), *Risk and the War on Terror* (Abingdon: Routledge,
   2008); Marieke de Goede and Samuel Randalls, 'Preemption, precaution: arts and
   technologies of the governable future', *Environment and Planning D: Society and
   Space*, 27:5 (2009), 859–878.
16 Marieke de Goede calls these type of security threats 'threat imaginaries'. See
   Marieke de Goede, 'European Security Culture: Preemption and Precaution in
   European Security', University of Amsterdam Inaugural Lecture (Vossiuspers
   UvA: Amsterdam University Press, 2011).
17 Bill Durodié, 'Fear and terror in a post-political age', *Government and
   Opposition*, 42:3 (2007), 441.

18 De Goede, 'European Security Culture', p. 10.
19 European Commission, *Communication from the Commission on the Precautionary Principle*, Brussels, 2 February 2000, COM (2000) 1.
20 Claudia Aradau and Rens van Munster, 'Taming the Future: The Dispositif of Risk in the War on Terror', in Louise Amoore and Marieke de Goede (eds), *Risk and the War on Terror* (Abingdon: Routledge, 2008), p. 24.
21 I will explore and outline precisely what I mean by term 'securitisation' in Chapter 2.
22 Paul Williams, *Security Studies: An Introduction*, 2nd edn (Abingdon: Routledge, 2013), p. 6.
23 A 'referent object of security' refers to the thing that is to be secured. Traditionally, this has meant the state. However, it might also refer to an individual, a group, a community or a society.
24 I have chosen to avoid defining terrorism for a specific reason. As I explain below, the term is so contested that no objective definition is possible. Instead, throughout the book I will analyse the way in which the meaning of terrorism is constructed through discourse. I do this in order to reflect upon the way in which terrorism functions discursively through the practice of counter-terrorism.
25 Croft, *Culture, Crisis and America's War on Terror*, p. 1.
26 Harald Müller, 'Security Cooperation', in Walter Carlsnaes, Thomas Risse and Beth Simmons (eds), *Handbook of International Relations* (London: Sage, 2002), p. 369.
27 Laura J. Shepherd and Jutta Weldes, 'Security: The State (of) Being Free from Danger?', in Hans Günter Brauch *et al.* (eds), *Globalisation and Environmental Challenges: Reconceptualising Security in the 21st Century* (Mosbach: AFES-Press, 2007), pp. 529–530.
28 Columba Peoples and Nick Vaughan-Williams (eds), *Critical Security Studies: An Introduction* (Routledge: New York, 2010).
29 The different approaches united under the umbrella of CSS and CTS adopt varying understandings of the term 'critical'. In the narrow sense, critical refers to the Critical Theory of the Frankfurt School (FSCT). These approaches go beyond critique of the weaknesses of traditional approaches to the study of security or terrorism and instead advocate a reconstructive agenda for security studies and terrorism studies. In particular, they advance a normative agenda for CSS/CTS arguing that security (or counter-terrorism) ought to be about human emancipation.
30 Steve Smith, 'The Contested Concept of Security', in Ken Booth (ed.), *Critical Security Studies and World Politics* (London: Lynne Rienner Publishers, 2005), p. 40.
31 Richard Jackson, Lee Jarvis, Marie Breen Smyth and Jeroen Gunning, *Terrorism: A Critical Introduction* (Basingstoke: Palgrave Macmillan, 2011).
32 Robert Cox, 'Social forces, states and world orders: beyond international relations theory', *Millennium: Journal of International Studies*, 10:2 (June 1981), 126–155.
33 Ibid., 128–129.
34 Ibid., 129.
35 Keith Krause and Michael C. Williams (eds), *Critical Security Studies: Concepts and Cases* (London: Routledge, 1997), p. xi.
36 Smith, 'The Contested Concept of Security'.

37 Jackson *et al.*, *Terrorism*. For the core commitments of CTS, see pp. 34–37. See also Richard Jackson, 'The core commitments of Critical Terrorism Studies', *European Political Science*, 'Symposium: The Case for Critical Terrorism Studies', 6:3 (2007), 244–251.
38 Walter B. Gallie, 'Essentially Contested Concepts', in *Proceedings of the Aristotelian Society* (London: Harrison & Sons, Ltd, 1955). By 'essentially contested' Gallie meant concepts 'the proper use of which inevitably involves endless disputes about their proper uses on the part of their users', p. 169.
39 Jackson, 'The core commitments'.
40 I will further elaborate on the theoretical and methodological commitments of this research in Chapter 2.
41 John Gerard Ruggie, 'Territoriality and beyond: problematizing modernity in International Relations', *International Organization*, 47:1 (1993), 140.
42 Jozef Batora and Brian Hocking, 'Bilateral Diplomacy in the European Union: Towards "Post-modern" Patterns', ECPR/SGIR 6th Pan-European Conference (Turin), 12–15 September 2007.
43 Traditionally, the concept of 'external security' refers to the measures taken by a state actor to ensure their own safety and survival within the international arena. This includes the use of military and foreign policy instruments to provide a feeling of safety from external security threats. 'Internal security', by way of contrast, refers to the keeping of peace within the domestic borders of a nation-state. It is provided for through the police, law enforcement and the judiciary.
44 Didier Bigo refers to this system of governance at the EU and other levels as a 'field of security' consisting of multiple actors engaged in competition over defining whose security is important and for what purpose. See Didier Bigo, 'Globalized (In)Security: The Field and the Ban-Opticon', in Didier Bigo and Anastassia Tsoukala (eds), *Terror, Insecurity and Liberty: Illiberal Practices of Liberal Regimes after 9/11* (Abingdon: Routledge, 2008), pp. 10–48.
45 Audie Klotz and Cecelia Lynch, *Strategies for Research in Constructivist International Relations* (London: M.E. Sharpe, 2007), p. 4.
46 Charlotte Bretherton and John Vogler, *The European Union as a Global Actor*, 2nd edn (London: Routledge, 2006); Thomas Christiansen, Knud Eric Jorgensen and Antje Weiner (eds), *The Social Construction of Europe* (London: Sage, 1999); Henrik Larsen, 'The EU: a global military actor?', *Cooperation and Conflict*, 37:3 (2002), 283–302; Henrik Larsen, *Analysing the Foreign Policy of Small States in the EU: The Case of Denmark* (Basingstoke: Palgrave, 2005).
47 Larsen, 'The EU', 287.
48 Henrik Larsen, 'Discourse Analysis in the Study of European Foreign Policy', in Ben Tonra and Thomas Christiansen (eds), *Rethinking European Foreign Policy* (Manchester: Manchester University Press, 2004), pp. 62–80.
49 Ian J. Manners and Richard G. Whitman, 'Towards identifying the international identity of the European Union: a framework for analysis of the EU's network of relationships', *Journal of European Integration*, 21:3 (1998), 246.
50 Ole Wæver, 'European security identities', *Journal of Common Market Studies*, 34:1 (1996), 103–132; Iver B. Neumann, 'European identity, EU expansion, and the integration/exclusion nexus', *Alternatives*, 23 (1998), 397–416; Larsen, 'The

EU'; Thomas Diez, 'Constructing the self and changing others: reconsidering "normative power Europe"', *Millennium: Journal of International Studies*, 33:3 (2005), 613–636; James Rogers, 'From "civilian power" to "global power": explicating the European Union's "grand strategy" through the articulation of discourse theory', *Journal of Common Market Studies*, 47:4 (2009), 831–862; Kamil Zwolski, 'The EU as an international security actor after Lisbon: finally a green light for a holistic approach?', *Cooperation and Conflict*, 47:1 (2012), 68–87.

51 Ben Rosamond, 'Conceptualizing the EU model of governance in world politics', *European Foreign Affairs Review*, 10 (2005), 470.

52 Ibid., 470.

53 Ian J. Manners and Richard G. Whitman, 'The "difference engine": constructing and representing the international identity of the European Union', *Journal of European Public Policy*, 10:3 (2003), 380–404.

54 Ibid., 400.

55 Richard Jackson, 'An analysis of EU counterterrorism policy discourse', *Cambridge Review of International Affairs*, 20:2 (2007), 233–247.

56 Ibid., 236.

57 Manners and Whitman, 'The "difference engine"', 396.

58 The European experience of terrorism differs greatly from country to country. Some members of the EU have never dealt with terrorism whereas others have had to deal with a significant amount of terrorist activity. What remains constant amongst the Europeans with regard to terrorism is that in response to this threat a solution based predominantly upon the enhancement of internal security measures has thus far been favoured.

59 Christopher Hill, 'The Political Dilemmas for Western Governments', in Lawrence Freedman (ed.), *Terrorism and International Order* (London: Routledge, 1986), p. 85.

60 Geoffrey Edwards and Christoph O. Meyer, 'Introduction: charting a contested transformation', *Journal of Common Market Studies*, 46:1 (2008), 15.

61 Christian Kaunert, 'Towards supranational governance in EU counter-terrorism? The role of the Commission and the Council Secretariat', *Central European Journal of International & Security Studies*, 4:1 (2010), 9.

62 Mark Rhinard, Arjen Boin and Magnus Ekengren, 'Managing Terrorism: Institutional Capacities and Counter-Terrorism Policy in the EU', in David Spence (ed.), *The European Union and Terrorism* (London: John Harper Publishing, 2007), pp. 93–97.

63 Monica den Boer, Claudia Hillebrand and Andreas Nölke, 'Legitimacy under pressure', *Journal of Common Market Studies*, 46:1 (2008), 101–124; Raphael Bossong, 'The Action Plan on Combating Terrorism', *Journal of Common Market Studies*, 46:1 (2008), 27–48; Oldrich Bures, 'EU counterterrorism policy: a paper tiger?', *Terrorism and Political Violence*, 18:1 (March 2006), 57–78; Rik Coolsaet, 'EU counterterrorism strategy: value added or chimera?', *International Affairs*, 86:4 (2010), 857–873.

64 Kim Eling, 'The EU, Terrorism and Effective Multilateralism', in David Spence (ed.), *The European Union and Terrorism* (London: John Harper Publishing, 2007), pp. 105–123.

65 Wyn Rees, *Transatlantic Counter-Terrorism Cooperation: The New Imperative* (London and New York: Routledge, 2006).
66 For further discussion of European and American counter-terrorism cooperation, see Karin von Hippel, *Europe Confronts Terrorism* (Basingstoke: Palgrave Macmillan, 2005); Fraser Cameron, 'Transatlantic Relations and Terrorism', in David Spence (ed.), *The European Union and Terrorism* (London: John Harper Publishing, 2007), pp. 124–144.
67 David Spence (ed.), *The European Union and Terrorism* (London: John Harper Publishing, 2007).
68 Daniel Keohane, 'The absent friend: EU foreign policy and counter terrorism', *Journal of Common Market Studies*, 46:1 (2008), 125–146.
69 Monica den Boer and Jörg Monar, 'Keynote article: 11 September and the challenge of global terrorism to the EU as a security actor', *Journal of Common Market Studies*, 40:1 (2002), 11–28.
70 Jörg Monar, 'Common threat and common response? The European Union's counter-terrorism strategy and its problems', *Government and Opposition*, 42:3 (2007), 292–313.
71 Oldrich Bures, *EU Counterterrorism Policy: A Paper Tiger?* (Farnham: Ashgate, 2011); Argomaniz, *The EU and Counter-Terrorism*; Raphael Bossong, *The Evolution of EU Counter-Terrorism: European Security Policy after 9/11* (Abingdon: Routledge, 2012).
72 For an in-depth critique of traditional, 'problem-solving' approaches to terrorism and counter-terrorism, see Richard Jackson, Marie Breen Smyth and Jeroen Gunning (eds), *Critical Terrorism Studies: A New Research Agenda* (Abingdon: Routledge, 2009), pp. 216–227.
73 Roxanne Lynn Doty, *Imperial Encounters: The Politics of Representation in North–South Relations* (Minneapolis: University of Minnesota Press, 1996), p. 4.
74 See, for example, Rees, *Transatlantic Counter-Terrorism Cooperation*; Monar, 'Common threat and common response?', 293–302; and Bures, *EU Counter-Terrorism Policy*, pp. 31–58, for discussions of the EU perception of the terrorist threat in the post-September 11 era.
75 Anastassia Tsoukala, 'Democracy against security: the debates about counter-terrorism in the European Parliament, September 2001–June 2003', *Alternatives: Global, Local, Political*, 29:4 (2004), 417–439.
76 Tsoukala differentiates between three narratives on EU counter-terrorism. First, the 'defence of the emergency rules' position, characterised by a focus on security, calls for exceptional measures and the linking of immigration and terrorism. Second, the 'two-fold' position, characterised by calls for counter-terrorism measures that reflect a compromise between liberty and security. Third, the 'defence of human rights' position, characterised by a belief that the fight against all forms of criminal behaviour should not go beyond the limits of the law, nor should it involve the breach of human rights or civil liberties.
77 Jackson, 'An analysis of EU counterterrorism policy discourse'.
78 Ibid., 233.

79 Oz Hassan, 'Constructing crises (in)securitising terror: the punctuated evolution of EU counter-terror strategy', *European Security*, 19:3 (2010), 445.

80 Ibid., 462.

81 Didier Bigo and Anastassia Tsoukala (eds), *Terror, Insecurity and Liberty: Illiberal Practices of Liberal Regimes after 9/11* (Abingdon: Routledge, 2008), p. 4. See also Bigo, 'Globalized (In)Security'. Bigo argues that terrorism is one of a number of threats (alongside war, organised crime or 'migratory invasion') contributing to a condition of 'global in-security' and reflected in what he call processes of 'in-securitisation'.

82 Bigo, 'Globalized (In)Security', p. 6.

83 Jef Huysmans and Anastassia Tsoukala, 'Introduction: the social construction and control of danger in counterterrorism', *Alternatives*, 33 (2008), 133–137.

84 Ibid., 133.

85 De Goede, 'European Security Culture'.

86 Ibid., p. 8.

87 Bigo and Tsoukala, *Terror, Insecurity and Liberty*, p. 4.

1

Investigating the language of EU counter-terrorism: analytical techniques

Introduction

Research on counter-terrorism is united by a concern with the way in which various actors define, understand and respond to the threat of terrorism. However, beyond this broad commitment it is possible to identify a variety of approaches to the study of counter-terrorism that differ as a direct result of the implicit and explicit assumptions that each individual researcher makes about the social world. Traditional approaches to counter-terrorism predominantly begin from a position whereby the meaning of terrorism is understood to be fixed or predefined, thereby constricting the type of research questions that can be asked. In terms of research on counter-terrorism policy, these approaches are generally concerned with explaining *why* certain actors made decisions that resulted in the development of particular policies.[1] For example, when we consider research on European Union (EU) counter-terrorism policy, the key texts in this area have been concerned with explaining: why EU counter-terrorism policy has been relatively ineffective as a counter-terrorism device; why EU counter-terrorism policy has suffered from serious consistency weaknesses and other shortcomings; and why the EU sought to become a significant counter-terrorism actor during the formative period of EU counter-terrorism policy between 2001 and 2005.[2]

Depending on the approach adopted, explanations for these questions range from the lack of power of the EU and its institutions relative to its member states, the actual legitimacy of the EU as a counter-terrorism actor, the varying degrees of authority that the different institutions and agencies of the EU have in the field of security and, importantly, the perceptions of the decision-makers involved in the policy process. As Roxanne Lynn Doty explains, approaches based upon this type of *why* questions are incomplete in the sense that 'they take as unproblematic the *possibility* that a particular course of action or decision could be taken'.[3] They start from a position whereby the social actors, the practices that they adopt and the meaning that makes those practices possible, as well as the meaning of terrorism itself, constitute an objectively identifiable social reality that can be accessed independently and in an impartial manner. Instead, I aim not to offer explanations for why particular counter-terrorism policies have been developed at the EU level or why they have been ineffective but rather to consider how EU counter-terrorism policy, or EU security policy more generally, has been made possible through the social construction of the threat of terrorism. In doing this, I borrow from Doty to ask a series of what she calls *how-possible* questions, about how terrorism has been socially constructed and how certain counter-responses were made possible as a result of that process of threat construction.

In order to explore this topic, I adopt an approach that is situated within a broader body of interpretive work in International Relations and the social sciences which, as I will argue, can be used to link the study of counter-terrorism and security with the concept of identity.[4] As Mark Bevir and Oliver Daddow explain, interpretive approaches can be used to offer explanation for political action in various policy areas, such as foreign and security policy, through a deeper contextual analysis of the social meanings that underpin that activity.[5] The interpretive approach I advocate, therefore, adopts a more fluid understanding of terrorism as a concept, the meaning of which changes depending upon the historical, social and cultural context within which it is being used. To start from this position is to make a series of assumptions about the social world and the way that it functions, including how to go about accessing that world for research purposes.

I argue that language is significant when analysing counter-terrorism policy in that it is constitutive of a particular social reality through the simultaneous construction of identity and difference. Starting from a position whereby it is assumed that representations of identity and counter-terrorism policy are mutually or co-constitutive, that is to suggest that they cannot be understood in simple cause-and-effect terms, it is argued that counter-terrorism policies need an account or a story of the issues that they are trying to address. There can be no formulation of a counter-terrorism response without a description (or interpretation) of who the terrorists are, what the terrorists want and the ways in which the terrorists differ from the actor responding to them. Identity is crucial here, as James Der Derian suggests, in that a 'terrorist' can only be identified through differentiation from, say, a 'state sanctioned soldier', a 'police-officer' or other agent of the national security state.[6] In essence, this is to propose that counter-terrorism responses are only made possible through a process of social construction and that both the public policy response to the threat of terrorism and the language that constructs terrorism as a threat are understood to be intimately linked.

This has implications for the analysis of EU counter-terrorism policy conducted in this book in the sense that, at the EU level, counter-terrorism policies are legitimised as in the 'European' interest through reference to identities. Yet, simultaneously, identities are produced and reproduced through the formulation of counter-terrorism policies. As Lene Hansen explains: 'Policies require identities, but identities do not exist as objective accounts of what people and places "really are", but as continuously restated, negotiated, and reshaped subjects and objects'.[7] It is argued throughout that EU counter-terrorism policy privileges an accepted knowledge about what terrorism is, who the terrorists are and what type of threat they represent in the post-September 11 era, promoting certain counter-terrorism responses as a 'natural' or 'common-sense' approach through representations of identity, whilst simultaneously silencing other alternative perspectives. To theorise counter-terrorism in this way, as discourse, is to argue that identity and policy are characterised by a mutually constitutive relationship that can be accessed through an analysis of the language and discourse of counter-terrorism policy.

In order to give context to these assumptions, in this chapter I reflect on the theoretical commitments that underpin this research and consider the techniques of discourse analysis that I have employed in order to conduct this analysis of the EU's counter-terrorism policy: the 'fight against terrorism'. The first part of the chapter introduces three interrelated concepts that I draw upon for the purpose of this research: discourse, representation and securitisation. I begin by discussing what I mean by the concept of discourse and explaining its relationship to contemporary understandings of terrorism. I then move on to consider the concept of representation, which I argue plays a key role in the reproduction of knowledge about terrorism. The final concept I explore is the Copenhagen School's notion of securitisation, making an argument that the securitisation framework needs to be reconceptualised in order to understand how securitisation processes work in the EU. For each concept I consider how it is understood for the purpose of this research, as well as its relationship with the concept of identity, which I argue is intrinsic to all three concepts. Having explored the interrelated and interlinked concepts of discourse, representation and securitisation, in the second part of the chapter I go on to consider how they can be operationalised through particular analytical techniques of discourse analysis. In particular, I introduce a three-step process of discourse analysis that I use to implement my analysis of the 'fight against terrorism' discourse. In this section I explain why various texts were selected for analysis, as well as how the analysis was itself completed. I conclude by offering some reflections on why this type of analysis of EU counter-terrorism policy is important and is necessary.

Discourse

I want to begin by outlining exactly what I mean by the notion of 'discourse', given that this concept is absolutely central to the analysis of EU counter-terrorism policy conducted in this book. Discourse generally refers to written or spoken communication, to processes of narration or discussion. It is, however, much more than this. Drawing on the works of Michel Foucault and other discourse scholars such as David Campbell, Roxanne Lynn Doty, Jennifer Milliken, Richard Jackson, Lene Hansen and Laura Shepherd, I understand discourse to refer to systems of thought composed of ideas, beliefs and practices, or 'performative, meaning-making attempts to make sense of the world through words and language', that structure how we think about a particular subject, topic or issue.[8] As Doty explains, 'A discourse delineates the terms of intelligibility whereby a particular "reality" can be known and acted upon. When we speak of a discourse we may be referring to a specific group of texts, but also importantly to the social practices to which those texts are inextricably linked.'[9] What this means in the context of a discussion of counter-terrorism is that a focus on the discourse of terrorism allows us to locate and identify precisely how understandings of terrorism are constructed and how they condition counter-terrorism responses by creating a particular reality that can be known and acted upon. I understand discourses as systems of meaning production that are more than just statements or language about a particular subject, topic or issue.

Discourses can be viewed as structures of signification that construct social realities, providing what Doty has termed *discursive spaces*. By this she means the concepts, categories, metaphors, analogies and identities through which meaning is created.[10] From this perspective meaning does not exist objectively but rather is created through a system of linguistic and/ or non-linguistic signs. Within this sign system discourse scholars focus on the relationship between different things, including specifically the way one subject or object is distinguished from another. Critically, the relationship between the different signs is constructed in terms of *binary oppositions*, which positions the different elements of the system in relation to each other.[11] Furthermore, as Milliken suggests, 'far from being neutral' these systems 'establish a relation of power such that one element in the binary is privileged'.[12] Some well-known examples of binaries include: good/evil, new/old and masculine/feminine. We can identify explicitly the way in which this system of signs operates through the language of counter-terrorism, including terms such as freedom/terror, moderate/extremist, state/non-state, peaceful/violent and civilisation/barbarian. For example, if we consider the first EU *Strategy for Combating Radicalisation and Recruitment to Terrorism*, from 2005, the document plays a key role in constructing two types of Muslim: the 'moderate' Muslim that needs to be engaged in order to prevent terrorism, the 'good' Muslim if you like; and the 'extremist' that needs to be challenged, the 'bad' Muslim then, who may potentially engage in acts of terrorism.[13]

Importantly, as the previous example suggests, discourse is understood to be productive of identity, which is itself constructed through processes of differentiation made possible through discourse. As Matthew Broad and Oliver Daddow argue, not only do discourses create *discursive spaces* by rendering things meaningful in certain ways, but 'discourses constitute the identities of social actors by carving out particular *subject-positions*, that is, sites from which the social actors can speak as the I/we of a discourse'.[14] Moreover, discourse confirms which social actors are authorised to speak and therefore to act. In the field of counter-terrorism this might include counter-terrorism officials, security practitioners, policy-makers and 'terrorism experts'. It is argued that these actors also operate within a discursive space that 'imposes meaning on their world'.[15] For the purpose of the research conducted in this book I am interested in revealing the discursive spaces that construct a 'European' or 'EU' sense of self in opposition to various 'others', including the figure of the 'terrorist' other, with a specific focus on how this influences the practice of EU counter-terrorism policy.

Therefore, I understand discourses as 'systems of truth' that have the potential to 'fix' meaning, if only temporarily, allowing us to make sense of the world at any given time.[16] Yet, whilst discourses attempt to fix meaning it is vital to recognise that 'neither absolute fixity nor absolute non-fixity is possible'.[17] Discourses are never completely fixed, closed or stable but are inherently open-ended, unstable, historically contingent and always in the process of changing. As Doty explains:

> A discourse is inherently open-ended and incomplete. Its exterior limits are constituted by other discourses that are themselves also open, inherently unstable, and always in the process of being articulated. This understanding of discourse implies an overlapping quality to different discourses. Any fixing of a discourse and the identities that are constructed by it, then, can only ever be of a partial nature.[18]

The partial fixing within discourse is important in the sense that it allows us to 'know' and act upon what we 'know'. As such, discourses require work to articulate and rearticulate their knowledge, to fix a particular 'system' of thought or 'regime of truth'.[19] If we apply this to terrorism it becomes clear that we can never really know what terrorism is in an objective sense. Indeed, the aim here is not to provide a typology or an account of the terrorist threat to Europe and the EU counter-response to that threat but rather to redirect the focus of study to the discourse within which the threat is constructed and a counter-response made possible. As Joseba Zulaika and William Douglass suggest: 'The challenge is not to learn the ultimate "truth" about terrorism, but to delve into the rhetorical bases of its powerful representations ... to scrutinise the discursive practices whereby this transpires.'[20] By focusing on terrorism and counter-terrorism as a form of discursive practice it becomes possible to identify the knowledges and representations of terrorism upon which the EU's 'fight against terrorism' rests, as well as to explore the practices that have been made possible through processes of identity and threat construction.

Representation

The second concept that has important implications for this research on EU counter-terrorism policy is the idea of 'representation'. If we take discourse to mean the systems of thought or 'regimes of truth' that structure and give meaning to how we think about a particular subject, topic or issue, then instances and practices of representation should be understood as the sites at which meaning is constituted. As I explained above, counter-terrorism is inextricably linked to discursive practices that put into circulation representations of terrorism that are taken as the 'truth'. The purpose of drawing attention to these practices is to demonstrate how particular representations underlie the production of knowledge about terrorism and make certain counter-terrorism policies possible.

If we think of the contemporary Western representation of a terrorist in the post-September 11 era; a *Google Images* search of the term 'terrorist' returns multiple images of gun-toting, bearded men, mainly of Arab, Asian or Middle-Eastern origin.[21] It also provides links to a series of other images entitled: 'Attacks', 'Al-Qaeda', 'Muslims', 'Bin Laden' and 'Beard'. This representation of what a 'terrorist' looks like is powerful in the sense that it contributes to a knowledge about terrorism that is constitutive of the social reality in which contemporary policy responses to terrorism are formulated. For example, in the United Kingdom (UK), Schedule 7 of the Terrorism Act 2000 gives police at the border powers of stop and detention for individuals suspected of involvement in terrorism, without the need for reasonable suspicion. Statistics suggest that these powers have led to the disproportionate targeting of individuals of Asian origin. In 2011/2012, of those individuals stopped for an examination 27 per cent were of Asian origin.[22] For individuals detained for more than an hour this rose to 38 per cent being of Asian origin. The current Asian population of England and Wales, according to the Census of 2011, is 6.9 per cent. I am not suggesting that the dominant contemporary representation of a 'terrorist' is a cause of these figures, but rather something more subtle. Instead, I am suggesting that this representation or perception of what a terrorist looks like provides the context within which counter-terrorism policies such as Schedule 7 operate and makes possible this disproportionate targeting of an ethnic minority.

Representation is therefore very important when we consider the practice of counter-terrorism. It should be understood as a source for the reproduction of knowledge, which is itself embedded in discourse.[23] Yet a focus on representation is not to deny the existence of a material world, nor is it to suggest that we can identify 'distinct realms of the discursive and the non-discursive'; rather it is to suggest that the material world can only ever be mediated through language and discourse, which are, if not prior to it, at least intrinsic to our accessing of it.[24] From this perspective, material realities are thought to be created or constituted through discourse and representation. For example, an individual travelling across a geographical territory from one place to another is certainly a material reality, but it means nothing outside of the discursive and representational practices that give the action meaning. It is only when 'Europe' and 'Syria' are applied to the geographical territories that the individual is travelling between that meaning is created. However, the purpose for which the individual is travelling remains uncertain until discursive practices constitute that individual as a 'refugee', an 'economic migrant' or a 'returning foreign fighter'.[25] As Doty tells us, what is really going on in this situation 'is inextricably linked to the discourse within which it is located'.[26]

Similarly, I draw attention to the idea of representation since, like discourse, it provides a framework through which to access the concept of identity. For Kathryn Woodward, representations can be understood as 'symbolic systems' that produce meaning through which we make sense of the world and furthermore 'create the possibilities of what we are and what we can become'.[27] If we accept that practices of representation are central to the constitution of all forms of identity then we can begin to theorise the constitutive relationship between representations of identity and counter-terrorism policy. It is argued here that security policies are dependent upon representations of the threat, country, security issue or crisis that they are designed to address.[28] This is certainly the case for counter-terrorism policies that require contextualisation through ascription of meaning to the situation and to the key actors or objects of the policy. As Hansen explains, counter-terrorism policies, like foreign policies, 'articulate and draw upon specific identities of other states, regions, peoples, and institutions as well as on the identity of a national, regional, or institutional self'.[29] For example, this is captured by the way in which the emergence of Islamic State in Iraq and Syria has been represented as a direct and growing threat to Europe by the EU. In September 2014, senior EU officials briefed newspapers that a terrorist attack on mainland Europe by 'returning foreign fighters' was 'almost inevitable' and 'pre-programmed', with the situation 'totally out of control' and time to mount an effective response running out.[30] In this case, the construction of a radically threatening 'other', the 'returning foreign fighter', is key to both the constitution of the EU's identity and the legitimisation of and justification for an immediate counter-terrorism response.

Yet, whilst security discourses are traditionally seen as producing identity through difference from a radical and threatening 'other', it is important to remember that identity can also be constituted through varying degrees of 'otherness' from radical difference to less than radical difference.[31] With this in mind, I have restricted the argument in this book to a focus on the representational practices of the main policy-making institutions of the EU, the European Council and the European Commission. I contend that these representations can be identified within the various security and counter-terrorism policy documents produced by the EU. Where appropriate I also draw out and highlight the representational practices of other EU institutions and agencies, such as the European Parliament or Europol, as well as the representational practices of EU politicians and policy-makers. Whilst the focus of the analysis is primarily concerned with the representations contained within these texts, I recognise that the notion of 'text' should not be restricted to purely written material and can be used to describe various modes of discourse or representation that can include diverse phenomena such as images, signs or symbols.

This focus on texts requires some consideration of the notion of *intertextuality*, which according to Doty can be defined as 'a complex and infinitely expanding web of possible meanings'.[32] In essence, all texts refer to other texts that also refer to other texts and so on. In this way, representations that create subjects and their identities can never be traced back to a fixed or stable centre, they are always in the process of becoming. This idea is important for understanding counter-terrorism in the sense that whilst some features of contemporary counter-terrorism discourses, such as the 'fight against terrorism' or the 'war on terror', are novel and new, other aspects of these discourse draw on and exhibit similarities with earlier political and security discourses.[33] In terms of the EU's 'fight against terrorism' what I am suggesting is that the discourse is constituted through a variety of narratives, discourses, representations and identities drawn from wider political and security discourses that play a key role in justifying and legitimising the counter-responses it makes possible, which I shall demonstrate go far beyond a mere focus on responding to terrorism.

Securitisation

The third concept that requires consideration for the purpose of the research conducted in this book is the notion of 'securitisation'. The discussion so far has proceeded to consider how counter-terrorism policy can be understood as discourse, as well as the ways in which the formulation of counter-terrorism policy draws upon and is constituted through representations of identity. Before moving forward to outline the analytical techniques that were employed in order to complete this research, I want to return to the discussion of the relationship between counter-terrorism and security that was first raised in the introductory chapter. Counter-terrorism policy, like all security policy, has in the classical sense been associated with the state and understood in terms of material factors, such as military, intelligence or policing capabilities, which provide defence against objectively identifiable threats. Following Hansen, I see no extra-discursive realm whereby material, objective facts become known, rather 'for problems or facts to become questions of security, they need therefore to be successfully constructed as such within political discourse'.[34] This entails a quite different commitment from the dominant realist approach to security in International Relations (IR), which has effectively tied the meaning of security to the nation-state.[35] Instead, this research is based on the belief that counter-terrorism can more appropriately be understood as a discursive form of security practice that cannot be separated out from the representational processes of identity and threat construction that make counter-terrorism possible.

This commitment has implications for our understanding of the relationship between identity and security. As Campbell suggests, the identity of 'the state', or of any other actor for that matter, is performatively constituted through the inscription of boundaries that delineate a 'self' from an 'other', the 'domestic' from the 'foreign' or 'security' from 'insecurity'.[36] What this means then is that the identity of an actor is inextricably bound up with security discourse in the sense that security is constitutive of identity, not because an actor needs to be protected from threats to their security but because their identity depends upon them. As Hansen explains, 'threats and insecurities are not just potentially undermining of the state and things that could be eliminated, they constitute the state: the state only knows who and what it is through its juxtaposition against the radical, threatening other.'[37] As I will go on to show in the following chapters, the identity of the EU is constituted through its delineation with a variety of 'internal' and 'external' others that are constructed as security threats through the formulation of EU counter-terrorism policy. For example, in the chapters that follow I discuss the way in which the identity of the EU is delineated from that of the 'terrorist' other (Chapter 3), the 'migrant' other (Chapter 4) and the 'Muslim' other (Chapter 5). In the classic realist understanding of security, when something or someone is identified as a threat to security the threat itself takes on an objective quality that masks the specific, historical, contestable and *socially constructed* nature of the security threat. To identify (or socially construct) something as a security threat is, in the words of the Copenhagen School of security analysts, to 'securitise' it, to present it as a threat to a 'referent object' of security such as a state, a society, a community or an individual. This then is the *securitisation theory*.

The concept of 'securitisation' has been acclaimed as one of the most prominent and influential of new approaches to international security developed since the mid-1990s.[38] Ken Booth has described securitisation theory as a 'curious theoretical mixture of liberal, poststructural, and neorealist assumptions'.[39] It is a commonly used way of understanding how 'security' is invoked by state actors to legitimise the use of special measures, contentious legislation or policies and practices that would otherwise have been deemed illegitimate.[40] According to Ole Wæver, securitisation starts from the premise that there are no security issues in and of themselves, only issues that have been constructed as security issues by certain actors.[41] He argues that:

> With the help of language theory, we can regard 'security' as a speech act. In this usage, security is not of interest as a sign that refers to something more real; the utterance itself is the act. By saying it, something is done (as in betting, giving a promise, naming a ship). By uttering 'security' a state- representative moves a particular development into a specific area, and thereby claims a special right to use whatever means are necessary to block it.[42]

Alongside the Copenhagen School's use of the term securitisation, what Stuart Croft has called the 'strict' meaning of the term, rests another, more lenient understanding of securitisation as a term used simply to describe or indicate when a subject, topic or issue has become the focus of a debate in security terms.[43] One way of distinguishing between the two types of securitisation is to think about what the term 'security' does in either instance. In the Copenhagen School approach the commitment to understanding security as a speech act reveals the performative nature of the act itself.[44] In the strict sense of the term, securitisation goes beyond providing a language for speaking about particular issues but is instead productive of the social world of which it speaks. In contrast, the lenient understanding of securitisation simply refers to a 'descriptive' process of labelling something a security issue, which provides no space for reflection on the implications the labelling process has in practice.[45]

In this book I adopt a 'performative' understanding of securitisation similar to that of the Copenhagen School. However, I follow Croft by creating a 'post-Copenhagen' approach to securitisation, which can be applied in the context of the EU, for the purpose of interpreting processes of securitisation that are evident in the 'fight against terrorism' discourse. In order to do this, like Croft, I relax a number of the key commitments to securitisation that the Copenhagen School make and reconceptualise the approach in order to make it applicable in the context of the EU.[46] In its traditional formulation the Copenhagen School's approach is based on five assumptions about how the process of securitisation works in practice. First, securitisation is understood to be a 'speech act'. Second, the securitising actor must have the authority to make a securitising move. In the Copenhagen School approach this normally refers to a 'top leader' or a representative of the state but can also refer to other actors with discourse-making power. Third, a securitising move must represent a specific issue as an existential threat to the security of an in-group (i.e. the citizens of a nation-state, a particular community, etc.) so that it threatens their survival. Fourth, the securitising move may or may not lead to the imposition of extraordinary or special measures designed to protect the in-group from the security threat that has been identified. Fifth, a securitising move is deemed to have led to a successful securitisation only when the audience (i.e. the in-group) accept the securitisation as such.[47] This approach has come to represent the dominant understanding of what is meant by the term securitisation, thus resulting in much criticism and debate over its usefulness and applicability in different situations.[48]

Like Croft, I draw on this traditional conceptualisation of securitisation, relaxing the various elements of the theory in order to demonstrate how I understand securitisation to work in a more general sense, as well as to show how I intend to interpret securitisation processes as they manifest through the EU's 'fight against terrorism'. Applying the securitisation framework to the EU is not as simple as applying it in the context of the nation-state. As Andrew Neal explains: 'Although the statements and discourses of the EU institutions may be identifiable as securitizing moves, the relationship between that discourse and the reception, discussion, legitimation and actual-ization of policy proposals and changes is less clear.'[49] Therefore, in order to apply securitisation in the context of the EU the traditional understanding of securitisation theory requires a degree of reconceptualisation. The initial step in this process requires slight amendments to the first two commitments of securitisation theory: the idea that securitisation is solely a 'speech act' and that the securitising actor must be a state representative.

First, this means recognising that security can be understood as more than just a 'speech act'. Securitisation when applied to the EU, therefore, must also take account of the multiple ways in which the meaning of security is trans-mitted through non-linguistic processes that can include silence, images and the actual practice of security. Although the primary focus of this analysis is on the language of the EU's 'fight against terrorism' discourse, in essence all I am simply arguing here is that I recognise that instances of securiti-sation in the discourse itself cannot be reduced to language alone and are interrelated with intertextual practices of counter-terrorism. Second, this means an acceptance that the actor undertaking the securitising move can be more than just a representative of the state, such as a top leader or elite.

The EU is made up of a complex array of institutional actors that make it difficult to identify the securitising actor in the classic Copenhagen School sense of the term. Instead, it is argued here that in the EU securitisation occurs at multiple sites, which include, but are not limited to, all of the main EU institution (the European Council, the European Commission and the European Parliament); EU politicians and policy-makers, such as the High Representative for Foreign and Security Policy and the Counter-Terrorism Coordinator; various EU agencies, such as Europol, the Intelligence Centre (IntCen) and Frontex; as well as all of the various working groups and technical committees involved in the policy process.[50]

The second step in this process requires substantial change to the final three commitments of securitisation theory: the notion that securitisation must involve an existential threat to a particular in-group, that it necessitates the introduction of special or extraordinary measures and that the audience must accept the securitising move. The idea that security is all about existential threats and survival may be correct in certain exceptional instances but it does not reflect the myriad ways in which security manifests itself on a regular basis, especially in the EU. A more appropriate way of thinking about the process of securitisation is to think of security issues moving across a continuum; where at one end we have the everyday, routine and 'normal' politics of security and on the other we have the idea of 'existential threats' to security and the notion of 'survival'.[51] The point is that there is very little about EU security policy, and specifically EU counter-terrorism policy, that can be defined as extraordinary or exceptional. As Neal points out: 'Much of what is being done in the name of security is quiet, technical and unspectacular, in the EU intensely so, and just as much again does not declare itself to be in the name of security at all.'[52]

By understanding security as something constituted through more than the identification of existential threat, there is a knock-on effect on the commitment to securitisation through the introduction of special measures. As Didier Bigo and Anastassia Tsoukala explain, the politics of terror is not so easy to separate from the simple threat and a more general feeling of unease. Instead, this process of *(in)securitisation*, as they call it, is not limited to the successful political speech act that transforms the decision-making process through a politics of exception and the use of extraordinary measures. It is also, above all, about the 'mundane bureaucratic decisions of everyday politics', the 'management of numbers instead of persons' and the 'use of technologies, especially the ones which allow for communication and surveillance at a distance through databases and the speed of exchange of information'.[53] The 'fight against terrorism' is therefore understood to span the entire space between the two approaches to securitisation outlined here: 'between exceptional measures and the immediacy of action on the one hand and the ordinary administrative, police or insurance measures on the other'.[54]

Finally, there is the question of the audience. Traditionally, the audience of a securitising move is thought to be the public (i.e. the electorate or citizenry) of the particular state where the securitising move is being made. In a national context securitisation moves can be identified more clearly because statements or securitising moves by securitising actors are much more widely reported, especially by the media. By way of contrast the communications of the EU are very different from that of the national context. They are not widely reported and 'often little debated beyond a very narrow specialist audience'.[55] Any link between a 'European' public and the securitising moves of EU institutions, politicians or policy-makers is therefore far less certain. However, as Neal points out, 'there is no methodological prescription which says the "audience" of security discourses must be "public" '.[56] As such, the audience of EU securitising moves is taken here to consist primarily of the bureaucrats, experts and political professionals working within the field of security at the EU level. In this way, securitisation processes in the EU are thought to have a self-reinforcing logic, whereby the security professionals responsible for the formulation of security policies engage in debates on security issues in and between themselves.

To summarise then, discourse, representation and securitisation can be understood as interrelated articulatory or intertextual practices that provide the conceptual and theoretical basis for the analytical techniques that I use to explore the EU's counter-terrorism response. The texts that I focused on were the key counter-terrorism and security policy documents produced by the main policy-making institutions of the EU, the European Council and the European Commission, between September 2001 and March 2015. Where appropriate I also included analysis of important speeches by important EU politicians and policy-makers, such as the High Representative of the Union for Foreign Affairs and Security Policy and the EU Counter-Terrorism Coordinator, produced during that same time period.[57] These documents were supplemented by and interrogated through discussion of a multiplicity of intertexts drawn from a variety of other sources, such as the media and academic scholarship on terrorism. In order to research the ways in which discourses of security, terrorism, identity and the 'European' are interrelated, mutually constitutive and simultaneously in conflict requires what Shepherd has called 'methods that engage with the production of meaning within and between texts'.[58] I refer to these methods as *analytical techniques*, which I outline below.

Analytical techniques

In conducting a discursive analysis of EU counter-terrorism policy it is important to state that the method of analysis that I employ in this study can be considered an amalgamation of various methods of *discourse analysis*, i.e. techniques of analysis, which are based upon the way in which I understand discourse to work in a theoretical sense. This attempt at constructing a discourse methodology is complicated by the fact that the notion of discourse is utilised by different discourse scholars in various ways both theoretically and in practical application. According to Milliken, discourse theorising 'crosses over and mixes divisions between poststructuralists, postmodernists and some feminists and social constructivists'.[59] Yet, whilst it is true that discourse scholars share a number of common research interests, there are clear dividing lines between different approaches over how discourses are thought to work. This distinction is captured most vividly in the differences that exist between Critical Discourse Analysis (CDA) and the technique of analysis that I employ here, which draws on the understanding of discourse that is central to the Discursive Practices Approach (DPA) and Discourse-Theoretical Analysis (DTA) methods of discourse analysis.[60] In order to highlight this division and explain why it is important, I contrast the understanding of discourse employed here with that of Richard Jackson and other CDA scholars.

CDA is based upon an empiricist understanding of discourse, which treats discourse as an instrument that can be used by people for ideological purposes. According to Teun van Dijk, CDA is a type of discourse analytical research that focuses primarily on 'the way social power abuse, dominance, and inequality are enacted, reproduced, and resisted by text and talk in the social and political context'.[61] Drawing on and inspired by the Frankfurt School of Critical Theory (FSCT), CDA is concerned with revealing how specific groups or institutions deploy social power through an instrumental use of language and discourse.[62] We can see this line of thinking in Jackson's analysis of US counter-terrorism policy, whereby he speaks of the 'war on terrorism' as 'deliberately' and 'meticulously composed', as a 'carefully constructed discourse – that is designed to achieve a number of key political goals'.[63] As Shepherd explains, this instrumental approach to discourse assumes that 'meaning is … identifiable through the discourse, rather than constituted by the discourse'.[64] What this means then is that CDA scholars start from a position whereby discourses are assumed to have causal effects that can be identified through discourse.[65] As Jackson argues, 'the practice of counter-terrorism is predicated on and *determined* by the language of counter-terrorism'.[66] Whilst I have a great deal of sympathy for the overall direction of Jackson's argument about the carefully constructed nature of the 'war on terrorism' discourse and the instrumental use of language by elites, I do not view discourses as causative.[67] Discourses are constitutive, they are contingent, they are performative, they produce interpretive possibilities but they are not in any way causative or deterministic.

Instead, I view discourse as something that makes possible the social world and the actors within it, including their beliefs, values and identities. Rainer Hülsse and Alexander Spencer have suggested that to view discourse in this way is to view discourse as something 'above' individual discourse participants.[68] They argue that from this perspective actors have little in the way of agency, i.e. they cannot manipulate discourses for their own purposes, but rather actors are bound by discourse, with what they say and do 'to a large extent *determined* by discourse'.[69] Whilst I certainly agree that discourses constitute actors and structures, I prefer to view discourse as mutually constitutive of actors and the social world rather than 'above' them. Discourses structure the social world and the actors within it but importantly actors have agency to change the social world. As I explained earlier, this is why discourse can only ever fix meaning on a temporary basis; discourses exist in constant flux and are always in the process of trans-formation. Adopting this approach to discourse, the research conducted in this book concerns itself with investigating the EU's counter-terrorism response, the 'fight against terrorism', as a form of *discursive practice*. In order to do this I borrow techniques from Doty, Jackson, Hansen, Milliken and Shepherd to create a methodological framework, i.e. a series of ana-lytical techniques, for investigating the 'fight against terrorism' discourse. Below I outline the three-step process that I implemented for the purpose of conducting this analysis.

Step one: selecting the texts

The selection of texts raises a number of questions about what exactly should provide the basis for this study. To what extent should the focus of the analysis be solely on the official EU counter-terrorism discourse? Should it consist of an analysis of intra-institutional opposition to the dominant narratives that underpin the 'fight against terrorism' discourse or include discussion of other marginal discourses? Should it focus on the national counter-terrorism discourses of the EU member states and to what extent they contribute to the ongoing construction of the 'fight against terrorism' discourse? As such, the first step involved asking the question:

What are the key texts that constitute the EU's 'fight against terrorism' discourse?

According to Hansen there are two sets of issues that need to be taken into consideration before selecting texts for the purpose of a discourse analysis of a particular topic.[70] First, the majority of the texts should be taken from the time period under study but with the caveat that historical texts should be included in as far as they present the researcher with the opportunity to trace the genealogy of dominant representations within the discourse. Second, the selected body of texts should include a series of key texts that provide signposts for stabilisation or transformation of dominant narratives (or 'nodal points') in the discourse, with a broader array of texts used to support the existence of the dominant narratives interpreted and identified by the researcher.[71]

Following these considerations I gave priority to the analysis of a number of primary texts that were taken as representative of the construction of a common EU language of counter-terrorism. These key documents were made up of twenty-seven security and counter-terrorism policy documents formulated by the European Council and the European Commission across the period from September 2001 to March 2015.[72] However, where appropriate texts from other institutions and agencies of the EU, as well as the speeches and statements of EU policy-makers and politicians, were used to substantiate the arguments put forward about the construction of the 'fight against terrorism' discourse. Furthermore, a multitude of secondary sources was also utilised to supplement the analysis of the primary sources. Where appropriate other texts (such as academic books, edited collections, journal articles, think-tank policy documents, media reports, etc.) were utilised for the purpose of understanding the conceptual histories of key representations within the 'fight against terrorism' discourse, as well as to analyse the main strands of the discourse that were identified as central to the constitution of the EU's counter-terrorism response.

Step two: mapping the discourse

The second step involved direct engagement with the chosen texts in order to discover how representational practices operate linguistically and discursively within the selected texts. I refer to this step as 'mapping the discourse'. In this stage the primary focus of the analysis was to understand how the 'fight against terrorism' discourse has been constructed. In line with a commitment to discourse as outlined above, each text was subjected to a process of reading and interpretation through the application of three analytical questions. First, each document was read with the purpose of identifying the most significant aspects of the language of the 'fight against terrorism' discourse. This involved asking the question:

What are the key words, terms, phrases, labels, metaphors, beliefs and assumptions, which are central to each of the texts?

Second, having identified the key words, terms, phrases, labels, metaphors, beliefs and assumptions that make up the language of EU counter-terrorism policy, the analysis then considered how this language, taken together, can be understood as contributing to the creation of various themes or categories, what I call discourse 'strands', that are central to the constitution of the overarching 'fight against terrorism' discourse. This involved asking the question:

What are the main strands of the discourse?

In order to do this, all of the texts were considered as an intertextual whole with discourse strands identified as each text was subjected to the process of reading and interpretation. In this phase of the analysis I sought to identify the various forms of thought that give meaning to the concepts that are central to the 'fight against terrorism' discourse. This form of interpretive analysis of texts is quite different from quantitative approaches to discourse analysis that involve 'coding', wherein the researcher applies preconceived codes to the data, with all codes planned before the researcher has even collected the data. Instead, the discourse strands were 'revealed' as the texts were interpreted. The analysis employed a 'grounded theory' approach, whereby the analysis was assumed to be complete when adding new texts created no new thematic categories beyond those identified in earlier texts.[73]

The third part of mapping the discourse involved exploring the texts for articulations and instances of identity construction in order to understand how the discourse constructs particular subjects and objects within it. This then is a form of *predicate analysis*, whereby subjects and objects are constructed through linguistic processes of differentiation. As Doty explains, predication involves the linking of subjects and objects to certain qualities by affirming 'a quality, attribute, or property of a person or thing'.[74] This technique fits smoothly into the understanding of identity that underpins this research in that identity is accepted as constructed through processes of differentiation and linking. This involved asking the question:

How does the discourse construct a 'European' sense of self in opposition to a notional 'terrorist' other?

For example, I looked at the way the identity of the EU is affirmed through the use of particular words like 'peaceful', 'democratic', 'free', 'secure' and 'prosperous' and set in opposition to the threat of terrorism. The 'terrorist' other, by way of contrast, is constructed as someone who 'puts lives at risk', is 'dangerous', is 'willing to use unlimited violence' and is focused on causing 'massive casualties'.[75] In addition to constructing subjects and objects discourse also works to establish a relationship between subjects (the EU) relative to other subjects (the 'terrorist' other). This is called *subject-positioning*.[76] By adopting this technique I was able to identify the various ways through which terrorism is constructed and positioned as a threat to European society, as well as to reveal the representational practices through which the identity of the EU is (re)articulated, (re)produced and (re) enforced.

Step three: analysing the functioning of the discourse

The third step of the analysis was concerned with understanding how the 'fight against terrorism' discourse functions. Again, I employed three analytical questions to conduct this part of the analysis. As with the previous analytical question, all of the texts were considered as an intertextual whole. However, the level of the analysis in this step went further in that it utilised a variety of intertexts on terrorism and security, drawn from various sources other than the EU texts, to reflect upon the wider political and social implications of the discourse. This process of wider intertextual analysis and reflection was considered important in the sense that simply considering the EU counter-terrorism texts on their own would not be 'sufficient ... to shed light on the relationship between discourse and social processes'.[77] Indeed, the purpose of discourse analysis is to 'reveal as much about the contexts as about the text'.[78] The first task in this process then was to reflect on how the discourse structures meaning. This involved asking the question:

> How does the discourse structure and/or fix the meaning, logic and policy response to the groups and/or the events that it describes?

This analytical question was based upon putting into practice Milliken's suggestion that discourses should be viewed as productive of the world they create.[79] By this she means that discourses go beyond establishing a language for speaking about certain things, in this case terrorism and European security; they also make 'logical' certain ways of acting towards these phenomena. Discourses define knowledgeable practices by subjects (such as the EU) towards other subjects (terrorists) or objects (terrorism) that are articulated through the discourse, in this way rendering logical and proper certain practices and excluding or preventing other possible courses of action. As Milliken explains, this focus on discourse productivity has 'clear political and ethical significance' in that by identifying processes of discourse productivity the researcher can 'potentially denaturalize dominant forms of knowledge and expose to critical questioning the practices that they enable'.[80] Conducting this critical reading of the EU 'fight against terrorism' discourse involved asking the question:

> What knowledge and/or practices are legitimised by the discourse and what knowledge and/or practices are excluded by the discourse?

In this way, the study of counter-terrorism as discursive practice is intended to address discourse productivity by analysing how knowledge about terrorism structures the policy response, making certain courses of action possible and others unworkable or improper. However, simply considering what knowledge and/or practices are made possible and which are excluded is not enough on its own to complete this analysis. It is also necessary to understand how discursive practices are operationalised through policy implementation.

The final part of the analysis involved discussion not just of the types of counter-terrorism policies made possible by the policy discourse but also reflection on the practice of EU counter-terrorism policy. What this means then is that categories such as 'European' or 'terrorist' have to be operationalised through actual practices that constitute the subjects which the discourse produces. For example, the *European Framework Decision on Combating Terrorism* from 2002 is representative of a practice made possible through the articulation of the 'fight against terrorism' discourse, which has had implications for the practice of counter-terrorism in EU member states ever since.[81] It is the two processes together, discourse through practice and vice versa, that allows for wider processes of political and social transformation to occur. Identifying these transformations involved asking the question:

> What are the wider political and societal implications of the operationalisation of the policy discourse?

In particular, I was interested here in drawing out instances and processes of securitisation, in line with the understanding of securitisation outlined above, that have been made possible through the 'fight against terrorism' discourse. This involved going beyond the identification of discursive instances of securitisation, i.e. given the nature of counter-terrorism, an issue was assumed to be discursively securitised when it was reproduced within EU counter-terrorism policy or more general security policy documents and speeches, and reflecting upon how the practice of counter-terrorism and security constitutes the identity of the EU itself, as well as considering the implications these practices have for European society more generally.

Identifying and analysing the 'fight against terrorism' discourse

As I have argued thus far, the EU's 'fight against terrorism' is both a set of counter-terrorism practices and a language or discourse about terrorism that co-exist as part of an interrelated and mutually constitutive relationship. I view the EU's 'fight against terrorism' as a discourse constituted at a multiplicity of sites where knowledge about terrorism, as well as the identity of the EU, is (re)articulated, (re)produced and (re)enforced. The language or discourse of the 'fight against terrorism', therefore, is made up of an extremely large corpus of 'texts' that primarily consists of written and spoken material but can also be expanded out to include diverse phenomena such as images, signs and symbols. Following Jackson's observation about the 'war on terror' as constituted through various layers of language, I view the 'fight against terrorism' as a discourse that also consists of various layers.[82]

The first layer is made up of all of the main EU institutions, such as the European Council, the European Commission and the European Parliament, central to the policy-making and implementation process, as well as the various EU agencies, such as Europol, IntCen and Frontex, that have been tasked with or have developed capacities for responding to the threat of terrorism. It consists of all of the main action plans, official reports, research papers and policy documents produced by these institutions and agencies for the purposes of counter-terrorism and security policy. The second layer consists of all of the public articulations made by key EU politicians and policy-makers, such as the High Representative for Foreign and Security Policy and the Counter-Terrorism Coordinator, which include speeches, press releases, media interviews, and radio and television addresses. The third layer consists of a much wider degree of material and is without doubt the largest layer of the 'fight against terrorism' discourse. It includes all of the briefing papers, intra-institutional memos, emails, letters, websites, departmental guidelines or, in other words, every text produced by the people working in the EU, for its various institutions and agencies, who are involved in the formulation of EU counter-terrorism and security policy. The final layer consists of all of the symbolic representations of terrorism, including all of the images, symbols and other visual or non-linguistic signs (such as memorials for victims of terrorism), which play a role in communicating knowledge about terrorism.

In this analysis of EU counter-terrorism policy I chose to focus predominantly on the counter-terrorism and security policy documents formulated by the main policy-making institutions of the EU, the European Council and the European Commission, across the period from September 2001 to March 2015. I chose to focus on one part of the first layer of the discourse for

two reason. First, for practical reasons, to investigate every document produced by the EU, to consider all of the various national counter-terrorism
discourses of member states, as well as the media iterations on terrorism
that contribute to a more general European discourse on terrorism, would
have produced a large and unmanageable volume of data. Second, and most
importantly, as the main policy-making institutions of the EU, the European
Council and the European Commission, represent the primary source of
the 'fight against terrorism' discourse. It is important to note at this juncture that whilst it is possible to identify differences within and between the
main EU institutions in relation to how they interpret the threat of terrorism, especially in terms of the discourses on terrorism articulated in the
European Parliament, there remains a degree of consistency in the choice of
language, across all of the institutions, that reflects a collective EU understanding of terrorism.[83]

With this in mind, I studied over 200 texts produced by the EU during this
period, which were taken as a representative sample from thousands of such
texts available on the EU public register of documents.[84] Within this body
of texts I identified a smaller number of sources that were selected as key
texts according to two criteria. First, key texts were chosen if they contained
either a substantial focus on the conceptualisation of terrorism or a dedicated section on how best to respond to terrorism. Second, they reflected,
on the one hand, either instances of stabilisation or partial fixing of the
meanings in the various strands that constitute the 'fight against terrorism'
discourse or, on the other, instances or processes of transformation in the
discourse. I outline the reasons for the choice of these texts in greater detail
in Chapter 2, which offers a genealogy of the historical emergence of the EU
terrorism as threat discourse.

In order to chart these processes of fixing and transformation in the discourse, the time period selected was broken into three shorter time periods that reflected potential moments of discursive rupture.[85] The reason for
this needs a little more explanation. When we consider the interrelationship
between security and discourse the notion of *crises* assumes great importance. As Croft explains, 'Crises often mark the origins of a particular discourse, and a discourse that emerges with credibility in a crisis – in a sense,
that which gives the crisis meaning – will soon take on the hallowed status
of "common sense" amongst those concerned with the issues raised and
threatened by that specific crisis.'[86] This is certainly the case when we consider responses to terrorism, which are very much event- or crisis-driven.
When a 'terrorist' attack occurs there is a degree of introspection on the
part of the actor targeted and a new wave of counter-terrorism responses
inevitably follows. Taking this into account, the 'fight against terrorism'
discourse was analysed across three periods each punctuated by incidents

of terrorism. First, the post-September 11 period (11 September 2001 to 11 March 2004); second, the post-Madrid period (12 March 2004 to 22 July 2011); and third, the post-Breivik period (23 July 2011 to 11 April 2014). It should be noted that splitting the development of EU counter-terrorism policy in this way was done solely for the purpose of analysis and in reality the 'boundaries' between each period are actually very fluid. The dates for each period were selected since they represented important instances at which the main themes of the 'fight against terrorism' discourse were either reinforced or transformed. By dividing the formulation of EU counter-terrorism policy and the construction of the 'fight against terrorism' discourse in this way, it was possible to establish: what the main themes (or 'strands') of the discourse were; how the discourse has changed across the time period analysed; and what aspects of the discourse have remained constant. Having selected the texts that I considered to be representative of key moments in the ongoing construction or (re)production of the 'fight against terrorism' discourse, I began the process of investigating the discourse through the analytical techniques outlined above.

Conclusion

This book takes the theoretical commitments and the analytical techniques outlined in this chapter and applies them to the EU's 'fight against terrorism' for the purpose of reflecting upon the relationship between the discursive construction of the threat of terrorism and the practice of EU counter-terrorism policy. Through this study I aim to encourage critical interpretation, analysis and reflection on the perceived terrorist threat to Europe, as well as the actual counter-terrorism and security policies made possible as a result of the articulation of that threat. In doing so I hope to challenge the 'conventional wisdom' of Western counter-terrorism that has simultaneously been reproduced through and come to underpin the EU response to terrorism. Following Shepherd, I view the purpose of discourse analysis to 'identify, problematize and challenge' dominant forms of knowledge and to demonstrate how this knowledge is both contingent and political rather than objective 'truth' that exists outside of the social context within which this knowledge has been created.[87] This is certainly the case with terrorism, where much of contemporary knowledge about terrorism is assumed to be fact. I intend to destabilise and disrupt this dominant knowledge about terrorism not to reveal the 'truth' about terrorism and responses to it but rather to reveal how it orders society through the practice of that knowledge. In doing so, I recognise that the analysis that I offer is itself an interpretation and that any claim I make is also 'contingent and open to challenge'.[88]

In the chapters that follow I aim to show how the 'fight against terrorism' has been constructed by revealing the main words, terms and phrases that make up the discourse. I intend to show how identity is central to the process of discursively constructing the threat of terrorism and how it affects the type of policy response that is made possible as a result of that process. As such, I am concerned with identifying the multiple sites where knowledge about terrorism, as well as the identity of the EU, is (re)articulated, (re)produced and (re)enforced. The chapters are organised around various themes that I have interpreted as the primary strands of the 'fight against terrorism' discourse. Again, by adopting this form of analysis I intend to show how these strands play a key role in the structuring of the EU counter-terrorism response. Finally, throughout this investigation of the 'fight against terrorism' I reflect on how the threat of terrorism is invoked consistently to justify or legitimise the EU's growing role as an actor in the field of security, including the formulation of broader security measures that go far beyond a mere focus on counter-terrorism.

Notes

1 Roxanne Doty, 'Foreign policy as social construction: a post-positivist analysis of US counterinsurgency policy in the Philippines', *International Studies Quarterly*, 37:3 (1993), 297–320.

2 Oldrich Bures, *EU Counterterrorism Policy: A Paper Tiger?* (Farnham: Ashgate, 2011); Javier Argomaniz, *The EU and Counter-Terrorism: Politics, Polity and Policies after 9/11* (Abingdon: Routledge, 2011); Raphael Bossong, *The Evolution of EU Counter-Terrorism: European Security Policy after 9/11* (Abingdon: Routledge, 2012).

3 Doty, 'Foreign policy as social construction', 298. Emphasis in original.

4 For an in-depth discussion of interpretive approaches as applied to the discipline of International Relations, see Cerwyn Moore and Chris Farrands (eds), *International Relations and Philosophy: Interpretive Dialogues* (Abingdon: Routledge, 2010). For an intriguing empirical analysis of the formation of armed resistance movements in Kosovo and Chechnya using interpretive methods, see Cerwyn Moore, *Contemporary Violence: Postmodern War in Kosovo and Chechnya* (Manchester: Manchester University Press, 2010). For interpretive analyses of various case studies involving global security, see Mark Bevir, Ian Hall and Oliver Daddow (eds), *Interpreting Global Security* (Abingdon: Routledge, 2013).

5 Mark Bevir and Oliver Daddow, 'Interpreting foreign policy: national, comparative, and regional studies', *International Relations*, 29:3 (2015), 273–287.

6 James Der Derian, *Antidiplomacy: Spies, Terror, Speed, and War* (Oxford: Basil Blackwell, 2002), pp. 92–126, cited in Lene Hansen, *Security as Practice: Discourse Analysis and the Bosnian War* (London and New York: Routledge, 2006), p. 17.

7 Hansen, *Security as Practice*, p. xiv.

8 See Matthew Broad and Oliver Daddow, 'Half-remembered quotations from mostly forgotten speeches: the limits of Labour's European policy discourse', *British Journal of Politics & International Relations*, 12 (2010), 208; Iara Lessa, 'Discursive struggles within social welfare: restaging teen motherhood', *British Journal of Social Work*, 36 (2006), 283–298.

9 Roxanne Lynn Doty, *Imperial Encounters: The Politics of Representation in North–South Relations* (Minneapolis: University of Minnesota Press, 1996), p. 6.

10 Doty, 'Foreign policy as social construction', see 302.

11 According to Jacques Derrida, the meaning of a sign (i.e. a subject or object) is never self-evident, it is always constructed through processes of differentiation whereby one sign is privileged over another. See Jacques Derrida, *Writing and Difference* (London: Routledge & Kegan Paul, 1978).

12 Jennifer Milliken, 'The study of discourse in International Relations: a critique of research and methods', *European Journal of International Relations*, 5:2 (1999), 229.

13 Council of the European Union, *The Strategy for Combating Radicalisation and Recruitment to Terrorism*, 24 November 2005, 12781/1/05.

14 Broad and Daddow, 'Half-remembered quotations from mostly forgotten speeches', 208.

15 Doty, 'Foreign policy as social construction', 303.

16 Michel Foucault, *Discipline and Punish*, trans. Alan Sheridan (New York: Vintage, 1979), p. 23.

17 Ernesto Laclau and Chantal Mouffe, *Hegemony and Socialist Strategy: Towards a Radical Democratic Politics* (London: Verso, 1985), p. 11.

18 Doty, *Imperial Encounters*, p. 6.

19 See Milliken, 'The study of discourse in International Relations', 230.

20 Joseba Zulaika and William A. Douglass, *Terror and Taboo: The Follies, Fables, and Faces of Terrorism* (London: Routledge, 1996), p. xi.

21 Google Images, 'Terrorist', available online at: www.google.co.uk/search?q=terrorist&biw=1355&bih=646&source=lnms&tbm=isch&sa=X&ei=YvD2VKWcCoTqaP-HgpgP&ved=0CAYQ_AUoAQ (accessed 4 March 2015).

22 Home Office, 'Operation of Police Powers under the Terrorism Act 2000 and Subsequent Legislation: Arrests, Outcomes and Stops and Searches', *Home Office Statistical Bulletin*, 13 September 2012, HOSB 11/12, p. 45, available online at: www.gov.uk/government/uploads/system/uploads/attachment_data/file/116756/hosb1112.pdf (accessed 27 March 2014).

23 Laura J. Shepherd, *Gender, Violence and Security: Discourse as Practice* (London: Zed Books, 2008).

24 David Campbell, *Writing Security: United States Foreign Policy and the Politics of Identity* (Manchester: Manchester University Press, 1992), p. 5.

25 The example I use is a reimaging of a similar example used by Doty, which I have reinterpreted in order to make it relevant to this study. See Doty, *Imperial Encounters*, p. 5.

26 Ibid., p. 6.

27 Kathryn Woodward, 'Concepts of Identity and Difference', in Kathryn Woodward (ed.), *Identity and Difference* (London: Sage, 1997), p. 14.
28 Hansen, *Security as Practice*.
29 Ibid., p. 5.
30 Ian Traynor, 'Major Terrorist Attack Is "Inevitable" as Isis Fighters Return, Say EU Officials', *Guardian* (25 September 2014), available online at: www.theguardian.com/world/2014/sep/25/major-terrorist-attack-inevitable-isis-eu (accessed 27 March 2014).
31 See Hansen, *Security as Practice*, pp. 6–10.
32 Doty, 'Foreign policy as social construction', 302.
33 Richard Jackson, *Writing the War on Terrorism: Language, Politics and Counter-Terrorism* (Manchester: Manchester University Press, 2005), see pp. 154–155 on intertextuality and counter-terrorism discourse.
34 Hansen, *Security as Practice*, p. 30.
35 Realists focus on security as a primary concern of the nation-state, as something measured through material factors, such as military capabilities, and focused on responding to objectively identifiable threats. See, for example, Stephen M. Walt, 'The renaissance of Security Studies', *International Studies Quarterly*, 35:2 (1991), 211–239.
36 Campbell, *Writing Security*, p. 8.
37 Hansen, *Security as Practice*, p. 30.
38 See Ole Wæver, 'Securitization and Desecuritization', in Ronnie D. Lipschutz (ed.), *On Security* (New York: Columbia University Press, 1995), pp. 46–86; Barry Buzan, Ole Wæver and Jaap de Wilde, *Security: A New Framework for Analysis* (Boulder, CO: Lynne Rienner, 1998). It was Bill McSweeny who used the title Copenhagen School for the work being done by Buzan, Wæver and others; for more, see Bill McSweeny, 'Identity and security: Buzan and the Copenhagen School', *Review of International Studies*, 22:1 (1996), 81–93. The work of Buzan and Wæver has been acclaimed by, amongst others, Jef Huysmans and Michael Williams; for more, see Jef Huysmans, 'Revisiting Copenhagen; or, on the creative development of a Security Studies agenda in Europe', *European Journal of International Relations*, 4:4 (1998), 479–505; Michael Williams, 'Words, images, enemies: securitization and international politics', *International Studies Quarterly*, 47:4 (2003), 511–531.
39 Ken Booth, *Theory of World Security* (Cambridge: Cambridge University Press, 2007), p. 163.
40 Andrew Neal, 'Securitization and risk at the EU border: the origins of Frontex', *Journal of Common Market Studies*, 47:2 (2009), 333–356.
41 Wæver, 'Securitization and Desecuritization'.
42 Ibid., p. 55.
43 Stuart Croft, *Securitizing Islam: Identity and the Search for Security* (Cambridge: Cambridge University Press, 2012), p. 78.
44 On the performative nature of speech acts in relation to securitisation theory, see Thierry Balzacq, 'A Theory of Securitization: Origins, Core Assumptions, and Variants', in Thierry Balzacq (ed.), *Securitization Theory: How Security Problems Emerge and Dissolve* (Abingdon: Routledge, 2011), pp. 4–8.

45 Croft, *Securitizing Islam*, p. 78.
46 For an exceptional, theoretically coherent and easily accessible reconceptualisa-
    tion of the securitisation framework along critical constructivist lines, see Croft,
    Securitizing Islam, pp. 79–94. I draw on Croft's reconceptualisation of the secu-
    ritisation framework in order to inform how I understand securitisation working
    in the context of the EU.
47 Buzan *et al.*, *Security*, see pp. 23–26. As a caveat to this process, Buzan *et al.* do
    not argue that the special measures have to be adopted, just that the existential
    nature of the threat has to be argued and gain enough resonance in the minds
    of the audience that a platform can be made from which to legitimise the use
    of special measures or other steps that would have been impossible without the
    construction of such a threat.
48 A sample of critiques that highlight the shortcomings of the Copenhagen
    School's approach to securitisation theory includes: Thierry Balzacq, 'The
    three faces of securitization', *European Journal of International Relations*,
    11:2 (2005), 171–202; Monica Barthwal-Datta, 'Securitisation threats without
    the state: a case study of misgovernance as a security threat in Bangladesh',
    Review of International Studies, 35:2 (2009), 277–300; Lene Hansen, 'The Little
    Mermaid's silent security dilemma and the absence of gender in the Copenhagen
    School', *Millennium: Journal of International Studies*, 29 (2000), 285–306; Olav
    F. Knudsen, 'Post-Copenhagen Security Studies', *Security Dialogue*, 32:3 (2001),
    355–368; Williams, 'Words, images, enemies'.
49 Neal, 'Securitization and Risk at the EU Border', 336.
50 I also recognise that securitisation can occur in wider society through the media,
    religious figures and cultural commentators. Where appropriate the securitisa-
    tion of terrorism at these sites will be drawn upon to reflect upon their implica-
    tions for understanding the 'fight against terrorism' discourse.
51 On the idea of a security continuum, see Sarah Leonard, 'The "Securitization" of
    Asylum and Migration in the European Union: Beyond the Copenhagen School's
    Framework', paper presented at the SGIR 6th Pan-European International
    Relations Conference (Turin), 12–15 September 2007, p. 13; Rita Abrahamsen,
    'Blair's Africa: the politics of securitization and fear', *Alternatives*, 30:1 (2005),
    59; Jef Huysmans, *The Politics of Insecurity: Fear, Migration and Asylum in the
    EU* (London: Routledge, 2006), p. 72.
52 Neal, 'Securitization and risk at the EU border', 352.
53 Didier Bigo and Anastassia Tsoukala, *Terror, Insecurity and Liberty: Illiberal
    Practices of Liberal Regimes after 9/11* (New York: Routledge, 2008), p. 5.
54 Claudia Aradau and Rens van Munster, 'Governing terrorism through risk: tak-
    ing precautions, (un)knowing the future', *European Journal of International
    Relations*, 13:1 (2007), 98.
55 Neal, 'Securitization and risk at the EU border', 336.
56 Ibid., 337.
57 The criteria for the selection of 'main' texts is outlined below and in
    Chapter 3.
58 Shepherd, *Gender, Violence and Security*, p. 26.
59 See Milliken, 'The study of discourse in International Relations', 225.

60 For an explanation of DPA, see Doty, 'Foreign policy as social construction', 302–309; for an explanation of DTA, see Shepherd, *Gender, Violence and Security*, pp. 19–33.

61 Teun A. van Dijk, 'Critical Discourse Analysis', in Deborah Schiffrin, Deborah Tannen and Heidi E. Hamilton (eds), *The Handbook of Discourse Analysis* (Oxford: Blackwell Publishing, 2003), p. 352.

62 The 'Frankfurt School' is the label given to an intellectual project associated with the critical theorising of thinkers such as Max Horkheimer, Theodor Adorno, Herbert Marcuse and, more recently, Jürgen Habermas. Scholars who embrace FSCT in their analysis of security issues go beyond traditional approaches to the study of security and instead advocate a reconstructive agenda for Security Studies. In particular, they advance a normative agenda whereby it is argued security ought to be about human emancipation. For an introduction to FSCT in international relations and security studies, see Ken Booth, 'Security and emancipation', *Review of International Studies*, 17:4 (1991), 313–326; Chris Brown, 'Turtles all the way down: anti-foundationalism, critical theory and International Relations', *Millennium: Journal of International Studies*, 23 (1994), 213–236; David Held, *Introduction to Critical Theory: Horkheimer to Habermas* (London: Hutchinson, 1980); Richard Wyn Jones, *Security, Strategy and Critical Theory* (Boulder, CO: Lynne Rienner, 1999).

63 Jackson, *Writing the War on Terrorism*, p. 2.

64 Shepherd, *Gender, Violence and Security*, p. 17.

65 For a discussion of discourse as a causal mechanism where the meaning of causality is reconceptualised in order to make it compatible with discourse analysis, see Benjamin Banta, 'Analysing discourse as a causal mechanism', *European Journal of International Relations*, 19:2 (2013), 379–402.

66 Jackson, *Writing the War on Terrorism*, p. 8. Emphasis added.

67 I accept that it is possible for actors to use discourse for instrumental purposes but I would argue that a focus on the instrumentality of discourse obscures the extent to which actors are also themselves a product of discourse. This is why I prefer to interpret discourse as constitutive of actors, institutions and social structures rather than causal.

68 Rainer Hülsse and Alexander Spencer, 'The metaphor of terror: terrorism studies and the constructivist turn', *Security Dialogue*, 39 (2008), 571–592.

69 Ibid., 577. Emphasis added.

70 Hansen provides an in-depth methodological framework for the selection of texts for the purpose of discourse analysis. See Hansen, *Security as Practice*, pp. 65–78.

71 Hansen uses the term 'nodes' to refer to key texts that are frequently quoted within the broader array of intertextual sources selected for analysis. She argues that it is possible to identify multiple 'nodal' points within a given discourse. Ibid., pp. 74, 198.

72 The analysis of primary texts included the two Council 'Framework Decisions on Combating Terrorism' from 2002 and 2008 respectively.

73 For discussion of 'grounded approaches' to discourse analysis, see Kathy Charmaz, 'Grounded Theory', in Jonathan Smith, Rom Harré and Luk van

Langenhove (eds), *Rethinking Methods in Psychology* (London: Sage, 1995), pp. 27–49; Richard Jackson, 'Constructing enemies: "Islamic terrorism" in political and academic discourse', *Government and Opposition*, 42:3 (2007), 394–426.

74 Doty, 'Foreign policy as social construction', 306.
75 All of these words that are used to describe the EU and terrorism can be found in the European Security Strategy. See Council of the European Union, *A Secure Europe in a Better World: European Security Strategy*, Brussels, 12 December 2003.
76 Doty, 'Foreign policy as social construction', 306.
77 Jackson, *Writing the War on Terrorism*, p. 25.
78 Paul Simpson and Geoff Hall, 'Discourse analysis and stylistics', *Annual Review of Applied Linguistics*, 22 (2002), 136.
79 On 'discourse productivity', see Milliken, 'The study of discourse in International Relations', 236–242.
80 Ibid., 236.
81 'Council Framework Decision of 13 June 2002 on Combating Terrorism' (2002/475/JHA), *Official Journal*, L164, 22/06/2002.
82 For discussion of the various 'layers' of the 'war on terror' discourse, see Jackson, *Writing the War on Terrorism*, pp. 16–18.
83 For a discussion of the different type of discourses on the threat of terrorism that have emerged in just one institution, the European Parliament, see Anastassia Tsoukala, 'Democracy against security: the debates about counter-terrorism in the European Parliament, September 2001–June 2003', *Alternatives: Global, Local, Political*, 29:4 (2004), 417–439.
84 A simple keyword search for 'terrorism' on the public register of documents for each of the main EU institutions, the European Council, the European Commission and the European Parliament, returns over 500, 200 and 12,000 relevant documents respectively.
85 By discursive rupture I simply mean instances where dominant meanings in the discourse are, potentially, either reinforced or transformed.
86 Stuart Croft, *Culture, Crisis and America's War on Terror* (New York: Cambridge University Press, 2006), p. 1.
87 Shepherd, *Gender, Violence and Security*.
88 Ibid., p. 33.

2

Constructing the threat of terrorism in Western Europe and the European Union: a genealogy

Introduction

There can be little doubt that EU politicians and policy-makers view terrorism as one of the most pervasive threats to the security of the EU, its member states and its citizens. Speaking in 2008, the EU Counter-Terrorism Coordinator (EU CTC) Gilles de Kerchove made this case by arguing that 'terrorism remains the most significant actual threat facing democratic societies'.[1] Drawing upon a 'biological life' metaphor, de Kerchove went on to state that the threat of 'terrorism is like a virus ... eradicated in some places it is continuing to adapt itself to new conditions and draw strength from ineffective measures to control it'. He noted that this would require 'cooperation', 'work across national boundaries' and a 'really comprehensive approach to counter terrorism' in order to effectively combat the threat. What is interesting is that this language and logic has changed little in the past forty years. Speaking in 1978, after the murder of the former Italian prime minister Aldo Moro by members of the Red Brigades, an Italian terrorist organisation, the vice president of the European Parliament, Carlo Meintz, argued that 'from now on, no one is safe from the fury of terrorism'. He went on to suggest that the only way to defeat terrorism would be to 'develop closer links across our national frontiers', 'to create a European judicial area' and to organise a 'fight against terrorism', thereby drawing a clear link between the threat of terrorism and the policy response needed to combat it.[2]

Nevertheless, there is a conundrum at the heart of this perception of terrorism, which is as significant today as it was in 1978: the statistical probability of any citizen of an EU member state actually becoming a victim of a terrorist incident is extremely low. The annual Europol Terrorist Situations and Trends report (TE-SAT) reveals that since the events of 11 September 2001 there have been roughly 380 deaths in Europe as a result of terrorism, or 32 deaths per year, in the period between 2001 and 2015.[3] To put these figures in perspective, according to a European Commission press release from 2013 there were 28,000 road accident fatalities in the EU in 2012, or 75 deaths per day.[4] Richard Jackson has argued that the figures for terrorism deaths appear minuscule when compared globally to 'the 40,000 people who die every day from hunger, the 500,000 people who are killed each year by light weapons and the millions who die annually from diseases like influenza'.[5] Regardless, the perception remains that terrorism is the most significant threat facing democratic countries.

This raises a question as to why it is that politicians and policy-makers continue to exaggerate and embellish the threat of terrorism when the statistics suggest the threat is relatively insignificant. Jessica Wolfendale has suggested that 'the discrepancy between the actual statistical threat of terrorism and the claims of politicians is not based just on what terrorists might do now, but also on what they might do in the future.'[6] It is the imagined and illusory threat of the future terrorist attack, which may potentially lead to major casualties, that fosters the creation of an extensive counter-terrorism and security apparatus in the present. For example, the Europol TE-SAT reports are replete with references to the perceived threat to Europe from 'Islamist terrorists' who aim to cause 'indiscriminate mass casualties'.[7] Yet even if we accept the rather problematic category of 'Islamist terrorism' it is clear that the primary victims of this 'type' of terrorism are citizens of non-Western countries and not Europeans, with some estimates putting the number of victims 'as high as forty times the number of victims in Western countries'.[8] As Stuart Croft contends, in political terms there is no objective power to statistics where the loss of a particular number of people leads to a given policy response.[9] Indeed, the power of the terrorism-as-threat discourse is evident in its durability in the face of statistics to the contrary. This is not to imply that terrorism is not a threat. Events in Europe across the past fifteen years from the terrorist attacks in Madrid, in March 2004, to the attack on the French satirical magazine *Charlie Hebdo*, in Paris, in January 2015, suggest that an obvious threat exists. Rather, the aim here is to explore how the threat of terrorism has been invoked by politicians and policy-makers at different points in time to justify and legitimise EU integration in the field of security and cooperation on counter-terrorism issues.

In order to trace the emergence and evolution of the terrorism discourse in Europe this chapter provides a genealogy of the threat of terrorism discourse, as it has been articulated in Western European, European Community (EC) and EU security discourses, across two main periods: from the 1970s until the events of 11 September 2001 and from 12 September 2001 until April 2015. The purpose of a genealogy is to reveal the historically contingent and subjective nature of an object of knowledge such as terrorism.[10] As Fred Chernoff explains, a genealogy should be understood as a critical examination of the way in which the standard origins or the history of an object of knowledge are represented, including the different ways that people have portrayed it over time and for what purposes. Therefore, 'a genealogy is intended to uncover aspects of the subject that other accounts of its origins exclude', meaning that 'there is not just one alternative to the accepted history, there are many'.[11] By adopting this method, a genealogy can help to reveal the ways in which terrorism has been invoked at different instances throughout European history to provide justification and legitimisation for the development of new security practices at the European level. I restrict the genealogical analysis to the discourse of terrorism as threat as it has emerged in European security policy circles since a complete genealogy of terrorism as an object of knowledge would cover more ground than is possible in a single study. The chapter is divided into two sections.

The first section investigates the intellectual and practical origins of the threat of terrorism discourse in Western Europe between the 1970s and the events of 11 September 2001. The purpose of this analysis is to demonstrate the contingent, event-driven nature of the entrenched ideas and practices that have come to form EU counter-terrorism policy. It shows how, once constituted, terrorism came to be understood by European governments as predominantly a specific type of *internal* security threat, one that would first require the development of a transnational framework for cooperation on matters of cross-border law enforcement (Trevi), and later a holistic system of governance for the provision of internal security under the auspices of the EU's Area of Freedom, Security and Justice (AFSJ). However, although the primary focus of counter-terrorism since the 1970s has been to respond to the threat of terrorism through the development of internal security policies, EC/EU counter-terrorism policy has retained an external dimension. Starting with the creation in 1970 of a forum for EC member-state cooperation on foreign policy matters, European Political Cooperation (EPC), the chapter also considers the relationship between the terrorism discourse and EC/EU external security policy.

The second half of the chapter explores the (re)emergence of the EU's 'fight against terrorism' discourse following the events of 11 September 2001 and its subsequent evolution across three periods: the post-September 11 period, the post-Madrid period and the post-Breivik period. The purpose for this is threefold. First, to identify the 'key texts' that 'are frequently quoted and function as nodes within the intertextual web of debate', which provide the basis for the analysis conducted in this book.[12] Second, in line with the methodological commitments highlighted in Chapter 1, to identify the 'nodal points' within the 'fight against terrorism' where processes of partial fixing or transformation in the terrorism as threat discourse occur. Third, to identify the main 'strands' of the EU's 'fight against terrorism' discourse. The first half of the chapter draws on empirical evidence taken from a number of EC/EU policy documents and speeches by EC/EU politicians, whilst the second half of the chapter focuses specifically on the policy documents produced by the European Council and the European Commission. These representative texts are selected in order to demonstrate the relationship between the terrorism as threat discourse and the formulation of security policy, which, it is argued, has played a key role in *making possible* the establishment of new modes of security governance at the European level.

The emergence of European cooperation on counter-terrorism: 1970–92

Historically, one of the defining features of the EU's 'fight against terrorism' has been to treat terrorism as primarily, although not exclusively, an internal security threat. Traditionally, at both national and European level, it has been interior ministers who have taken the lead in the formulation of counter-terrorism policy, helping to explain why the EU has developed a deeply embedded perception of terrorism as crime, or as a form of criminal activity.[13] Initially, cooperation between European states in matters of internal security governance was limited to the strictly intergovernmental framework of the Council of Europe.[14] Since its creation the Council of Europe has agreed a number of conventions that the EC/EU considered so important to the development of its internal security sphere that they have subsequently been defined as part of the *acquis communautaire*.[15] These include the European Convention on Extradition (1957) and the European Convention on the Suppression of Terrorism (1977). Valsamis Mitsilegas *et al.* note that these conventions have 'become points of departure for the more comprehensive measures adopted by the EC member states or (later) by the EU' in the field of internal security.[16] Regardless of the progress made through the Council of Europe, much stronger incentives were needed for EC member states to move towards a greater level of cooperation.

These incentives arrived in the 1970s, during a period in which Western Europe was plagued by a wave of terrorism that effectively catapulted it 'to the top of all world regions in incidence of terrorist activity'.[17] The murder of 11 Israeli athletes at the Olympic Games in Munich in 1972, combined with heightening tensions in the Middle East, drastically increased the perceived threat from transnational terrorist organisations in Europe. During this period groups such as the Irish Republican Army (IRA), the West German Red Army Faction (the Baader–Meinhoff group), the Italian Red Brigades and the Basque separatists ETA intensified their activities. Thus it was a series of crises involving terrorism, and more specifically the threat of further incidents of terrorism, that provided the motivation for greater cooperation amongst European states on matters of internal security. At a Council of Ministers meeting in December 1975, a proposal by the UK Prime Minister Harold Wilson 'that Community Ministers for the Interior (or Ministers with similar responsibilities) should meet to discuss matters coming within their competence, in particular with regard to law and order' was adopted.[18] Tony Bunyan has noted that at the same meeting a proposal for the establishment of a specific working group to combat terrorism was also agreed upon.[19] This led to the formation of the Trevi group by the nine members of the EC in June 1976, created for the purpose of countering transnational terrorist activity in Europe and improving coordination between police forces of EC member states.[20]

It was therefore terrorism that provided the initial justification for the development of the intergovernmental Trevi group.[21] An even weaker institution than the Council of Europe, and remaining outside the EC institutional structure, it operated on an ad hoc basis. It consisted initially of only two groups: TREVI I, dealing with 'international terrorism'; and TREVI II, dealing with public order and the training of police forces. The Trevi group had its own telex system separate from EPC and the foreign ministries, for circulation amongst interior ministries, police forces and the security services.[22] Although initially set up to deal with 'international terrorism' and to help facilitate cooperation amongst European governments and their police forces, the focus of the Trevi group soon switched to other perceived security concerns. In the 1980s a third group (TREVI III) was set up to tackle drug trafficking and organised crime. Furthermore, by the end of the 1980s and the start of the 1990s the question of international migration had also found its way onto the Trevi agenda.

The establishment of these new ad hoc practices of European internal security cooperation were accompanied by a justificatory narrative emphasising the *extreme* threat of terrorism, reflected in a series of statements made at the time by EC politicians. In his opening address to the European Parliament in January 1975, the President Cornelius Berkhouwer asserted that 'the Western world is afflicted with a number of diseases that are a serious threat to its continued existence', of which he identified a 'constant increase in terror and aggressiveness' as one of the most prevalent concerns that 'threaten to destroy the structures of Western society'.[23] He warned that all EC member states could potentially 'fall victim to this terrorism', arguing that the threat would require all EC member states to work together to 'jointly protect ourselves, [to] put a stop to this terror and destroy it root and branch'.[24] This perception of terrorism, as a potentially existential threat, led the European Council at a meeting in July 1976 to issue a declaration on combating terrorism that was unequivocal in its condemnation of terrorism, and which emphasised the need for cooperation to counter the threat.[25]

The statement declared the taking of hostages by terrorists, for the purpose of putting political pressure on a particular state or government, to be an 'inhuman practice' that was 'completely unacceptable'. It further noted that it was 'in the interests of all governments to cooperate in combating the evil of terrorism'.

In a speech to the United Nations (UN) in September 1976, addressing the General Assembly in his role as the president of EPC, the Dutch Foreign Minister Max van der Stoel made reference to the threat of 'international terrorism' as a matter of deep concern for the nine members of the EC, which would also require an external dimension to the counter-terrorism response.[26] Van der Stoel echoed many of the claims made in the 1976 European Council declaration on terrorism, arguing that Europe had begun to witness an 'increasing frequency of acts of violence which endanger or take innocent human life'; noting that what was particular about these incidents was their 'international dimension'.[27] Acts of 'international terrorism', such as hostage taking, were described as 'one of the most heinous crimes against human life' and a form of 'insidious violence against the innocent', whilst the actors who engaged in this type of activity were thought to be 'evil' or 'inhuman'. Van der Stoel went on to argue that there were 'serious indications that we are confronted with a growing danger of a worldwide network of professional criminal terrorism ready to strike at any moment against any state and its citizens'.[28] In response, van der Stoel called for 'all governments' to 'set up effective world-wide measures to eradicate and prevent international terrorism' as well as promote 'international action' and 'cooperation' in this area.

At this point the EC interpretation of the threat of terrorism was characterised by four main assumptions. First, the threat of terrorism was thought to be not just 'domestic' but 'international' in dimension, therefore necessitating some type of coordinated pan-European response. Second, terrorism was viewed as an activity carried out by 'criminals'. Third, the argument that terrorism should be viewed as a threat to 'any state and its citizens' can be interpreted as a belief that the EC considered terrorism to be an act perpetrated by non-state actors. Fourth, running throughout this discourse on terrorism was the belief that terrorism should be viewed as a potentially existential or extreme threat to the EC and its member states. Importantly, the threat of terrorism was also portrayed as a threat to European 'values' like 'freedom', 'liberty' and the 'rule of law', marking the start of a nascent European (security) identity.[29] In contrast, the terrorists were described as 'evil' and 'inhuman', an immoral, illegitimate and radically threatening 'other' against which this nascent European identity would be produced and reproduced. There can be little doubt therefore that the terrorism as threat discourse shaped the counter-terrorism response of European governments, necessitating and *making possible* the creation of new intergovernmental and ad hoc structures designed to facilitate cooperation in this policy area.

Having provided the initial impetus for the creation of the informal modes of internal security cooperation established through the Trevi structure, an interesting transformation in the accompanying terrorism as threat discourse occurred. As cooperation progressed through the 1980s, with the security structures becoming more entrenched, terrorism was no longer referred to as a single identifiable threat but was invoked as one of a number of interlinked threats alongside 'organised crime', 'drug trafficking' and 'illegal immigration'.[30] Between 1987 and 1992 the EC and its various working groups on internal security formulated a number of policy documents that were designed to smooth the transfer of the existing informal security structures into the legal structure of the soon-to-be-established European Union. These included: the 'Palma Document', Madrid, June 1989; the 'Declaration of Trevi Group Ministers', Paris, 15 December 1989; and the 'Programme of Action', Dublin, June 1990.[31] In particular, the release of the Palma document in June 1989 marked the beginning of a transformation from ad hoc structures of cooperation to the more permanent structure of intergovernmental cooperation created with the establishment of the EU in 1993. The document highlighted the progressive development of policies designed to combat terrorism, organised crime and drug-trafficking, establishing their association with policing and immigration control. The repetitive and frequent reference to the series of interlinked security threats (terrorism, crime, drug-trafficking and illegal immigration) and the perceived need for coordination and cooperation of policy responses demonstrated the constitutive relationship between the articulation of security threats and the development of new security practices.

The pre-September 11 period: 1 November 1993–11 September 2001

On 1 November 1993 the Treaty on European Union (TEU), signed the previous year in February 1992, entered into force.[32] Operating under a pillar structure, the newly signed treaty established, for the first time, formal intergovernmental cooperation between member states in the fields of external security, Title V 'A Common Foreign and Security Policy' (CFSP), and internal security, Title VI 'Cooperation in the Fields of Justice and Home Affairs' (JHA). The CFSP and the field of JHA were established on the basis of integrating into the treaty framework the informal structures of security cooperation set up under EPC and Trevi respectively. In the TEU, where it made reference to terrorism it did so not as an area of focus for the CFSP but as part of one 'area of common interest' in the field of JHA, below asylum and immigration policy, control of external borders and judicial cooperation in civil and criminal matters, and as part of 'police cooperation for the purposes of preventing and combating terrorism, unlawful drug trafficking and other serious forms of international crime'.[33] Terrorism was not considered to be unique or to warrant its own policy provision but instead thought to be one of a number of similar internal security problems facing member states.

In 1995, at the European Council meeting in Madrid, the EU identified a series of 'challenges' that it would have to overcome in order to reach the goal of 'ever closer union', which it had set out as a priority objective under the TEU.[34] In particular, one of these challenges was to 'contribute to establishing the new European security architecture' with a requirement that the EU 'bring added value to all its citizens and to shoulder its responsibilities adequately, both internally and externally'.[35] Externally, the document provided the framework for 'a new transatlantic agenda' between the EU and the United States (US) focused upon responding to global challenges that included 'international crime, drug-trafficking and terrorism'.[36] The European Council also affirmed its commitment to the La Gomera declaration, which reiterated the EU's pledge to further develop cooperation between member states for the purposes of combating and preventing terrorism. The declaration rearticulated many of the assumptions about terrorism that had been expressed in earlier speeches and policy documents.[37] Yet, internally, whilst terrorism was seen as an issue, the focus had switched to the creation of 'an area of freedom and security' based upon responding to other security issues, such as drugs, organised crime, racism, immigration and asylum.[38] These developments gave credence to Monica den Boer's assertion that the work of Trevi had by this point become absorbed into the 'executive-driven Third Pillar hierarchy' and that terrorism had been 'demoted to a position amidst other internal security concerns, [alongside] illegal immigration and organised crime'.[39] In terms of the perceived threat from terrorism 'the issue ... had temporarily disappeared from the stage'.[40]

In relation to the goal of increased cooperation in the field of internal security, the 1997 Amsterdam Treaty was of particular importance in that it marked the creation of the EU's internal security sphere: the 'area of freedom, security and justice' (AFSJ). The treaty set out the objective of providing 'a high level' of safety for EU citizens through cooperation in police, judicial and criminal matters.[41] The treaty stated that preventing and combating crime – organised or otherwise – was essential in order to meet this objective. The treaty mentioned the threat of terrorism just twice, in relation to efforts to increase police and judicial cooperation. Where it was discussed, it was identified as one of a number of security problems facing the EU that also included 'organised crime' and 'drug trafficking'. It is therefore clear that the driving factor behind the creation of the AFSJ was not terrorism. Instead, the accompanying discourse in support of these developments, before the events of 11 September 2001, continually emphasised the need to combat 'organised crime' and better coordinate policy relating to 'criminal matters'. Terrorism was almost completely excluded from the discourse. The Presidency Conclusions from the European Council meeting in Vienna in 1998 support this line of argument in that whilst they set out the plan of action to be taken to ensure the successful development of the ASFJ, they did not mention terrorism as a key issue in the creation of this policy area.[42]

The Presidency Conclusions from the European Council meeting in Tampere in October 1999, also known as the *Tampere Milestones*, were absolutely central to the development of the EU as a security actor in that they provided the conceptual basis for the EU's internal security programme, with many of the measures later being adapted to form a central part of the EU's counter-terrorism policy.[43] The main aim of the Council was the deepening of cooperative action in the areas of policing, judicial cooperation, migration and asylum policy. Interestingly, the opening articles of the document outlined the values that the identity of the EU, as an emerging security actor in the internal sphere of security, would be based upon, stating that

> From its very beginning European integration has been firmly rooted in a shared commitment to freedom based on human rights, democratic institutions and the rule of law ... the challenge ... is now to ensure that freedom, which includes the right to move freely throughout the Union, can be enjoyed in conditions of security and justice accessible to all.[44]

The document set out a whole range of policy proposals including: a common EU asylum and migration policy; policy instruments for creating a genuine area of justice; a Union-wide fight against crime; and recognition of an external dimension to these internal policies. These proposals were identified as essential to ensuring the creation of an environment of security and justice for all EU citizens. Again, it is curious to note that terrorism was not mentioned in this document until Article 43 and was highlighted only in relation to the union's fight against crime, with a specific focus on the creation of joint investigative teams to combat human trafficking, drug trafficking and terrorism. This was the only time terrorism was mentioned in the whole document, supporting the line of argument that terrorism was, at this point, little more than an afterthought for the EU in the formulation of its internal security policy.

To summarise, in the periods before the events of 11 September 2001, the EU began to develop a nascent form of counter-terrorism policy through the creation of the Trevi group, which operated informally, outside of the treaty structure and focused primarily on terrorism as an internal security issue. Thus, originally it was the threat of terrorism, or more specifically 'international terrorism', which was invoked to justify and legitimise the creation of new security structures and modes of governance at the EU level. In terms of external security, terrorism was viewed as an issue but not one of primary importance given the more substantive nature of foreign policy issues facing the EU during these periods. Although the perceived threat of terrorism provided the initial justification for the development of the EU as an internal security actor, as time progressed and the new security arrangements were formalised as part of the legal structure of the TEU, the discourse switched from a focus on terrorism to other security concerns, such as 'organised crime' and 'illegal immigration'.

At the start of 2001, the EU viewed terrorism as one of a number of related internal security issues. It was not perceived to be a major problem and the phrase 'fight against terrorism' had yet to re-enter the vocabulary of the EU. The events of 11 September 2001, had a transformative impact on the formulation of EU security policy, both internally and externally, necessitating a perceived need for the development of an EU counter-terrorism policy. In particular, after these events the language of the 'fight against terrorism' was continually invoked to justify and legitimise the EU's role as a security actor both in terms of counter-terrorism policy specifically and security policy (internal and external) more generally. The following section develops this genealogy in two ways. First, it identifies the key texts that were selected for analysis, which when taken together, it is argued, constitute the EU's 'fight against terrorism' discourse, across the period from 11 September 2001 until 11 March 2015. Second, it traces the continued development of the terrorism as threat discourse as it is articulated in these texts.

The post-September 11 period: 11 September 2001–11 March 2004

The period following the events of 11 September 2001, witnessed a flurry of institutional activity that set the basis for the direction of the EU counter-terrorism response. I begin by showing how in the immediate aftermath of the terrorist attacks the terrorism as threat discourse was characterised by two main themes. First, the threat from terrorism was perceived to be predominantly an external threat, albeit one that required, rather counter-intuitively, the development of a series of internal security measures.

Second, the language adopted by EU politicians and policy-makers and contained in the various policy documents, action plans and legal texts was a language of emergency, which emphasised the necessity of swiftly implementing the various measures agreed upon as central to the EU counter-terrorism response. However, I go on to argue that by the end of the period the 'fight against terrorism' discourse had really begun to take shape, with the EU offering a more developed perception of what exactly the terrorist threat to Europe was thought to look like.

In response to the terrorist attacks the first action undertaken by the EU was to release two declarations, the first on 12 September, and the second, a unique joint statement by the heads of state of EU governments, the presidents of the European Commission and the European Parliament and the High Representative for the CFSP, on 14 September expressing solidarity with the US.[45] Both statements were quick to condemn the actions of the terrorists as acts of 'barbarism', 'savagery' and 'evil', whilst emphasising that the terrorist attacks were acts of violence 'against humanity itself' and 'directed against us all'. Importantly, the second statement outlined a series of internal and external measures that would require 'urgent decisions', such as 'accelerat[ing] the implementation of a genuine European judicial area ... in accordance with the Tampere conclusions', as well as representing the first instance in which the phrase 'the fight against terrorism' re-entered the vocabulary of the EU.[46]

According to Raphael Bossong, the European Commission in particular seized the opportunity presented by the terrorist attacks to position itself as the key actor in the formulation of EU counter-terrorism policy.[47] At a meeting on 17 September the Commission reached an agreement that two initiatives, which had been under preparation since 1999, would form the central pillar of the EU counter-terrorism response: the European Arrest Warrant (EAW) and the 'Framework Decision on Combating Terrorism'. The following day the Commission went on to release a strategy paper titled *Increasing the Capacity of the EU to Fight International Terrorism* that listed eighteen further areas of 'possible action' for coordinated EU efforts to combat terrorism.[48] Invoking the 'international' dimension of the terrorist threat, the document called for action in areas that had rather vague links to terrorism, including provisions on 'organised crime' and 'border control'. As Bossong points out, 'at least 14 of the 18 proposals went clearly beyond, or had rather tenuous links to, counter-terrorism'.[49] By 20 September the perception of an immediate and quite different type of terrorist threat led the JHA Council to agree upon a series of measures that reflected many of the objectives set out in the earlier proposal by the Commission.[50] The language was clear, the aim of the Council was to develop 'the necessary measures to maintain the highest level of security and any other measures needed to combat terrorism', with 'the seriousness of recent events' leading the EU to 'speed up' the creation of the AFSJ.[51] It was at this meeting that a whole range of measures were agreed upon, including the use of Europol and Eurojust for counter-terrorism purposes, the setting up of an EU Police Chiefs Task Force, improvements in intelligence cooperation, the development of an annual report by Europol on terrorism within the EU area – the *Terrorism Situations and Trends Report* (TE-SAT) – and proposals intended to disrupt terrorist funding, to name but a few. Beyond this, agreement was also reached on measures to be taken at EU borders.

On 21 September an extraordinary session of the European Council was held in which it was confirmed that the 'fight against terrorism' would, 'more than ever, be a priority objective of the European Union'.[52] The EU reaffirmed its commitment to and solidarity with the US, as well as highlighting five priority areas that would shape the 'European policy to combat terrorism'. These included: 'enhancing police and judicial cooperation', 'developing international legal instruments', 'putting to an end the funding of terrorism', 'strengthening air security' and 'coordinating the European Union's global action'. Importantly, the document established the threat as primarily an external one, stating that any counter-terrorism response by the US to the attacks in New York would be justified. The headline goals were the completion of the aforementioned EAW and the adoption of the common definition of terrorism. Interestingly, in addition to this the European Council reiterated the call of the Commission for the JHA Council to 'implement as quickly as possible the entire package of measures decided on at the European Council meeting in Tampere' that had been scheduled to be reviewed at the end of 2001.[53]

Given that the threat of terrorism had barely featured in any of the policy documents central to the creation of the AFSJ, this assertion that the *Tampere Milestones* needed to be implemented 'as quickly as possible' adds weight to Monica den Boer's argument that 'the terrorist attacks ... provided a window of opportunity for outstanding JHA business', which was taken advantage of by the EU to further develop its capacities as a security actor.[54] Throughout the formulation of EU counter-terrorism policy, during this initial period phrases such as 'at the earliest opportunity', 'speed up', 'as soon as possible' and 'implement as quickly as possible' were commonplace and contributed to a sense of emergency. This perception therefore *made possible* the development of a coordinated response to the threat of terrorism, as well as calls for the completion of the AFSJ and the implementation of various internal security measures that went far beyond the sole purpose of combating terrorism. Beyond a recognition that terrorism presented some type of external security threat to the EU that would require an immediate or quick response, exactly what the threat consisted of was at this early point less well defined. However, this began to change as a result of two developments. First, progress on the question of defining terrorism was made with the signing into law of the EU 'Framework Decision on Combating Terrorism', on 13 June 2002, which established a common EU legal definition of terrorism for the first time.[55] Second, having established a common legal definition of terrorism, the first text to offer a more comprehensive assessment of terrorism, identifying it as an explicit security threat, was the *European Security Strategy* (ESS) in December 2003.[56]

The ESS played a central role in articulating the EU interpretation of the terrorist threat, identifying terrorism as one of five key threats to the security of the EU; the others being proliferation of weapons of mass destruction (WMD), regional conflict, state failure and organised crime.[57] The ESS contributed to the construction of the 'fight against terrorism' discourse by offering a more developed perception of the terrorist threat identifying the various elements that I refer to as the 'strands' of the discourse. First, it defined the threat of terrorism as one of a number of 'new' and 'growing' threats, which were perceived to be more diverse, less visible and less 'predictable'.[58] Indeed, the document contained a reference to a catastrophic vision of the future where the 'new' terrorists could *potentially* be willing 'to use unlimited violence to cause massive casualties'.[59] Second, the strategy also introduced for the first time another discourse strand that was linked to the perception of terrorism as a 'new' and dangerous threat: that actual and potential terrorists may seek to acquire and use WMD.

This aspect of the terrorist threat was outlined more clearly in a document titled the *EU Strategy against Proliferation of Weapons of Mass Destruction*, which had been released two days prior to the ESS.[60] Third, the document constructed the 'openness' of European societies as a potential security challenge by stating that terrorism impacts upon 'the openness and tolerance of our societies' and 'poses a growing strategic threat to the whole of Europe'. Fourth, the ESS drew attention to a perceived need to combat the 'root causes' of terrorism. It stated that the 'current wave' of terrorism was 'global in scope' and related to 'violent religious extremism', noting that this type of terrorism 'arises out of complex causes' that include 'the pressures of modernisation, cultural, social and political crises, and the alienation of young people living in foreign societies', arguing that this type of terrorism should be acknowledged as emanating from Europe itself and recognised as 'part of our own society'.[61]

By the end of this period, the EU had begun to offer a more developed perception of the terrorist threat to Europe, with the 'fight against terrorism' discourse characterised by a number of themes that have remained constant throughout the formulation of EU counter-terrorism policy. These strands of the 'fight against terrorism' discourse are:

1. terrorism as a threat to the 'values' of the EU;
2. terrorism as a form of crime;
3. terrorism as an act primarily perpetrated by non-state actors;
4. terrorism as a 'new' and 'growing' threat;
5. terrorism as connected to 'violent religious extremism';
6. terrorists as seeking to obtain and use WMD or CBRN materials;
7. the 'openness' of EU society as an environment terrorists would seek to take advantage of;
8. the threat of terrorism as having both an internal and external dimension;
9. the threat of terrorism as requiring a coordinated EU response, including the development of various internal and external security measures.

Although these strands of the discourse have remained constant throughout the evolution of the EU's counter-terrorism response, the discourse has continued to evolve in relation to events. During this period two minor changes to the discourse could be identified. First, this period witnessed a move away from the language of emergency, a trait that was a central characteristic of the speeches given by EU politicians and the policy documents adopted by the EU in the immediate aftermath of the September 11 attacks. The policy documents in particular began to adopt a more technocratic language that emphasised the importance of the various internal and external measures suggested as the most appropriate responses to the threat of terrorism. Second, the EU perception of the terrorist threat evolved from one that viewed terrorism, in the weeks following the events of 11 September 2001, as primarily an external security threat, to a perception that the 'current wave' of terrorism was now 'part of our own society', and therefore a 'domestic' as well as an external threat that had important implications for the internal security of EU member states. This perception was seemingly confirmed by the events in Madrid on 11 March 2004.

The post-Madrid period: 12 March 2004–22 July 2011

The attacks in Madrid provided further incentive for the formulation of EU counter-terrorism policy. By this point a number of concerns had begun to develop amongst policy-makers over the direction of the policy. Only three days prior to the Madrid bombings Javier Solana, the High Representative for the CFSP, had finished an internal report on the EU's counter-terrorism response. The report identified three principle areas of concern with respect to the policy: member states were failing to implement EU agreements such as the EAW; the EU was lacking the resources to play an effective role in combating terrorism; and

coordination between EU officials working in the fields of law enforcement, foreign and defence policies was poor.[62] Although the Madrid
attacks did not directly lead to greater or quicker implementation of
policy, they were important in terms of refining the shared perception
of the terrorist threat. As such, the first policy document released in
the aftermath of the attack, the *Declaration on Combating Terrorism*,
aimed to improve policy cohesion and present a clearer unity of purpose.
The document did this by developing the EU counter-terrorism policy in
three key ways. First, agreement was reached on a solidarity declaration
designed to enhance the political legitimacy and cohesiveness of the EU's
counter-terrorism response. The second development was the establishment of the position of EU Counter-Terrorism Coordinator (CTC). The
third was to extend and revise the anti-terrorism Action Plan that had
to date provided the cornerstone of the EU's counter-terrorism policy.[63]

In December 2004 the European Council adopted the *Hague Programme*
as its new internal security programme, replacing the *Tampere Milestones*.
Since the Tampere Council in 1999, significant progress had been made in
relation to the development of the AFSJ. The agreement at Tampere provided the foundations for a common asylum and immigration policy, the
harmonisation of border controls and improved police cooperation, and
laid the groundwork for judicial cooperation on the basis of mutual recognition of judicial decisions and judgments. Yet, whereas the *Tampere
Milestones* invoked the threat of organised crime as a justification for the
development of the EU's internal security area, in the post-September 11 and
post-Madrid periods the real driving force behind increased cooperation in
this field has been the spectre of further terrorist attacks. This was made
clear in the opening preamble of the *Hague Programme*, which stated that:

> The security of the European Union and its Member States has acquired
> a new urgency, especially in the light of the terrorist attacks in the United
> States on 11 September 2001 and in Madrid on 11 March 2004. The citizens
> of Europe rightly expect the European Union, while guaranteeing respect for
> fundamental freedoms and rights, to take a more effective, joint approach to
> cross-border problems such as illegal migration, trafficking in and smuggling
> of human beings, terrorism and organised crime, as well as the prevention
> thereof.[64]

The focus on terrorism as a key justification for the need for the *Hague
Programme* was in marked contrast to the arguments put forth in support of the
Tampere Milestones. Discursively, the focus had shifted from problems such as
'organised crime' or 'illegal immigration', which although still important had
been downgraded, to a focus on the threat of terrorism. Terrorism was elevated

to a central concern within the internal security programme, with the document stating that 'a key element in the near future will be the prevention and suppression of terrorism', indeed developing a cross-border approach to 'repress', 'prevent' or 'suppress' the threat of terrorism was mentioned several times in the introduction to the document.[65] There were also a number of measures put forward under the section on 'strengthening security' that dealt specifically with terrorism, a change that was in contrast to the *Tampere Milestones*, which, as noted previously, made only passing reference to terrorism.

The *Hague Programme* witnessed several important changes in relation to the evolution of the 'fight against terrorism' discourse. It began to expand on and reinforce the idea that the internal and external aspects of security policy should be considered a unified field of action. It stated that in 'the field of security, the coordination and coherence between the internal and the external dimension has been growing in importance and needs to continue to be vigorously pursued'.[66] The document went on to make the argument that the EU considered 'freedom, justice, control at the external borders, internal security and the prevention of terrorism' to 'henceforth be considered indivisible within the Union as a whole'.[67] The document also contributed significantly to the discursive meshing of the perceived threat of terrorism with the need for more substantial migration and border control policies. Furthermore, beyond the claim that the security of the Union had 'acquired a new urgency' there was a move away from the language of emergency to a more holistic approach that recommended 'a clear need for adequate and timely implementation and evaluation of all types of measures in the area of freedom, security and justice'.[68] The one major change that occurred at this point was that the *Hague Programme* represented the first instance in which a security policy document placed some emphasis on formulating security policies that would be developed with 'respect for the basic values of the European Union and fundamental human rights'.[69] However, no specific policy provisions for the protection of 'fundamental human rights' were put forward.

The next major step in the development of EU counter-terrorism policy followed soon after the terrorist attacks in London on 7 July 2005. In November 2005, the EU released its first *Counter-Terrorism Strategy*, which cut across both the internal and external dimensions of EU security policy and articulated the strategic commitment that would govern the EU counter-terrorism response moving forward: 'To combat terrorism globally while respecting human rights, and make Europe safer, allowing its citizens to live in an area of freedom, security and justice.'[70] The strategy covered four elements of work: Prevent, Protect, Pursue and Respond. The main aim of the strategy was to add value to national counter-terrorism efforts by 'strengthening national capabilities', 'facilitating European cooperation',

'developing collective capability' and 'promoting international partner-
ship'. Each element of work contained a series of 'key priorities' that would
provide the focus for the policy response moving forward, as well as contributing to the development of the terrorist threat perception through the
articulation of different strands of the 'fight against terrorism' discourse.
The Prevent dimension of the EU *Counter-Terrorism Strategy* essentially
reproduced the main arguments set out in the *Strategy for Combating
Radicalisation and Recruitment to Terrorism*.[71] The strategy for the first
time framed the threat posed by terrorism as a problem implicitly linked
to the 'Muslim community' within Europe. The counter-radicalisation
strategy represented an evolution in the 'terrorism as connected to violent
religious extremism' strand of the EU's 'fight against terrorism' discourse
by claiming that: the threat of 'terrorism perpetrated by Al-Qa'ida and
extremists inspired by Al-Qa'ida has become the main terrorist threat to
the Union'.[72] This perception that the terrorist threat also had important
internal characteristics and was 'part of our own society' had seemingly
been confirmed with the terrorist attacks by UK nationals in London.[73] The
radicalisation strategy recommended that the most prescient way to tackle
this form of terrorism would be through the engagement of the 'Muslim
community' in Europe, as well as 'empowering moderate voices' within
that community. The language of preventing or 'combating radicalisation
and recruitment' into terrorism has since come to represent a central theme
of the 'fight against terrorism' discourse.

Similarly, the Protect dimension of the strategy referred to the objective
of protecting EU citizens and infrastructure from terrorist attack, reinforcing two discourse strands. First, the document stated that the EU must
seek 'to enhance protection of our external borders to make it harder for
known or suspected terrorists to enter or operate within the EU', rearticulating an assumption that terrorists might take advantage of the EU migration and asylum system.[74] Second, the assumption that terrorists might seek
to acquire and use chemical, biological, radiological and nuclear (CBRN)
materials was also strengthened. The concept of 'protection' against terrorism was therefore constructed as primarily achievable through border
security. The Pursue and Respond dimensions of the strategy emphasised
the need for cooperation and coordination of policy alongside the effective
implementation of policy proposals and legislative measures. They focused
on developing 'cooperation in law enforcement', 'exchange of information
and intelligence', 'mutual recognition of judicial decisions', surveillance
through the 'development of new IT systems' and the 'retention of telecommunications data' and 'tackling terrorist financing'.[75] Interestingly, many
of the policy proposals contained in the EU *Counter-Terrorism Strategy*
were policies designed as part of the EU's internal security programme, the

Hague Programme. These measures were now being reproduced as central elements of the EU *Counter-Terrorism Strategy*, with the 'fight against terrorism' providing the justification for their adoption and implementation by EU member states. The *Counter-Terrorism Strategy* also contained a commitment to promoting counter-terrorism through external action, which was strengthened through the *Strategy for the External Dimension of JHA*, released on the same day in November 2005.[76]

With the EU *Counter-Terrorism Strategy* in place and no significant terrorist attack occurring on European soil in the period directly after the London bombings in 2005, the next key 'fight against terrorism' policy document was not released until the end of November 2008. During this period the EU CTC was particularly active, giving a series of speeches and providing a number of reports to the European Council on the implementation of the *Counter-Terrorism Strategy*. Likewise, the annual Europol TE-SAT reports were also adding significantly to the development of the EU terrorism threat perception. However, it was the release of the *Revised Strategy for Combating Radicalisation and Recruitment to Terrorism* that really contributed to the continuing evolution of the 'fight against terrorism' discourse.[77] This document was significant in that it solidified 'counter-radicalisation' as the priority objective of the EU's counter-terrorism response, moving away from a specific focus on combating forms of terrorism inspired by Al-Qaida to a 'desire to combat all forms of terrorism' and suggesting that 'radicalisation and recruitment is a common factor of all ideologies that predicate terrorist action'.[78]

This was followed a month later in December 2008 by an updated version of the ESS, which identified the threats thought to represent the most pressing concerns for the foreign policy of the EU. The *Report on the Implementation of the European Security Strategy* set out how the EU could be 'more capable', 'more coherent' and 'more active', as an external provider of security, in a global environment characterised by 'increasingly complex threats and challenges'.[79] Whilst the focus of the document was primarily on progression of the implementation of the original ESS, it contributed to the evolution of the 'fight against terrorism' discourse in two important ways. First, it strengthened the claim that terrorists had sought to acquire and use WMD or CBRN, suggesting that over the previous five years the potential threat from terrorists acquiring WMD had 'increased'. Again, this demonstrates the way in which the EU terrorism as threat discourse has relied upon the imagination of catastrophic terrorist events as a way of justifying and legitimising increased cooperation in the field of security. Second, terrorism and organised crime were again grouped together as one universal threat that was stated to have 'evolved with new menace, including within our own societies'.[80]

In December 2009 the EU released the next iteration of it multi-annual internal security programme, for the period 2009–14, the *Stockholm Programme*. Like the *Hague Programme* that had preceded it, the focus of the new policy document was on the development of the EU's AFSJ as a whole.[81] However, it also had important implications for the continued evolution of the 'fight against terrorism' discourse. Terrorism was dealt with primarily under the section on 'a Europe that protects'. The headline policy goal of this 'political priority' was the creation of 'an internal security strategy' designed to tackle the interrelated threats of terrorism and organised crime. The document made frequent references to the threat posed by 'terrorism and organised crime' with the document treating the problems as synonymous with one another. The perceived threat of 'terrorism and organised crime' again played a powerful role in the justification of the policy proposals contained within the document.[82] Importantly, the document also outlined, for the very first time, a number of proposals that expanded on how the EU would promote the 'fundamental rights' of its citizens in relation to the measures that had been agreed upon and adopted in the field of internal security, including counter-terrorism, since the events of 11 September 2001.[83]

The last major documents produced during this period were the *Internal Security Strategy* (ISS), which was endorsed by the European Council in March 2010, and the European Commission's review of the main achievements and future challenges of EU counter-terrorism policy, which was released in July 2010.[84] This was followed in November 2010 by a series of proposals by the European Commission on how to ensure the successful implementation of the ISS.[85] The ISS identified a number of threats to the internal security of the EU that included: terrorism, all forms of serious or organised crime and natural or man-made disasters. The Commission communication set out five strategic objectives that would underpin the response to these threats. Terrorism was dealt with under the second strategic objective to 'prevent terrorism and address radicalisation and recruitment'. Interestingly, the document represented one of the first instances in which the EU began to focus not just on the threat from traditional 'organised terrorists' but also from so-called 'lone wolves', with the document citing the case of Umar Farouk Abdulmutallab, a Nigerian citizen who attempted to bomb a flight from Amsterdam to Detroit on Christmas Day in 2009, as representative of this 'evolving' threat.[86] The response to terrorism in the ISS was organised around three key actions. These were to 'empower communities to prevent radicalisation and recruitment', 'cut off terrorists' access to funding and materials and follow their transactions' and 'protect transport', with the aim of 'preventing future attacks'.[87]

Throughout the post-Madrid period the EU continued to cultivate a more holistic role as an actor in the fields of internal and external security, with the invocation of the threat of terrorism lending legitimacy to this development. Likewise, the EU's counter-terrorism strategy and the accompanying political discourse of a 'fight against terrorism' continued to develop. In particular, the nine discourse strands identified in the previous section as central to the 'fight against terrorism' discourse remained stable across the post-Madrid period. However, certain aspects of the discourse began to evolve with differing degrees of complexity. Most notably, the perception that the type of terrorism facing the EU since the events of 11 September 2001 was somehow 'new' and potentially more 'violent' than other past forms of terrorism was again strengthened, in particular through the sustained use of terms such as 'new', 'evolving', 'growing' and 'increasing' to describe the terrorist threat or the ongoing rearticulating of the threat posed by CBRN terrorism.

Significantly, major changes could be identified within four of the strands that constitute the EU's terrorism as threat discourse:

1. terrorism as perpetrated not just by organised groups but also by individuals or 'lone wolves' (linked to the 'new' and 'growing' threat of terrorism discourse strand);
2. terrorism and organised crime as intertwined threats (linked to the terrorism as crime discourse strand);
3. terrorism as occurring through processes of 'radicalisation' (linked to the terrorism as connected to violent religious extremism discourse strand);
4. counter-terrorism as requiring measures that respect 'human rights' (linked to threat of terrorism as requiring a coordinated EU response discourse strand).

First, a new type of terrorist threat, the 'lone wolf' or 'lone actor' who could potentially strike anywhere and at any time, was introduced. Second, whilst the EU continued to define terrorism as a 'criminal act', the overarching discourse of a 'fight against terrorism' began to merge with the 'fight against organised crime', treating each as mutually constitutive policy goals. This reflected the way in which the issues of 'terrorism' and 'organised crime' were treated by the EU as just two of a number of internal security issues of common interest in the pre-September 11 period. The discursive meshing of these two distinct areas of internal security presents a number of issues that shall be analysed further in Chapter 3. The third change related to the strand of the discourse that suggests there is a religious dimension to the threat posed by contemporary forms of terrorism, with the EU directing the focus of its counter-terrorism response towards the threat of 'violent radicalisation' and the development of a counter-radicalisation strategy to combat that threat. The final change was the introduction of a new strand of the 'fight against terrorism' discourse that has since helped to direct focus towards 'respect' for 'human rights' and 'fundamental freedoms' in the formulation of EU counter-terrorism policies.

The post-Breivik period: 23 July 2011–11 April 2015

The terrorist attacks in Norway by the right-wing extremist Anders Breivik in July 2011 provided context for the continued evolution of the EU's 'fight against terrorism' discourse. In this period the EU increased its focus on the threat posed by so-called 'lone actor' terrorists as a new area of attention for its counter-terrorism response. The key document here was a discussion paper put forward to the European Council from the EU CTC in April 2012 titled *Preventing Lone Actor Terrorism: Food for Thought*.[88] The document highlighted the cases of Breivik and Mohammed Merah, a French citizen of Algerian decent and the perpetrator of a series of terrorist attacks in Toulouse and Montauban in France during March 2012, as confirmation of this threat. It went on to explain that 'although lone actor terrorists only account for a small percentage of the total number of terrorist attacks', it was essential for the EU to facilitate 'further research' in order to develop a policy response that would 'reduce the threat or limit the impact' of 'lone actor' terrorist attacks.[89]

Noting the difficulty of defending against this type of terrorism, the document outlined a number of recommendations for dealing with 'lone actor' terrorism, primarily through the Prevent work strand of the counter-terrorism strategy. The threat from 'lone actor' terrorism was invoked to justify the continued expansion of the EU's counter-radicalisation programme, including the suggestion that public sector workers (such as health professionals) could be involved in the process of identifying those individuals within society who might be vulnerable to involvement in terrorism. Importantly, the document concluded with a section on the threat posed to Europe by 'foreign fighters and returnees', stating that a number of lone actors had travelled to 'conflict areas' or 'attended terrorist training camps' before returning to Europe.[90] This new dimension to the terrorist threat led the EU CTC to suggest eight areas of response that were specifically linked to strengthening EU border security, including through the use of the Schengen Information System (SIS).

Since 2012, and as a result of ongoing conflicts in countries like Yemen, Somalia, Iraq and Syria, the EU 'fight against terrorism' has become ever more focused on the threat posed by 'lone actors' and 'returning foreign fighters'. In May 2013 the European Council invited the European Commission to provide a communication on the updating of the EU *Strategy for Combating Radicalisation and Recruitment to Terrorism* to take into account these 'new' threats.[91] The third *Strategy for Combating Radicalisation and Recruitment to Terrorism* was released a year later in May 2014.[92] The strategy outlined a number of terrorist threats, including 'home grown terrorists, individuals supporting extremist ideology linked to terrorism, lone actors, foreign fighters and any other form of terrorism', which would need to be the focus of counter-radicalisation policies moving forward.[93] Significantly, the final section of the strategy called for the alignment of the 'internal' and 'external' dimensions of counter-radicalisation work, noting that 'domestic and international terrorism are often inextricably linked'.[94] The threat from returning 'foreign fighters' was again invoked to legitimise the further development and integration of 'border management' policies, including visa policies.

The ongoing conflict in Iraq and Syria, and the emergence of Islamic State in July 2014, appeared to offer further confirmation of the terrorist threat to the EU posed by 'returning foreign fighters', with evidence suggesting that a number of European citizens have travelled to fight in the conflict. The major fear that now drives the formulation of EU counter-terrorism policy is that European citizens who have travelled to fight for extremist groups in Iraq and Syria, such as Islamic State, could potentially return home and launch a terrorist attack against their country of origin. On 20 October 2014 the foreign ministers of the EU member states agreed upon a *Counter-Terrorism Strategy for Syria and Iraq, with Particular Focus on Foreign Fighters*, which was later updated in January 2015.[95] A terrorist attack in France against the satirical magazine *Charlie Hebdo* on 7 January 2015 also seemed to confirm another aspect of the evolving threat perception: that individuals or small groups inspired or 'radicalised' by the actions and messages of Islamic State were also now to be considered a major threat to the EU. These events led the JHA ministers meeting at the European Council to release the *Riga Joint Statement* on 30 January 2015, which declared the EU's ongoing commitment to the development of counter-terrorism policies designed to combat 'the growing threat posed by the phenomenon of foreign terrorist fighters'.[96] The final document selected for analysis was a guiding strategy for EU foreign policy in Iraq and Syria, the *Council Conclusions on the EU Regional Strategy for Syria and Iraq*, released on 16 March 2015, which set out the external counter-terrorism strategy the EU would put in place to respond to the threat posed by 'foreign fighters' in Iraq and Syria.[97]

In the post-Breivik period the EU perception of the terrorist threat continued to develop in new and different ways. A wave of terrorist attacks across Europe by individuals and small groups, a number of disrupted plots and the perceived threat posed by European citizens who had travelled to and returned from conflict zones all contributed to the perception of a 'growing' or 'evolving' threat. As such, three strands of the 'fight against terrorism' discourse were considerably strengthened during this period:

1. terrorism as perpetrated by 'lone actors' (linked to the 'new' and 'growing' threat of terrorism discourse strand);
2. terrorism as perpetrated by 'returning foreign fighters' (linked to the 'openness' of EU society as an environment terrorists would seek to take advantage of);
3. counter-terrorism as requiring counter-radicalisation policies (linked to threat of terrorism as requiring a coordinated EU response discourse strand).

There can be little doubt that the threat of 'lone actor' or 'returning foreign fighter' terrorism has come to represent the contemporary security threat that the EU is most concerned with. Since the emergence of Islamic State in July 2014 the EU has released a large number of policy documents and EU politicians have given a number of speeches detailing the threat and the suggested EU response to that threat. The European Council has also listed the 'response to foreign fighters' as one of its priority areas of action in the 'fight against terrorism'.[98] This perception of the terrorist threat has come to be framed through the lens of 'radicalisation', which is now viewed by the EU as the most appropriate and effective way of preventing future terrorist attacks. As well as this, the threat of 'returning foreign fighters' has also been invoked to legitimise the continued expansion and development of EU border security policy.

Conclusion

This chapter has offered a genealogy of the terrorism as threat discourse in Europe as it has been articulated through the formulation of EU counter-terrorism and security policy from the 1970s to the present day. The genealogy has helped to reveal the way that the EU has constructed the threat of terrorism as predominantly an internal security issue, albeit one with important external dimensions, which has led the EU to focus primarily on the internal dimension of the security response to terrorism. Indeed, throughout the chapter I have sought to demonstrate how the threat of terrorism was invoked at various points in the history of the EU to justify and legitimise the continued expansion of the EU's role as a security actor. Beyond this, the chapter had two further aims. The first aim was to trace the formulation of EU counter-terrorism policy and the evolution of the 'fight against terrorism' discourse from the post-September 11 period through to the present day. This was done in order to identify the 'nodal points' within the 'fight against terrorism' discourse (i.e. the key counter-terrorism policy documents) where processes of partial fixing or transformation in the terrorism as threat discourse have occurred. Across the period analysed, twenty-seven security and counter-terrorism documents were identified: these documents provide the basis for the discourse analysis of the EU's 'fight against terrorism' conducted in this book.

The second aim was to identify the different themes, or discourse 'strands' – articulated through the various counter-terrorism and security policy documents – that, it was argued, taken together, constitute the 'fight against terrorism' discourse. In particular, in the chapters that follow an argument will be made that many of the strands of the 'fight against terrorism' discourse are a reflection of a pre-existing 'accepted knowledge' about terrorism that can be critiqued in various ways. The following chapters now turn to an analysis of the discourse strands identified above in order to map further how they have been constructed and to analyse how they make sense of the world for policy-makers, politicians, academics and others influenced by anti-terrorist or counter-terrorism discourses, as well as the novel interpretations they provide for understanding and explaining EU counter-terrorism policy. Finally, it will be demonstrated throughout this analysis that the process of constructing the 'fight against terrorism' discourse has played an intrinsic role in the construction of the identity of the EU and vice versa.

Notes

1 Gilles de Kerchove, 'EU Policy in the Fight against Terrorism: From Formulation to Implementation', paper presented at 'World Summit on Counter-Terrorism: Terrorism's Global Impact', ICT's 8th International Conference, 8–11 September 2008, available online at: www.consilium.europa.eu/uedocs/cmsUpload/SPEECH_FOR_HERZLIYA_CONFERENCE.pdf (accessed March 2015).

2 European Parliament, 'Tribute to Aldo Moro', Strasbourg, 11 May 1978, available online at: http://aei.pitt.edu/44325/1/A7215.pdf (accessed March 2015).

3 The TE-SAT is based mainly on information contributed by the EU member states and from 'open sources'. The reports do not clearly state the number of deaths/fatalities, which can in part be explained by the lack of consistency in the reporting of these figures by the member states. Therefore the figures may be slightly inaccurate. The TE-SAT reports are available online at: www.europol.3europa.eu/latest_publications/37.

4 European Commission, 'Road Safety: EU Reports Lowest Ever Number of Road Deaths and Takes First Step towards an Injuries Strategy', press release, Brussels, 19 March 2013, IP/13/236.
5 Richard Jackson, *Writing the War on Terrorism: Language, Politics and Counter-Terrorism* (Manchester: Manchester University Press, 2005), p. 92.
6 Jessica Wolfendale, 'Terrorism, security, and the threat of counterterrorism', *Studies in Conflict & Terrorism*, 30 (2008), 78.
7 Europol, *TE-SAT 2009: EU Terrorism Situation and Trends Report* (The Hague, 2009), p. 19.
8 Rik Coolsaet (ed.), *Jihadi Terrorism and the Radicalisation Challenge in Europe* (Aldershot: Ashgate, 2008), p. 1.
9 Stuart Croft, *Culture, Crisis and America's War on Terror* (New York: Cambridge University Press, 2006), pp. 41–42.
10 On the genealogy of terrorism, see Michael Blain, *The Sociology of Terrorism: Studies in Power, Subjection and Victimage Ritual* (Boca Raton, FL: Universal Publishers, 2009), pp. 105–134.
11 Fred Chernoff, *Theory and Metatheory in International Relations: Concepts and Contending Accounts* (Basingstoke: Palgrave Macmillan, 2007), p. 160.
12 Lene Hansen, *Security as Practice: Discourse Analysis and the Bosnian War* (London and New York: Routledge, 2006), p. 74.
13 Geoffrey Edwards and Christoph O. Meyer, 'Introduction: charting a contested transformation', *Journal of Common Market Studies*, 46:1 (2008), 1–25; Richard Jackson, 'An analysis of EU counterterrorism policy discourse', *Cambridge Review of International Affairs*, 20:2 (2007), 233–247.
14 The Council of Europe is an intergovernmental organisation, which is separate from the EU. It is made up of 47 member states including all 28 EU member states. It promotes human rights, democracy and the rule of law in Europe.
15 The *acquis* is the body of law that binds all the member states together within the EU.
16 Valsamis Mitsilegas, Jörg Monar and Wyn Rees, *The European Union and Internal Security: Guardian of the People?* (Basingstoke: Palgrave Macmillan, 2003), p. 20.
17 Raymond R. Corrado and Rebecca Evans, 'Ethnic and Ideological Terrorism in Western Europe', in Michael Stohl (ed.), *The Politics of Terrorism*, 3rd edn (New York: Marcel Dekker, 1988), p. 373.
18 European Council, 'Summary of the Conclusions of the Meeting of the European Council Held in Rome on 1 and 2 December', *Bulletin of the European Communities*, 11 (1975).
19 Tony Bunyan, 'Trevi, Europol and the European State', in Tony Bunyan (ed.), *Statewatching the New Europe: A Handbook on the European State* (London: Statewatch, 1993).
20 It should be noted that meetings in this area were conducted in secrecy between 1976 and 1986. Therefore, information on the workings of these security structures is very limited. According to Tony Bunyan, the policies and practices adopted during this period were subject to little or no democratic scrutiny in

the European or national parliaments, with many of the policies developed 'in secret by Interior Ministry officials, police, customs, and immigration officials, and officers of the internal security services'. See ibid., p. 1.

21 The Trevi group was formally established by the Justice and Home Affairs ministers of the EC member states following a resolution in Luxembourg on 29 June 1976.

22 Edwards and Meyer, 'Introduction', 9.

23 European Parliament, 'Twenty-First Joint Meeting of the Members of the Parliamentary Assembly of the Council of Europe and the Members of the European Parliament', Strasbourg, 21 January 1975, available online at: http://aei.pitt.edu/34159/1/A643.pdf (accessed April 2015).

24 Ibid.

25 European Council, 'Session of the European Council: Conclusions', the European Council, Brussels, 12–13 July 1976.

26 Max van der Stoel, 'Speech by Mr van der Stoel, Netherlands Foreign Minister, at the Thirty-first General Assembly of the United Nations (New York, 28 September 1976)', in *European Political Co-operation*, 3rd edn (Bonn: Press and Information Office, Federal Republic of Germany, 1978).

27 Ibid.

28 Ibid.

29 This type of language punctuated the addresses to the parliament by Members of the European Parliament (MEPs) in 1978 after the murder of Aldo Moro. See European Parliament, 'Tribute to Aldo Moro'.

30 Incidentally, it should be noted that the first time the EC used the phrase 'fight against terrorism' in an official policy document was in the conclusions of the London European Council meeting in December 1986. See European Council, 'Session of the European Council: Conclusions', London European Council, 5–6 December 1986.

31 All of these documents are available in Tony Bunyan (ed.), *Statewatching the New Europe: A Handbook on the European State* (London: Statewatch, 1993).

32 The Treaty on European Union, 1992.

33 Ibid.

34 European Council, 'Presidency Conclusions', Madrid European Council, 16 December 1995.

35 Ibid., p. 9.

36 Ibid., Annex 10.

37 Ibid., Annex 3.

38 Ibid., p. 16.

39 Monica den Boer, '9/11 and the Europeanisation of anti-terrorism policy: a critical assessment', *Notre Europe Policy Paper*, 6 (2003), 1.

40 Ibid.

41 Treaty of Amsterdam Amending the Treaty on the European Union, the Treaties Establishing the European Communities and Certain Related Acts, 1997, p. 16.

42 European Council, 'Presidency Conclusions', Vienna European Council, 10–11 December 1998, 00300/1/98 REV.

43 European Council, 'Presidency Conclusions', Tampere European Council, 15–16 October 1999, 200/1/99. From this point on the 'Tampere Conclusions' will be referred to as the *Tampere Milestones*. The *Tampere Milestones* (1999–2004) were the first iteration of the EU's multi-annual internal security programme, which has since included the *Hague Programme* (2004–09) and the *Stockholm Programme* (2009–14).

44 Ibid., Articles 1 and 2.

45 Council of the European Union, *Declaration by the European Union*, CL01-053EN, 12 September 2001; Council of the European Union, *Joint Declaration by Heads of State and Government of the European Union, President of the European Parliament, President of the European Commission, High Representative for the Common Foreign and Security Policy*, CL01-054EN, 14 September 2001.

46 Council, *Joint Declaration*, para. 5.

47 Raphael Bossong, 'The Action Plan on Combating Terrorism', *Journal of Common Market Studies*, 46:1 (2008), 27–48.

48 European Commission, *Increasing the Capacity of the EU to Fight International Terrorism*, 18 September 2001, SEC (2001) 1429/3.

49 Bossong, 'The Action Plan on Combating Terrorism', 35.

50 Council of the European Union, *Conclusions Adopted by the Council (Justice and Home Affairs)*, Brussels, 20 September 2001, SN3926/6/01 Rev 6.

51 Ibid., p. 1.

52 Council of the European Union, *Conclusions and Plan of Action of the Extraordinary European Council Meeting on 21 September*, 2001, SN 140/01, p. 1.

53 Ibid., p. 2.

54 Monica den Boer, 'The EU Counter-Terrorism Wave: Window of Opportunity or Profound Policy Transformation', in Marianne van Leeuwen (ed.), *Confronting Terrorism: European Experiences, Threat Perceptions and Policies* (New York: Kluwer Law International, 2003).

55 'Council Framework Decision of 13 June 2002 on Combating Terrorism' (2002/475/JHA), *Official Journal*, L164, 22/06/2002. The framework decision was updated in 2008 after a proposal by the European Council, see Council of the European Union, *Council Framework Decision Amending Framework Decision 2002/475/JHA on Combating Terrorism*, Brussels, 6 November 2007, SEC (2007) 1424; 'Council Framework Decision of 28 November 2008 Amending Framework Decision 2002/475/JHA on Combating Terrorism' (2008/919/JHA), *Official Journal*, L330/21, 09/12/2008.

56 Council of the European Union, *A Secure Europe in a Better World: European Security Strategy*, Brussels, 12 December 2003. It should be noted that the ESS is based upon the text of a speech given by Javier Solana in May 2003. The speech and the text of ESS are very similar, with only minor differences in the use of language in each document.

57 Council, *European Security Strategy*, pp. 4–6.

58 Ibid., p. 3.

59 Ibid., p. 4.
60 Council of the European Union, *EU Strategy against Proliferation of Weapons of Mass Destruction*, Brussels, 10 December 2003, 15708/03.
61 Council, *European Security Strategy*, p. 3.
62 Daniel Keohane, 'The EU and Counter-Terrorism', *CER Working Paper* (May 2005), p. 18.
63 Council of the European Union, *Declaration on Combating Terrorism*, Brussels, 25 March 2004, 7906/04; Council of the European Union, *EU Action Plan on Combating Terrorism*, Brussels, June 2004, 10010/04.
64 Council of the European Union, *The Hague Programme: Strengthening Freedom, Security and Justice in the European Union*, Brussels, 13 December 2004, 16054/04, p. 3.
65 Ibid., pp. 2–4.
66 Ibid., p. 3.
67 Ibid., p. 4.
68 Ibid., p. 5.
69 Ibid., p. 21.
70 Council of the European Union, *The European Union Counter-Terrorism Strategy*, Brussels, 30 November 2005, 14469/4/05, p. 3.
71 See European Commission, *Communication Concerning Terrorist Recruitment: Addressing the Factors Contributing to Violent Radicalisation*, Brussels, 21 September 2005, COM (2005) 313 final; Council of the European Union, *The Strategy for Combating Radicalisation and Recruitment to Terrorism*, 24 November 2005, 12781/1/05.
72 Ibid., p. 2.
73 Council, *European Security Strategy*, p. 3.
74 Council, *Counter-Terrorism Strategy*, p. 10.
75 Ibid., pp. 12–14.
76 Council of the European Union, *A Strategy for the External Dimension of JHA: Global Freedom, Security and Justice*, Brussels, 30 November 2005, 14366/3/05.
77 Council of the European Union, *Revised EU Strategy for Combating Radicalisation and Recruitment to Terrorism*, Brussels, 14 November 2008, 15175/08.
78 Ibid., p. 2.
79 Council of the European Union, *Report on the Implementation of the European Security Strategy: Providing Security in a Changing World*, Brussels, 11 December 2008, S407/08.
80 Ibid., p. 1.
81 Council of the European Union, *The Stockholm Programme: An Open and Secure Europe Serving and Protecting Citizens*, Brussels, 2 December 2009, 17024/09.
82 The implications of this meshing of terrorism and organised crime will be considered in greater detail in the following chapter.
83 For a list of these measures, see Council, *The Stockholm Programme*, pp. 11–20.

84 Council of the European Union, *Draft Internal Security Strategy for the European Union: Towards a European Security Model*, Brussels, 8 March 2010, 7120/10; European Commission, *The EU Counter-Terrorism Policy: Main Achievements and Future Challenges*, Brussels, 20 July 2010, COM (2010) 386 final.

85 European Commission, *The EU Internal Security Strategy in Action: Five Steps towards a More Secure Europe*, Brussels, 22 November 2010, COM (2010) 673 final.

86 Ibid., p. 8.

87 Ibid., pp. 8–10 and p. 4.

88 Council of the European Union, *Preventing Lone Actor Terrorism: Food for Thought*, Brussels, 23 April 2012, 9090/12.

89 Ibid., p. 1.

90 Ibid., pp. 8–10.

91 Council of the European Union, *Draft Council Conclusions Calling for an Update of the EU Strategy for Combating Radicalisation and Recruitment to Terrorism*, Brussels, 15 May 2013, 9447/13.

92 Council of the European Union, *Revised EU Strategy for Combating Radicalisation and Recruitment to Terrorism*, Brussels, 19 May 2014, 9956/14.

93 Ibid., p. 4.

94 Ibid., p. 13.

95 Council of the European Union, *Outline of the Counter-Terrorism Strategy for Syria and Iraq, with Particular Focus on Foreign Fighters*, Brussels, 16 January 2015, 5369/15.

96 Council of the European Union, *Riga Joint Statement*, Brussels, 29–30 January 2015.

97 Council of the European Union, *Council Conclusions on the EU Regional Strategy for Syria and Iraq as well as the ISIL/Da'esh Threat*, Brussels, 16 March 2015, 7267/15.

98 See the European Union website: www.consilium.europa.eu/en/policies/fight-against-terrorism/foreign-fighters (accessed April 2015).

3

Constructing the 'terrorist' other: a 'new' and 'evolving' threat to the European Union

Introduction

This chapter builds on the genealogy of the European Union's (EU) terrorism as threat discourse that was conducted in Chapter 2, attempting to extend our understanding of the way in which the 'fight against terrorism' has been constructed. It does this by analysing four of the discourse strands in a detailed and thematic manner. This is done for four reasons. First, to explore how the four discourse strands contribute to a specific EU understanding of the threat posed by terrorism in the post-September 11 era. Second, to demonstrate the role that each strand of the discourse plays in the discursive construction of the radically threatening figure of the 'terrorist' other. Third, to highlight the way in which the identity of the EU is constituted in opposition to and through differentiation from the terrorist 'other'. Fourth, to show how, when invoked together, the various strands of the discourse takes on a performative quality in that they help to shape the type of policy that the EU conducts in response to the perceived threat of terrorism. It should be noted that although the four discourse strands analysed in this chapter are separated for analytical purposes, in reality the boundaries between each overlap. Therefore, although the four discourse strands are analysed in a thematic manner, it is important to recognise that they incorporate elements from other discourse strands identified in Chapter 2.

The first half of the chapter begins by mapping each of the four discourse strands: terrorism as a threat to the 'values' of the EU, terrorism as a 'new' and 'evolving' threat, terrorism as a form of crime and terrorism as an act perpetrated by non-state actors, in order to show how they help to construct the radically threatening figure of the 'terrorist' other. In doing so, I draw on representative examples from many of the documents identified in Chapter 2. I also highlight instances of securitisation and point out where the 'fight against terrorism' adopts the language of future-oriented threats, which I argue makes possible a precautionary approach to security. The second half of the chapter explores the functioning of the discourse, with a specific focus on how the discourse makes possible the practice of EU counter-terrorism policy. Drawing attention to the representations of identity that were prevalent throughout the texts analysed, I show how the EU has constructed itself as a particular type of counter-terrorism actor. I argue that the 'fight against terrorism' discourse makes possible a criminal justice-based approach to counter-terrorism, which reflects its own self-perception as a 'civilian' or 'normative' power. Significantly, I demonstrate the contested nature of the knowledge upon which the EU counter-terrorism discourse is based and reflect upon the 'silences' within the discourse. I conclude by considering some of the political and societal implications of the discourse, highlighting questions that arise over effectiveness and the consequences of the 'fight against terrorism' for human rights and civil liberties.

Terrorism as a threat to the 'values' of the European Union

Since the events of 11 September 2001, one of the most significant themes of the 'fight against terrorism' discourse has been the belief that terrorism was a threat to the values of the EU. From this perspective terrorism was viewed as more than just a material threat to the EU, its member states and its citizens; it was also a threat to the very ideals that the EU itself was founded upon. In particular, this strand of the discourse was characterised by the use of an emotive and condemnatory moral language that has been key to the construction of the identity of the EU and the creation of a radically threatening 'other' against which that identity has been affirmed and reaffirmed.

Throughout the texts analysed, terrorism was described as 'deadly', 'an assault', 'a challenge to the conscience of each human being' and 'barbaric'. The terrorists themselves were portrayed as a 'scourge' on society, as well as 'murderous', 'dangerous', 'lethal', 'ruthless' and 'violent'. In contrast, the EU and its allies were often described in positive terms that were in direct opposition to the 'terrorist' other, such as 'open', 'democratic', 'tolerant', 'multicultural', 'prosperous', 'secure' and 'free'. There were numerous instances in the texts analysed where the identity and the values of the EU were presented as vulnerable to the threat of terrorism. In the immediate aftermath of the terrorist attacks on 11 September 2001, the way in which the dilemma posed by terrorism would be constructed through the prism of identity, as a threat to the 'values' of the EU, was evident. The EU *Joint Statement* of 14 September 2001, spoke of the terrorist attacks as 'an assault on humanity', as an attack 'directed against us all, against open, democratic, multicultural and tolerant societies' and called on 'all countries' that shared these 'universal ideals and values to join together' to combat terrorism.[1] The *Conclusions and Plan of Action of the Extraordinary European Council*

Meeting continued this line of thought, describing the events as an attack on 'our open, democratic, tolerant and multicultural societies' and suggested the need for the creation of a 'global coalition against terrorism' that should consist of any country ready to 'defend our common values'.[2]

Equally, the *European Security Strategy* of 2003 described Europe as a place that had 'never been so prosperous, so secure nor so free', with terrorism presented as a direct and major threat to that prosperity, that security and that freedom.[3] Terrorism was constructed as a phenomenon that sought to undermine 'the openness and tolerance of our societies' and one that posed 'a growing strategic threat to the whole of Europe'.[4] Similarly, the EU *Counter-Terrorism Strategy* of 2005 presented terrorism as a threat to the 'values of our democratic societies and to the rights and freedoms of our citizens'.[5] The strategy stated that the EU would seek to develop counter-terrorism policies that would respect 'human rights', 'make Europe safer' and allow 'its citizens to live in an area of freedom, security and justice'.[6] Again, this type of language was evident in the amended 'Framework Decision on Combating Terrorism', from 2008, which demonstrated clearly how the 'fight against terrorism' discourse has served to construct an 'EU' self in opposition to a 'terrorist' other. The document stated that: 'Terrorism constitutes one of the most serious violations of the universal values of human dignity, liberty, equality and solidarity, respect for human rights and fundamental freedoms on which the European Union is founded.'[7]

This aspect of the discourse has remained remarkably consistent throughout the evolution of the 'fight against terrorism' discourse. For example, the *Riga Joint Statement* by the European Council from January 2015, which was released shortly after the terrorist attacks in France on the cartoonists of the magazine *Charlie Hebdo*, stated that the acts of terrorism had once again 'endangered the core values of EU'.[8] The document led the EU to reaffirm its 'unfailing attachment to the freedom of expression, to fundamental rights, to pluralism, to democracy, to tolerance and to the rule of law'.[9] This language is revealing in the sense that it shows the way in which EU identity has continually been produced and reproduced through the articulation of these values, which include 'liberty', 'equality' and 'respect for human rights', whilst the acts of terrorism engaged in by the 'terrorist' other have been constructed in direct opposition, as a 'violation' of those values and a threat to the identity of the EU.

Alongside the perception of terrorism as a threat to the 'values' of the EU has been the use of an emotive and condemnatory moral language to describe acts of terrorism and the terrorists themselves. Across all of the key documents released since the events of 11 September 2001, the EU has at different points referred to terrorism as 'acts of barbarism', 'savagery', 'deadly', 'an assault', 'horrific', 'violent', 'unjustifiable' and a 'scourge' on society, with terms and phrases such as 'faceless killers', 'fanatical', 'evil', 'heinous', 'extremist', 'murderous', 'dangerous' and 'criminal' used to describe the terrorists themselves. It is important to recognise two aspects about the use of this type of language. First, the use of emotive language has had a tendency to occur – and was more prevalent – in the immediate aftermath of a terrorist attack. For example, in the post-September 11 period *The Conclusions and Plan of Action of the Extraordinary European Council Meeting*, released on 21 September 2001, referred to the 'deadly terrorist attacks' as 'barbaric acts' that posed a challenge to 'the conscience of each human being'.[10] Similarly, in the period after the Madrid bombings in March 2004, the *Declaration on Combating Terrorism* described the acts of terrorism as 'outrages', using the phrase 'callous and cowardly' to describe the terrorists themselves.[11]

Second, the use of this type of emotive language has remained more prevalent in the speeches of EU politicians and policy-makers. For example, in the immediate aftermath of the London bombings in July 2005, Olli Rehn, the EU Commissioner for Enlargement, in a speech to the Institute for European Policy asked that 'the cowardly acts of terrorism in London last Thursday … be condemned by the whole civilised world', and furthermore stated that the terrorist attacks were 'a crime against humanity'.[12] Although the use of emotive words, terms and phrases to describe terrorism have appeared in the key policy texts with less frequency since 2004, this does not mean that this language has completely disappeared from the discourse, only that the EU has become more restrained in the use of such language in its key security and counter-terrorism policy documents. The EU's strategy for combating Islamic State and 'returning foreign fighters' demonstrated this, wherein it again invoked the civilisation/barbarian dichotomy by stating that the EU must do all within its power to combat Islamic State, a group that had 'committed barbaric acts against the peoples of Syria and Iraq'.[13] The perception of terrorism as a threat to the values of the EU has been underpinned by another strand of the discourse that has constructed terrorism as a 'new' type of threat.

Terrorism as a 'new' and 'evolving' threat

As I have suggested above, another of the more ubiquitous features of the EU's 'fight against terrorism' discourse in the post-September 11 period has been the idea that the contemporary terrorist threat to Europe was a 'new' threat that was somehow different from the 'old' forms of terrorism that occurred in the past. Whilst the EU recognised that terrorism was 'not a new phenomenon in Europe', the language that constitutes this strand of the discourse included multiple references to the threat of terrorism as something that was 'new', 'evolving', 'growing' or 'increasing'.[14] The 'new' threat of terrorism has also been continuously linked to the threat of weapons of mass destruction (WMD), as well as thought to be predominantly religious in nature and to occur through processes of 'radicalisation'. Since the start of the Syrian civil war in 2011, in the post-Breivik period, the 'new' and 'evolving' threat of terrorism has been linked to the emergence of 'lone actor' terrorists and is now focused predominantly on the threat posed by so-called 'returning foreign fighters'. I contend that this strand of the discourse can be understood as a clear representation of the process through which the EU has discursively securitised the threat of terrorism.

In the first few months after the events of 11 September 2001, the EU did not refer to the threat of terrorism as 'new'. The *European Security Strategy*, in December 2003, was the first document to frame the threat of terrorism as somehow 'new' and different from the terrorism of the past.[15] The document stated that whilst traditional forms of military conflict, defined as 'large-scale aggression' against any of the member states, was thought to be 'improbable', it was argued that 'Europe faces new threats which are more diverse, less visible and less predictable'.[16] Terrorism was considered to be the most prevalent of these threats, alongside organised crime and WMD. The document articulated a number of features that were thought to make the contemporary terrorist threat 'new' and more 'dangerous' than the terrorism of the past, in essence discursively securitising the threat. It stated that 'increasingly, terrorist movements are well resourced, connected by electronic networks, and are willing to use unlimited violence to cause massive casualties'. The threat of terrorism was assumed to be 'global in scope', to pose 'a growing strategic threat' and to have links to 'violent religious extremism'. This type of 'new' terrorism was considered to be 'dynamic', with the discourse making possible concerted European action through the claim that 'left alone, terrorist networks will become ever more dangerous'. The document also linked this 'new' form of terrorism to the threat posed by WMD, again articulating the imagined threat of the future terrorist attack. It stated that 'we are now, however, entering a new and dangerous period' in which a proliferation of these weapons may occur, and furthermore 'the most frightening scenario is one in which terrorist groups acquire weapons of mass destruction'.[17] In a speech to the US House of Representatives, the EU Counter-Terrorism Co-ordinator (EU CTC) even used the phrase 'the rise of the new terrorism' to convey the perceived gravity of the threat.[18]

This discourse strand of a 'new' and 'evolving' threat of terrorism has been strengthened in three ways in the periods since the September 11 attacks. First, the idea of 'new' terrorism was underpinned by a perception that the main terrorist threat to the EU in the post-September 11 period was from 'religiously inspired' groups such as Al-Qaida, who unlike the politically motivated groups of the past were willing to use 'unlimited violence' and were concerned primarily with killing as many people as possible. The EU counter-terrorism discourse constructed this type of terrorism as the main threat to the EU, stating in the *Strategy for Combating Radicalisation and Recruitment to Terrorism* that although 'Europe has experienced different types of terrorism in its history ... the terrorism perpetrated by Al-Qaida and extremists inspired by Al-Qaida has become the main terrorist threat to the Union'.[19] Accompanying the articulation of a religious dimension to the terrorist threat was since 2004 an ever-present assumption that the prevention of terrorism could be achieved through tackling the processes that lead to 'radicalisation and recruitment' into terrorism. Introduced first as a policy priority in the *Declaration on Combating Terrorism*, responding to 'radicalisation and recruitment' into terrorism has become the central most preventative dimension of EU counter-terrorism policy.[20] The counter-terrorism as requiring counter-radicalisation policies strand of the discourse will be explored in greater detail in Chapter 5.

Second, the discourse explicitly linked the 'new' terrorism threat to the dilemma posed by WMD. The *EU Strategy against Proliferation of Weapons of Mass Destruction* was particularly revealing in the sense that it demonstrated quite clearly the way WMD and terrorism have been discursively linked.[21] The document argued that there was a very real 'risk that terrorists will acquire chemical, biological, radiological or fissile materials', adding 'a new critical dimension to this threat', and furthermore 'the possibility of WMD being used by terrorists' on EU territory 'present[s] a direct and growing threat to our societies'.[22] Across the period analysed, the discourse articulated numerous references to the potential threat posed by terrorists in possession of WMD. For example, in 2009, the EU released the *EU CBRN Action Plan*, the aim of which was to strengthen chemical, biological, radiological and nuclear (CBRN) security in the EU.[23] The document set out a precautionary approach designed for the purpose of reducing 'the threat of and damage from CBRN incidents of accidental, natural or intentional origin, including acts of terrorism', with particular 'priority' given 'to the terrorist threat'.[24] The European Commission website clearly highlighted the future-oriented fear that underpinned this strand of the discourse, stating that 'There is a possibility that terrorist organisations might eventually turn to unconventional weapons, such as chemical, biological, radiological or nuclear (CBRN) materials, potentially leading to a high number of casualties and causing huge socio-economic damage.'[25] In 2012 the European Commission released a report on the implementation of the *CBRN Action Plan*, which made ten references to the threat of 'CBRN terrorism', including the use of phrases such as 'animal bioterrorism', 'nuclear terrorism' and

'CBRN terrorism'.[26] The document offered a review of the policies put in place for the purpose of 'CBRN security', with a particular focus on policies designed to protect and prepare against 'CBRN terrorism'. This discursive meshing of the threat of terrorism with proliferation of WMD has become a central element of the EU's terrorism as threat discourse.

Third, from 2005 onwards, there have been fewer direct references to the threat of terrorism as 'new', and instead more references to terrorism as a threat that was 'growing', 'increasing' or 'continually evolving'. The first report on the *Implementation of the Action Plan to Combat Terrorism* from the EU CTC to the European Council, in December 2005, captured this aspect of the 'fight against terrorism', demonstrating the way in which it was interlinked with other strands of the discourse, by stating that 'The nature of the terrorist threat facing Europe is evolving. In addition to the threat from outside, Europe is confronted with informal loose networks of extremists operating within its borders. Other challenges include the way terrorists use the Internet, and the efforts by some to obtain and employ non-conventional weapons.'[27] There are numerous examples of this emphasis on terrorism as 'evolving', which has contributed to the perception of con-temporary terrorism as a 'new' and different type of threat. The *Report on the Implementation of the European Security Strategy* stated that 'terrorism and organised crime have evolved with new menace'; whilst the *Stockholm Programme* argued that 'the threat from terrorists remains significant and is constantly evolving'.[28] Since 2011, the 'evolving' nature of the terrorism threat was thought to be confirmed by events in Europe and the Middle East with the emergence of 'lone actor' terrorists and so-called 'returning foreign fighters'. The EU CTC report from April 2012 on *Preventing Lone Actor Terrorism: Food for Thought* spoke of the 'continuing' threat from and the 'growth of the autodidact lone actor terrorist', clearly linking this threat to Al-Qaida and 'foreign fighters and returnees'.[29]

Likewise, the threat from 'returning foreign fighters' has come to form the central preoccupation of the EU with regard to the 'evolving' threat of ter-rorism. The 2014 TE-SAT report clearly stated that the EU was now faced with a 'growing threat from EU citizens, who, having travelled to conflict zones to engage in terrorist activity', might 'return to the European Union with a willingness to commit acts of terrorism'.[30] Again, this perception of the potential future risk from the threat of the 'returning foreign fighter' led the EU to develop a raft of reports, guidelines and strategies aimed at 'redu-cing the flow of individuals who may depart to Syria or Iraq to participate in fighting'.[31] The 2014 *Revised EU Strategy for Combating Radicalisation and Recruitment to Terrorism* was also significant in this respect in that it clearly linked the threat from 'returning foreign fighters' to efforts to combat 'rad-icalisation'.[32] The document suggested that because 'the means and patterns of radicalisation and terrorism' were thought to be 'constantly evolving', further work would need to be done to prevent the radicalisation of 'people who have been trained abroad (such as foreign fighters)'.[33]

Terrorism as a form of crime

Another key theme of the EU 'fight against terrorism' discourse has been the construction of an act of terrorism, in both a legal and a political sense, as a criminal act. The perception of terrorism as crime has remained consistent throughout the evolution of the 'fight against terrorism' discourse, reflecting how terrorism was understood during the pre-September 11 periods and was borne out by analysis of the key EU security and counter-terrorism policy documents. The relationship between terrorism and criminality was reinforced in two ways: first, by direct statements in policy documents and in speeches that terrorism was or should be considered a criminal act; and second, by the discursive meshing of 'terrorism' and 'organised crime' as similar activities that required similar counter-responses. In respect of both these techniques by which the relationship between terrorism and crime has been constituted, there are numerous examples that could be drawn from the texts analysed.[34]

In relation to the first technique, in the immediate aftermath of the attacks on New York in September 2001, the Justice and Home Affairs Council met to discuss certain measures to be taken in order to 'step up the fight against terrorism' within the EU. One set of proposals related to increasing judicial cooperation and the need for 'approximation of Member States' criminal laws with a view to establishing a common definition of a terrorist act and laying down common criminal sanctions'.[35] The social construction of terrorism as a criminal act was reinforced by the legal institutionalisation of this discourse strand in the EU 'Framework Decision on Combating Terrorism'.[36] For example, the framework decision identified efforts taken by the EU to 'deal with crimes committed or likely to be committed in the course of terrorist activities against life, limb, personal freedom or property'.[37] The decision also identified a list of intentional acts that would be 'defined as offences under national law', thereby criminalising those offences as acts of terrorism. In the introduction to the *EU Counter-Terrorism Strategy* there was a clear inference that terrorism should be considered synonymous with criminal activity, with the document stating that 'terrorism is criminal and unjustifiable under any circumstances'.[38] This line of reasoning was strengthened by the EU CTC, Gilles de Kerchove, who in a speech in 2008 argued that members should 'consider terrorism a crime – an odious crime – which should be prevented, prosecuted and punished according to the ordinary rules and procedures of criminal law'.[39] The EU's third multi-annual internal security programme, the *Stockholm Programme*, also contributed to the discursive construction of terrorism as crime by referring to terrorists as 'heinous criminals'.[40] In the post-Breivik period, the EU has maintained such an embedded perception of terrorism as crime that in 2012 it suggested that attending a 'terrorist training camp' abroad should be considered a criminal offence, with a recommendation that the 2002 'Framework Decision on Terrorism' be amended in order 'to make it a crime to attend a terrorist training camp in the EU or abroad'.[41]

In terms of the second technique, since the re-emergence of the 'fight against terrorism' discourse in September 2001 there has been a consistent meshing of the threat posed by 'terrorism' with the threat posed by 'organised crime'. In the initial aftermath of the September 11 attacks the threats posed by 'terrorism' and 'organised crime' were considered to be distinct enough to warrant their own policy approaches. The *European Security Strategy* identified 'terrorism' and 'organised crime' as two of five 'key threats' that the EU would face in the 'coming decades', stating with reference to 'organised crime' that in certain ways 'it can have links with terrorism'.[42] Since 2004, and in the wake of the terrorist attacks in Madrid, this meshing of the two threats has become more apparent, with terrorism, organised crime and responses to those threats now considered to be almost synonymous with one another. The EU's second internal security programme, the *Hague Programme*, reinforced this interlocking of the two threats by making numerous references to the need for a cross-border approach to deal with 'terrorism and organised crime' or the 'fight against serious cross-border (organised) crime and terrorism'.[43] This blurring of 'terrorism' and 'organised crime' as one holistic threat was further strengthened by the 2008 *Report on the Implementation of the European Security Strategy*, which identified 'Terrorism and Organised Crime' as one of four 'Global Challenges and Key Threats' to the security of the EU.[44] In 2012 a report by the EU CTC spoke of the need to develop policies directed at the 'nexus between terrorism and organised crime', with the term 'nexus' hinting that the EU believed that there exists some type of mutually constitutive relationship between organised crime and terrorism.[45]

Terrorism as an act perpetrated by non-state actors

Given the intergovernmental nature of EU counter-terrorism cooperation and the state-centric nature of policy initiated by the European Council, it was unsurprising to find that within the 'fight against terrorism' discourse acts of terrorism were constructed solely as acts perpetrated by non-state actors. This aspect of the counter-terrorism discourse constructed the 'terrorist' other as primarily a non-state group or individual through two techniques. First, there was continued and consistent reference to sub-state terrorist actors as the main terrorist threat to the EU; and second, by either failing or denying space within the discourse to include or define acts of state terrorism. It should be noted that although the EU placed some emphasis on combating state-sponsored terrorism, this form of terrorism was only defined with reference to the threat posed by those state sponsors who support acts of terrorism directed against the EU and its allies. It is argued that this element of the 'fight against terrorism' demonstrates clearly how EU identity is constituted through the counter-terrorism discourse, with particular reference to the construction of both an internal and external dimension to the terrorist threat.

In relation to the first technique, continued and consistent references to sub-state terrorist actors, there was a multitude of instances that could be identified within the texts analysed. From the initial move in September 2001 to formulate an EU counter-terrorism response, the 'fight against terrorism' discourse offered numerous references to the need for a state-based response to terrorist 'groups' or 'individuals'. The *Conclusions Adopted by the Council* from September 2001 referred to the importance of national state intelligence agencies in relation to the 'fight against terrorism', particularly with regard to 'disclosing possible terrorist threats and intentions of terrorists and terrorist groups at an early stage'.[46] The document referred to the development of 'national anti-terrorist arrangements' and the creation of 'lists of terrorist organisations', as well as working with the United States to assess 'the terrorist threat' and 'in particular the identification of terrorist organisations'. The *European Security Strategy* played an important role in strengthening this strand of the discourse.[47] The document stated that the 'open borders' of the EU and processes of globalisation had 'increased the scope for non-state groups to play a part in international affairs'.[48] The document emphasised the notion that the 'most recent wave of terrorism' was characterised by 'terrorist movements' that were 'well-resourced' and 'connected by electronic networks'. It also focused specifically on a particular terrorist group, Al-Qaida, noting that 'logistical bases for Al Qaeda have been uncovered in the UK, Italy, Germany, Spain and Belgium'.[49] The document also suggested that if sub-state terrorist groups were able to acquire WMD then 'in this event, a small group would be able to inflict damage on a scale previously possible only for States and armies'.[50]

This type of language has remained consistent throughout the evolution of the 'fight against terrorism' discourse. In the post-Madrid period, in the introduction to the 2005 *EU Counter-Terrorism Strategy*, for example, it was stated clearly that 'terrorism is a threat to all States and to all peoples'.[51]

Importantly, the language of 'radicalisation' has also contributed to the construction of terrorism as primarily a non-state phenomenon by drawing attention to the role of the individual in committing acts of terrorism. The 2008 report on the *Actualisation of the European Union Strategy for Combating Radicalisation and Recruitment to Terrorism* argued that 'the decision to become involved in terrorism is an individual one' and suggested in response the development of policies that would 'disrupt the activities of the networks and individuals who draw people into terrorism'.[52] Likewise, in the post-Breivik period the EU switched its focus to 'understanding the threat' posed by 'the emergence of self-starting "lone wolves" (or small groups) that have no organisational connections, but work entirely from material they find for themselves on the internet'.[53] The April 2012 report, *Preventing Lone Actor Terrorism: Food for Thought*, was also significant with regard to the strengthening of this discourse strand.[54] The document highlighted 'lone actor' terrorism and 'returning foreign fighters' as examples of individual sub-state actors that could potentially threaten the EU in the future. The May 2014 *Revised EU Strategy for Combating Radicalisation and Recruitment to Terrorism* provided a list of the types of sub-state terrorists threats thought to be the most threatening to the EU, including 'home grown terrorists, individuals supporting extremist ideology linked to terrorism, lone actors, foreign fighters and any other form of terrorism'.[55]

In relation to the second technique, where state terrorism was discussed within the policy discourse it was only ever to refer to instances of state-sponsored terrorism that could potentially be directed against the EU and its allies. This externalisation of the terrorist threat was most prominent during the earliest phase of the formulation of EU counter-terrorism policy, in the immediate aftermath of the September 11 attacks. For example, the European Council's *Conclusions and Plan of Action of the Extraordinary European Council Meeting* in September 2001 emphasised the need to punish 'the perpetrators, sponsors and accomplices' of the September 11 terrorist attacks by taking action that 'must be targeted and may also be directed against States abetting, supporting or harbouring terrorists'.[56] There was also reference to a re-evaluation of EU relations 'with third countries in the light of the support which those countries might give to terrorism', as well as the need to develop 'an in-depth political dialogue with those countries and regions of the world in which terrorism comes into being'.[57]

However, this framing of terrorism as predominantly an external threat, which occurred immediately after the terrorist attacks in September 2001, was to undergo an important discursive evolution. From 2003, with the release of the *European Security Strategy*, the policy discourse began to focus on both the internal and external dimensions of the terrorist threat.[58] Whilst direct threats of action or intervention against states 'abetting, supporting or harbouring terrorists' no longer appeared within the 'fight against terrorism' discourse, the external dimension of the counter-terrorism discourse continued to emphasise that there remained a potential threat of terrorism emanating from sub-state actors operating within third countries. For example, the *EU Counter-Terrorism Strategy* argued that since 'The current international terrorist threat affects and has roots in many parts of the world beyond the EU, co-operation with and the provision of assistance to priority third countries – including in North Africa, the Middle East and South East Asia – will be vital.'[59]

Similarly, a European Commission document from 2010, the *EU Counter-Terrorism Policy: Main Achievements and Future Challenges*, identified a number of regions that would require 'reinforced cooperation' between the EU and its counter-terrorism allies (such as the US). The document named a number of countries 'as common priorities in combating terrorist threats', including 'Afghanistan, Pakistan, Iraq, Yemen, Somalia [and] the Sahel region'.[60] In the post-Breivik period, with the emergence of Islamic State in Syria and Iraq, the perception of an external threat from terrorism, including potential state-sponsored terrorism, was seemingly confirmed and as such took on renewed importance. In January 2015 the EU released an *Outline of the Counter-Terrorism Strategy for Syria and Iraq*. The document again adopted the language of precaution and risk, focusing attention on minimising 'the risks to Europe and European interests ... from terrorism emanating from Syria and Iraq', ensuring 'the strategic defeat of ISIL/Da'ish and Jabhat al-Nusra, including of their violent ideology' and working 'with and in third countries that are significant sources of foreign fighters, particularly the Maghreb, or transit countries'.[61] The construction of the external dimension of the terrorist threat will be considered in greater detail in Chapter 4.

Analysing the functioning of the discourse

The previous section dealt with how the various interlinked strands of the 'fight against terrorism' discourse construct the 'terrorist' other. This section deals with the ways in which these elements of the discourse relate to the practice of counter-terrorism policy by offering a critical analysis of how the discourse functions. It does this in three ways: first, by considering the ways in which the different strands of the discourse structure the logic and policy response to the threat of the 'terrorist' other, as well as highlighting the ways in which certain security practices are legitimised; second, by revealing the contested nature of the knowledge that the various strands of the EU counter-terrorism discourse are based upon; and third, by reflecting on the wider political and societal implications of the operationalisation of the policy discourse.

Structuring the policy response, legitimising security practice

The first function of the discourse is related to two of the discourse strands identified above: the notion that the EU is a particular type of actor in the international system with specific 'values' that are threatened by terrorism and the EU's deeply embedded perception of terrorism as a form of crime. Taken together, these strands of the discourse serve to structure the EU approach to terrorism in terms of a criminal justice-based response. A critical reading of the 'fight against terrorism' discourse reveals that the EU approach to counter-terrorism reflects an EU self-perception of the type of actor it aspires to be; in this context the 'fight against terrorism' discourse contributes to the construction of the EU as both a 'civilian' and a 'normative power'. There is an extensive literature debating the concept of 'civilian power' or 'normative power' as applied to the EU.[62] On the one hand, the idea of 'civilian power' is used primarily to describe the external or 'international identity' of the EU, as well as to conceptualise the means and ends of EU foreign policy objectives, with the EU said to prioritise 'civilian' policy instruments over military means in order to achieve its goals. On the other hand, the conceptualisation of the EU as a 'normative power' is used to explain the way in which the EU has adopted particular 'norms' in the development of its policies, such as the pooling of sovereignty or the pursuit of human rights.[63]

The discourse contains numerous instances in which it reveals an approach that is supposedly based on and constitutive of a 'civilian' or a 'normative power'. For example, this primarily 'civilian' or norm-based approach to counter-terrorism was expressed in a report from 2011 by the European Parliament, which stated that the threat of terrorism 'Requires a globally coordinated response which fully respects human rights and fundamental freedoms; [and emphasising] that counter-terrorism requires a comprehensive approach based on intelligence, police, judiciary, political and – in some limited cases – military means.'[64] The expression of an approach developed in accordance with 'human rights' and 'fundamental freedoms', with a particular focus on an important role for the police and judiciary in the external dimension of EU counter-terrorism, is particularly revealing in this sense. This type of language was articulated frequently across all of the key texts analysed, with the 'fight against terrorism' representing not just the external projection of the 'civilian' or 'normative' ideals that underpin EU identity but, as I suggest below, representing the internal projection of that identity as well.

Similarly, the focus on terrorism as crime plays an important role in the functioning of the EU counter-terrorism response, differentiating it from that of the US 'war on terror'. As Henrik Larsen explains, 'the basic difference between the EU and the US on this issue has been the EU's tendency to frame the problem of terrorism as an economic, political and social problem', whereas the US has 'focused on terrorism as a military threat that could and should be addressed by military means'.[65] By framing terrorism as a criminal act the EU has at least ensured that terrorism would be dealt with through the criminal justice system, thereby avoiding the worst excesses made possible by the war-based discourse of the US. This war-based discourse has given rise to numerous practices that include the illegitimate invasion of other countries, torture, extraordinary rendition and extrajudicial or 'targeted' killings.[66] As was explained in the introduction, the reason for framing the EU response to terrorism in this way can be traced back to the key role of interior ministers in the policy-making process and the past experiences of key member states, such as France, Germany, Italy, Spain and the United Kingdom (UK), who have historically had to deal with terrorism as an internal or domestic security threat. The past experiences of internal security cooperation between EC/EU countries through the forum of Trevi made possible the criminal justice-based approach adopted by the EU. Furthermore, in the cooperative process of formulating a counter-terrorism response, the 'fight against terrorism' has come to represent a holistic security response centred on the ideals that are assumed to be constitutive of EU identity and that are a reflection of the EU's own self-perception as a 'civilian' or 'normative power'.

The second function of the 'fight against terrorism' discourse is that it provides a dominant discursive framework through which the problem of terrorism has been interpreted. From this perspective it can be observed that the overarching discourse of a 'fight against terrorism' constructs the threat of terrorism in a particular way. The 'terrorist' other is potentially: a 'criminal' with links to 'organised crime'; a 'new' and 'evolving' type of threat, which is predominantly 'religious' in nature; or a non-state actor, a member of a group or an individual, such as a 'lone actor' or a 'returning foreign fighter'. Flowing from this is a perception that the 'new' type of terrorist is committed to inflicting 'massive casualties' on European societies, possibly through the acquisition and application of WMD or CBRN materials. As was noted in Chapter 1, each of these strands that make up the 'fight against terrorism' discourse are not 'new' but reflect an 'accepted knowledge' or 'conventional wisdom' about terrorism.[67] The focus on the 'terrorist' other as a 'new' and constantly 'evolving' threat, in the post-September 11 security environment, can be viewed as the key unifying element that helps to tie the various strands of the 'fight against terrorism' discourse together.

Additionally, within this threat discourse, the EU has adopted an approach structured around the future-oriented fear of potential terrorist attacks. As I have shown in the analysis above, the policy documents contain various references to imagined scenarios of potentially devastating terrorist events. As well as this, in the documents analysed there were multiple references to the need to adopt measures to reduce the 'risk' of further attacks. In this way, the figure of the 'terrorist' other has made possible EU practices of counter-terrorism that are representative of precautionary responses to risk.[68] By framing terrorism in this way, the discourse has strengthened the political legitimacy of the EU as an important security actor responsible for ensuring the security of EU citizens.

A third function of the discourse is that it provides legitimacy to the practice of security and the EU's growing role as a security actor. What this means then is that in the context of EU policy-making, the threat of terrorism has provided the basis not just for the emergence of an EU counter-terrorism response but for the furtherance of the EU's broader security agenda. In this context, the threat of terrorism has been invoked in order to push through a wide range of security policies that are not limited to counter-terrorism. According to Geoffrey Edwards and Christoph Meyer, the belief that the EU was confronted with a 'new' type of terrorist threat coupled with the 'the window of opportunity [that presented itself] after 9/11 (and [the] subsequent attacks in Madrid and London)' provided the political will 'to accelerate and eventually pass stalled legislation in JHA'.[69] For example, in the immediate aftermath of the attacks in New York in 2001, the EU released the *Anti-Terrorism Roadmap*.[70] Raphael Bossong has argued that many of the measures contained in this plan were already on the EU security agenda before 11 September 2001, noting that of the eleven legislative measures on the roadmap only the investigation of immigration and asylum policy in respect of terrorist threats was a new item.[71] Similarly, unlike the *Tampere Milestones*, which focused specifically on the threat from 'organised crime' and contained only one minor reference to terrorism, the subsequent EU internal security programmes released in the periods after 11 September, the *Hague Programme* and the *Stockholm Programme*, invoked the threat of terrorism in order to legitimise the policies outlined in each document. Ben Hayes and Chris Jones have shown that by 2013 'at least 239 specific EU laws and policy documents … [had] been adopted in the name of "counter-terrorism" … 88 of which are legally binding (or "hard law")'.[72] According to Hayes and Jones, many of the specific 'counter-terrorism' measures, such as the retention of telecommunications traffic data for law-enforcement purposes, the establishment of the Visa Information System (VIS) and the EU framework for critical infrastructure protection, were all originally developed for purposes other than counter-terrorism.[73]

I argue therefore that the construction of terrorism as an all-encompassing and multifaceted threat has played a key role in structuring, justifying and legitimising a whole range of EU security measures that cut across the various dimensions of internal and external security policy, which are not limited to a sole focus on counter-terrorism. Significantly, the emphasis on terrorism as a 'new' and potentially serious threat has: helped to speed up the development of new EU agencies such as Eurojust (coordinated judicial cooperation); led to an expansion of responsibilities (in matters of counter-terrorism) for existing EU agencies such as Europol; enhanced bilateral cooperation with the US, including the Passenger Names Record (PNR) agreement; influenced the strengthening of external border checks, including the use of pre-existing border control databases for counter-terrorism purposes; and played a key role in the agreement of measures such as the European Arrest Warrant (EAW), to name but a few of the policy provisions adopted since 11 September 2001 that have a broader focus than simply counter-terrorism. These developments support the assertion that one of the most important functions of the 'fight against terrorism' discourse is the legitimising role it plays in promoting the adoption of more general EU security policies and the strengthening of the EU's role as a *provider of security* in the fields of internal and external security.[74]

Contested nature of the discourse

This section highlights the contested nature of knowledge about terrorism that the discourse is based upon, as well as pointing to knowledge that is 'excluded' from the discourse. As I explained in the opening chapter, terrorism is an 'essentially contested' concept.[75] One academic study by Alex P. Schmid and Albert Jongman documented over 100 different definitions of terrorism, yet still reached the conclusion that 'the search for an adequate definition of terrorism is still on'.[76] Bruce Hoffman has suggested that one compelling reason for this difficulty in reaching an acceptable definition 'is because the meaning of the term has changed so frequently over the past two hundred years'.[77] Indeed, Louise Richardson has argued that the only certainty about terrorism is the pejorative nature with which the word is used.[78]

Not only is the meaning of terrorism contested and difficult to pin down but in addition the strand of the discourse that constructs terrorism as a 'new' type of threat is one of the most contested aspects of knowledge about contemporary terrorism. This strand is built on a quite substantial academic literature developed in the period before 11 September 2001, which argued that what was being witnessed was in fact a 'new' phase in respect of the terrorist threat.[79] It assumed that with its potential for destruction, its commitment to the acquisition and use of CBRN materials, its links to extremist religious doctrine and its increased lethality, the 'new' terrorism rendered much of the 'previous analysis of terrorism based on established groups obsolete, and complicates the task of intelligence-gathering and counter-terrorism'.[80] However, the extent to which the present threat of terrorism can be considered 'new' is also highly problematic. Martha Crenshaw has argued that the departure from the past is not quite as pronounced as these accounts make it out to be and that today's terrorism is not a fundamentally or qualitatively 'new' phenomenon; instead, like all other historical instances of terrorism, how terrorism is understood must always be grounded in the historical, social and cultural context within which it emerges.[81]

Likewise, the assumption that terrorists are seeking to acquire and use WMD or CBRN materials seems at best misplaced. This fear first gained momentum with the 1995 Aum Shinrikyo sarin gas attack on the Tokyo subway, which is often cited as demonstrative of the link between the 'new' terrorism and WMDs.[82] Alexander Spencer has argued that 'the possible use of WMDs as a characteristic of new terrorism is debatable', noting, for example, the limited use of chemical weapons by groups representative of the 'old', more traditional forms of terrorism.[83] Crenshaw supports this line of argument, highlighting that the Aum Shinrikyo attack on the Tokyo subway remains the only example of the deliberate use of chemical weapons against a civilian population. She also points out that 'terrorists have not used nuclear or radiological weapons despite official concern over the prospect since at least 1976'.[84] The EU's continued insistence that there is a 'possibility of WMD being used by terrorists' on EU territory and that this represents 'a direct and growing threat to our societies' is based on a lack of evidence and a certain degree of imagination on the part of policy-makers.[85] Indeed, Sonia Kittelsen has argued with respect to the EU's response to bioterrorism that the significance of the threat lies not in the likelihood of mass casualties in the event of an attack but rather in the fear that it generates.[86] Studies in the US modelling the consequences of CBRN or WMD terrorism have shown that the direct effects of such an attack would be little different from those of conventional terrorism and that in all probability 'would not kill many people'.[87] Instead, the main consequences would be economic and psychological.

The discourse strand that constructs terrorism as crime can also be contested on the basis that it serves a particular purpose. It plays a role in delegitimizing the actions of the 'terrorist' other, whilst simultaneously obscuring the political dimension of the act itself. Michael Stohl has been particularly critical of this element of terrorism knowledge, arguing that it is in fact a 'myth' related to the psychological explanations of terrorism that is subscribed to by virtually all governments.[88] He does not make this point in order to argue that terrorism should not be conceived as crime, or to argue that it can ever be legitimate; instead he makes this point in order to highlight the hypocrisy of governments that engage in activities that could conceivably be labelled 'terrorist' (torture, 'targeted killings'), which are then defended by the government in question as acts central to 'national security'. This critique ties into the contested nature of the term 'terrorism', a description that has almost never been voluntarily adopted by an individual or group. It is a label that is applied to 'terrorists' by others, first and foremost by the governments of the states they attack. As Charles Townshend explains, the delegitimising role of the label terrorism is power-ful in the sense that 'states have not been slow to brand violent opponents with this title, with its clear implications of inhumanity, criminality, and – perhaps most crucially – lack of real political support'.[89]

Similarly, the conflation of terrorism with organised crime can also be challenged. This element of the discourse reflects a quite substantial aca-demic literature in support of a convergence thesis between organised crime and terrorism in what is referred to as the 'crime–terror nexus'.[90] This aspect of the discourse is contested in the sense that these 'links' are far from obvious. As Alex P. Schmid explains, whilst in a small number of instances there has been a limited degree of cooperation between certain terrorist and criminal organisations, it is imprudent to lump these two dis-tinct phenomena together, pointing out that 'there are links … but there are also important motivational and operational differences between ter-rorist groups and organised crime groups'.[91] John Rollins and Liana Sun Wyler doubt the existence of any link between either phenomenon, point-ing out that where such evidence exists, it consists of 'limited anecdotal evidence [which] largely serves as the basis for the current understanding of criminal-terrorist connections'.[92] However, the linking of terrorism and organised crime serves an important purpose in that it provides legitimacy for taking counter-measures designed for one area (organised crime/crimin-ality) and applying them in another (terrorism); as such, policies designed to tackle one issue may be introduced on the basis of one set of criteria and justified on the basis of quite another. Wyn Rees has noted that this practice might result in a 'significant impact upon civil liberties if new crim-inal measures are brought into effect on the grounds of fighting terrorism'.[93] In such a situation he contends that it will be 'more difficult to maintain accountability over security policies if a mutually self-sustaining discourse of domestic and international threats becomes deeply entrenched'.[94]

Finally, as Jackson has highlighted, the notion that states may employ ter-ror as an instrument of foreign or domestic policy, what is referred to as 'state terror', is absent from the EU 'fight against terrorism' discourse.[95] Within the counter-terrorism discourse, terrorism is 'understood very narrowly as referring primarily to forms of illegitimate violence committed by individuals and small groups, and not as a repressive form of governance or counter-insurgency by state actors'.[96] Furthermore, the 'fight against terrorism' constructs the threat posed by sub-state terrorist actors as, if not an existential threat, then, at the very least, an extreme threat to European society and in particular EU citizens. This has become even more evident since 2011, in the post-Breivik period, with the EU counter-terrorism policy focusing specifically on the threat posed by 'lone actors' and 'returning foreign fighters'.

Both of these assumptions are based upon a rather narrow understanding of the nature, characteristics and causes of terrorism. In the first instance the policy discourse ignores or fails to acknowledge the problem of state terrorism. Indeed, Jackson suggests that if we understand terrorism as 'violence directed towards or threatened against civilians designed to instil terror or [to] intimidate a population for political reasons' then it can also be argued that 'state terrorism is arguably a much greater security issue than dissident or nonstate terrorism'.[97] Without seeking to pass judgement on the policy discourse, it is possible to acknowledge that this narrow conceptualisation of terrorism plays a key role in constructing or conditioning the type of policy responses advocated for combating terrorism. Michael Stohl supports this proposition by arguing that the primary purpose of terrorism, as practised by those who seek to challenge governmental authority, is the production of chaos to accelerate social disintegration and demonstrate the inability of government to govern. He states that 'it remains the case that the most persistent and successful use of terror both in the past and the modern era has been demonstrated by governments for the purpose of creating, maintaining, and imposing order'.[98]

Political and societal implications

Whilst the EU's criminal justice-based approach to terrorism may have helped the EU to avoid the worst excesses of the United States' war-based discourse, this does not mean that it is without consequence. It is argued here that the EU 'fight against terrorism' discourse has a number of important political and societal implications. First, the discourse is significant in the sense that it simultaneously creates – and is created upon – the basis of knowledge about terrorism that structures the policy response, thereby making certain types of policy possible and others unworkable or improper. As Jackson points out, there is an issue here in that if we concede that the 'accepted knowledge' or 'conventional wisdom' about terrorism is based upon a series of incomplete, contested or flawed assumptions, flowing from this is a direct policy implication that the task of formulating an effective counter-terrorism response becomes increasingly more difficult.[99]

If we take the EU's acceptance of the 'new' terrorism thesis as an example, this criticism becomes clearer. As Martha Crenshaw explains, the structuring of the threat in this way offers policy-makers a simplistic, 'top-down' model for the processing of information, which often results in a failure to take into account the 'contradictory and confusing reality' of terrorism.[100] Instead, by developing policies based upon the conventional wisdom of the supposed threat of 'new' terrorism, the discourse provides policy-makers with a 'set of simple assumptions about terrorism' that they can rely upon to formulate a response.[101] By focusing on the notion of 'new' terrorism, which is committed to 'unlimited violence' and the causing of 'massive casualties', as the main terrorist threat to the EU, the discourse reflects a failure on the part of the EU to recognise the nuances and complexity of terrorism as a form of political violence.[102] Furthermore, the formulation of policy based upon what is essentially contested knowledge suggests that the counter-terrorism policies developed by the EU may turn out to be 'ineffectual at best and counterproductive at worst'.[103]

Second, the perceived threat of the 'terrorist' other has led the EU and its member states to adopt measures that have been argued to be potentially harmful for civil liberties and basic human rights. In essence, the formulation of EU counter-terrorism policy has contributed to a reconceptualisation of the understanding of 'freedom', which has certain political and social implications. According to Anastassia Tsoukala, 'freedom' is no longer defined 'in positive terms, i.e. as a freedom to act, but in negative terms, i.e. as a release from a threat'.[104] From this perspective 'freedom' no longer refers 'to civil rights and liberties' but instead 'legitimizes the very restriction of these civil rights and liberties' in order to protect people from the threats to which discourses of insecurity say they are prey.[105] Significantly, the EU has developed a number of policies based around border control, the processing of personal data, the tracking of financial transactions and the creation of lists of terrorist organisations, which all raise serious questions for civil liberties, human rights and the EU's attempts to strike a balance between liberty and security in the creation of its counter-terrorism response.

In the documents analysed, the EU counter-terrorism discourse contained numerous references to the development of policies that would continue 'to respect human rights and international law'.[106] Yet, as Hayes and Jones have shown, not only has there been little in the way of public consultation on the dozens of legally binding measures agreed upon by the EU for counter-terrorism purposes, but the EU has failed to explain exactly how these commitments to civil liberties would be met in practice.[107] Hayes and Jones suggest that 'there is certainly no shortage of expertise available to the EU to properly assess the impact, legitimacy and effectiveness of its counter-terrorism policies', but that 'these resources are at best underutilised and at worst applied in a manner that ultimately ignores crucial issues of civil liberties and human rights, necessity and proportionality, accountability and democratic control'.[108] Indeed, they suggest that the EU appears to have developed numerous policies without taking account of the extent to which they would actually be effective in preventing terrorism. In the 'fight against terrorism' it is the construction of the radically threatening figure of the 'terrorist' other that has made this possible.

A third implication of the 'fight against terrorism' discourse is that it serves to obscure the potential for the state to be considered a 'terrorist' actor, with particular reference to the hypocrisy of governments that engage in activities that, if we were to take a different viewpoint, might be labelled 'terrorist'. The EU counter-terrorism discourse as articulated through the main policy-making institutions of the EU, the European Council and the European Commission, has been characterised by silence on the issue of state terrorism involving the allies of the EU, which includes complicity by EU member states in acts of state terrorism. A report published by Amnesty International in 2010 compiled evidence of collusion by a number of European countries, including Germany, Italy, Lithuania, Poland, Romania, Sweden and the UK, in the unlawful rendition and secret detention programmes of the Central Intelligence Agency (CIA), which have led to the enforced disappearance, torture and ill-treatment of a number of people.[109]

It should be noted that the European Parliament has been active in drawing attention to these issues. For example, in 2007 the European Parliament adopted a report, by the Parliamentary Assembly of the Council of Europe (PACE) Committee on Legal Affairs and Human Rights, on the complicity of the aforementioned European countries in the illegal transfer of individuals to places where they were at risk of torture.[110] The European Parliament has continued to call for an examination of EU member states' role in these practices, in 2011 asking that 'the EU and its Member States must fully clarify their role in the CIA programme of renditions and black sites'. However, beyond this there has been little in the way of official EU criticism of the practice of extraordinary rendition, with no reference made to the issue in any of the European Council or European Commission texts analysed.[111] Indeed, the Director of Amnesty International's European Institutions Office, Nicolas Berger, commented that 'the EU has utterly failed to hold member states accountable for the abuses they've committed'.[112]

Nathalie Van Raemdonck has also highlighted the US 'counter-terrorism' policy of 'targeted killings' in Pakistan and surrounding regions through the use of unmanned aerial vehicles (UAVs), or 'drones' as they are more commonly known, which she has argued have been conducted on a questionable legal basis and have set a controversial precedent for covert warfare, which conflicts with the stated counter-terrorism priorities of the EU.[113] In her opinion the EU has opted not just for silence, but has elected against developing a policy on the matter in order to prevent a potentially harmful rift with the US in relation to counter-terrorism cooperation. In a report for the Human Rights Council of the UN General Assembly, special rapporteur Philip Alston was heavily critical of the US policy of 'targeted killings'.[114] He argued that the claim of self-defence against alleged terrorists is a highly controversial practice that rests on a 'disturbing tendency' to permit violations of International Human Rights Law (IHL) on the basis that the cause is 'just', and furthermore, that these practices are 'tantamount to abandoning IHL'.[115] In support of Van Raemdonck's assertion that the EU has no policy on the US practice of 'targeted killings', there was no mention of 'targeted killings' or any criticism of US counter-terrorism policy in any of the documents analysed.

Conclusion

The aim of this chapter has been to demonstrate how the EU's 'fight against terrorism' discourse contributes to a particular conceptualisation of terrorism, which helps to both shape and make possible the EU's counter-terrorism response. It has been argued that this is achieved through four interlinked discourse strands that, when taken together, construct the 'terrorist' other, against which the identity of the EU is produced and reproduced. Although each strand of the discourse has evolved with varying degrees of complexity, they have also remained consistent across the period analysed and can therefore be understood as continuities within the 'fight against terrorism' discourse. These four strands of the discourse construct terrorism: first, as a threat to the 'values' of the European Union; second, as a 'new' and 'evolving' threat; third, as a form of crime or a criminal act; and fourth, as an act committed primarily by non-state actors, wherein the state is the primary victim and never the perpetrator. It has been argued that these strands tie into other aspects of the discourse including the fear that terrorists are seeking to acquire and/or use WMDs or CBRN material, as well as the perceived threat from 'lone actor' terrorism or, since the emergence of Islamic State in Iraq and Syria in 2014, the threat from 'returning foreign fighters'. As I noted earlier in the chapter, these discourse strands help to construct the image of the 'terrorist' other, a radical threat to the EU who is potentially a 'criminal' with links to 'organised crime', a 'new' and 'evolving' type of threat that is predominantly 'religious' in nature, a non-state actor, a member of a group or an individual, such as a 'lone actor' or a 'returning foreign fighter', who seeks to inflict 'massive casualties' against the EU and its member states. This is a particularly powerful image that structures EU policy around the future-oriented fear of potential terrorist attacks and imagined scenarios of potentially devastating terrorist events. It is a representation of threat that the EU has invoked at regular instances, throughout the period analysed, to justify the development of its role not just as an actor in counter-terrorism but also to legitimise its ever-increasing role as a security actor in various aspects of internal and external security.

The chapter argued that the 'fight against terrorism' discourse has played a key role in structuring the EU approach as a criminal justice-based approach to counter-terrorism, which has differentiated it from the war-based approach of the US. Throughout the formulation of its counter-terrorism response the EU has articulated the need to develop policies that are consistent with EU values, such as the protection of human rights and civil liberties, reflecting the EU's own self-perception as a 'civilian' or 'normative' power. It has been argued that this conceptualisation of EU identity, which is normally used to explain the external projection of EU identity, can also be used to explore and understand the internal projection of EU identity and to recognise various 'others' against which EU identity is produced and reproduced. However, it has been also shown that much of the 'accepted knowledge' upon which the EU counter-terrorism response has been built is based on knowledge about terrorism that is highly contestable. Although the EU response has been structured around a criminal justice-based, precautionary approach to counter-terrorism, this does not mean it has been without consequence. In particular, the discourse raises a number of significant political and social implications. Importantly, there is the implication that developing policies based upon contested, inaccurate or incomplete knowledge can lead to ineffective or counter-productive policies. It has been argued that the construction of the radically threatening figure of the 'terrorist' other has led the EU to develop counter-terrorism policies that challenge the intrinsic values of EU identity, such as freedom, human rights and civil liberties. Indeed, I have argued that the threat of terrorism has led the EU to develop numerous policies without giving due consideration to the extent to which they are actually *effective* counter-terrorism measures. Furthermore, as I will show in the following chapters, the adoption of a precautionary approach to counter-terrorism has further implications for those 'others' identified as a potential source of terrorist threat.

Notes

1 Council of the European Union, *Joint Declaration by Heads of State and Government of the European Union, President of the European Parliament, President of the European Commission, High Representative for the Common Foreign and Security Policy*, CL01-054EN, 14 September 2001.

2 Council of the European Union, *Conclusions and Plan of Action of the Extraordinary European Council Meeting on 21 September*, 2001, SN 140/01, p. 1.
3 Council of the European Union, *A Secure Europe in a Better World: European Security Strategy*, Brussels, 12 December 2003, p. 2.
4 Ibid., p. 5.
5 Council of the European Union, *The European Union Counter-Terrorism Strategy*, Brussels, 30 November 2005, 14469/4/05, p. 2.
6 Ibid., p. 6.
7 'Council Framework Decision of 28 November 2008 Amending Framework Decision 2002/475/JHA on Combating Terrorism' (2008/919/JHA), *Official Journal*, L330/21, 09/12/2008.
8 Council of the European Union, *Riga Joint Statement*, Brussels, 29–30 January 2015, p. 1.
9 Ibid.
10 Council, *Conclusions and Plan of Action*, p. 1.
11 Council of the European Union, *Declaration on Combating Terrorism*, Brussels, 25 March 2004, 7906/04, p. 1.
12 Olli Rehn, 'EU Enlargement under Stress: The Policy of Consolidation, Conditionality and Communication', speech delivered at the Institute for European Policy, Berlin, 12 July 2005, SPEECH/05/438.
13 Council of the European Union, *Council Conclusions on the EU Regional Strategy for Syria and Iraq as well as the ISIL/Da'esh Threat*, Brussels, 16 March 2015, 7267/15, p. 2.
14 Gijs de Vries, 'Seminar on EU Cooperation in Preparing for Attacks with CBRN-agents', Ministry of Foreign Affairs, The Hague, 7 July 2004, available online at: www.consilium.europa.eu/uedocs/cmsUpload/Hague7July2004.pdf (accessed May 2015).
15 Council, *European Security Strategy*.
16 Ibid., p. 3.
17 Ibid., p. 4.
18 Gijs de Vries, 'Contribution by Gijs de Vries, European Union Counter-Terrorism Coordinator, to the Hearing by the Subcommittee on Europe of the Committee on International Relations, U.S. House of Representatives', Washington, DC, 14 September 2004, available online at: www.consilium.europa.eu/uedocs/cmsUp-load/WashingtonSeptember14.2004.pdf (accessed May 2015).
19 Council of the European Union, *The Strategy for Combating Radicalisation and Recruitment to Terrorism*, 24 November 2005, 12781/1/05, p. 2.
20 Council, *Declaration on Combating Terrorism*.
21 Council of the European Union, *EU Strategy against Proliferation of Weapons of Mass Destruction*, Brussels, 10 December 2003, 15708/03.
22 Ibid., pp. 1–4.
23 Council of the European Union, *Council Conclusions on Strengthening Chemical, Biological, Radiological and Nuclear (CBRN) Security in the European Union: An EU CBRN Action Plan*, Brussels, 12 November 2009, 15505/1/09.

24 Ibid., pp. 2–5.
25 European Commission, 'Securing Dangerous Material', DG Migration and Home Affairs, available online at: http://ec.europa.eu/dgs/home-affairs/what-we-do/policies/crisis-and-terrorism/securing-dangerous-material/index_en.htm (accessed May 2015).
26 European Commission, *Progress Report on the Implementation of the EU CBRN Action Plan*, Brussels, May 2012.
27 Council of the European Union, *Implementation of the Action Plan to Combat Terrorism*, Brussels, 12 December 2005, 15704/05.
28 Council of the European Union, *Report on the Implementation of the European Security Strategy: Providing Security in a Changing World*, Brussels, 11 December 2008, S407/08, p. 1; Council of the European Union, *The Stockholm Programme: An Open and Secure Europe Serving and Protecting Citizens*, Brussels, 2 December 2009, 17024/09, p. 50.
29 Council of the European Union, *Preventing Lone Actor Terrorism: Food for Thought*, Brussels, 23 April 2012, 9090/12.
30 Europol, *EU Terrorism Situation and Trends Report 2014*, The Hague, 2014, p. 7.
31 Council of the European Union, *Foreign Fighters and Returnees: Implementation of the Measures Decided by the JHA Council on 9–10 October 2014*, Brussels, 24 November 2014, 16002/14.
32 Council of the European Union, *Revised EU Strategy for Combating Radicalisation and Recruitment to Terrorism*, Brussels, 19 May 2014, 9956/14.
33 Ibid., p. 13.
34 In the context of this analysis, the use of the term technique is not intended to convey instrumentality on the part of the EU. The term is used to demonstrate the ways in which elements of the discourse are constructed.
35 Council of the European Union, *Conclusions Adopted by the Council (Justice and Home Affairs)*, Brussels, 20 September 2001, SN3926/6/01 Rev 6, p. 1.
36 'Council Framework Decision of 13 June 2002 on Combating Terrorism' (2002/475/JHA), *Official Journal*, L164, 22/06/2002.
37 Ibid., para. 5.
38 Council, *The European Union Counter-Terrorism Strategy*, p. 6.
39 Gilles de Kerchove, 'Speech by the European Counter-Terrorism Coordinator, Gilles de Kerchove, to the United Nations General Assembly on the Occasion of the Review of the UN Global Counter-Terrorism Strategy', New York, 4–5 September 2008, available online at: www.consilium.europa.eu/uedocs/cmsUpload/speechGANYengldef.pdf (accessed May 2015).
40 Council, *The Stockholm Programme*, p. 50.
41 Council, *Preventing Lone Actor Terrorism*.
42 Council, *European Security Strategy*.
43 Council of the European Union, *The Hague Programme: Strengthening Freedom, Security and Justice in the European Union*, Brussels, 13 December 2004, 16054/04.
44 Council, *Report on the Implementation of the European Security Strategy*, p. 4.
45 Council of the European Union, *EU Counter-Terrorism Strategy: Discussion Paper*, Brussels, 23 May 2012, 9990/12.

46 Council, *Conclusions Adopted by the Council (Justice and Home Affairs)*, p. 6.
47 Council, *European Security Strategy*.
48 Ibid., p. 3.
49 Ibid., p. 4.
50 Ibid., p. 5.
51 Council, *The European Union Counter-Terrorism Strategy*, p. 6.
52 Council of the European Union, *Actualisation of the European Union Strategy for Combating Radicalisation and Recruitment to Terrorism*, Brussels, 16 October 2008, 14294/08, p. 3.
53 Council of the European Union, *EU Counter-Terrorism Strategy: Discussion Paper*, Brussels, 28 November 2011, 17595/11, p. 2.
54 Council, *Preventing Lone Actor Terrorism*.
55 Council, *Revised EU Strategy for Combating Radicalisation and Recruitment to Terrorism*, 19 May 2014.
56 Council, *Conclusions and Plan of Action*, p. 1.
57 Ibid., p. 3.
58 Council, *European Security Strategy*.
59 Council, *The European Union Counter-Terrorism Strategy*, p. 7.
60 European Commission, *The EU Counter-Terrorism Policy: Main Achievements and Future Challenges*, Brussels, 20 July 2010, COM (2010) 386 final, SEC (2010) 911, p. 12.
61 Council of the European Union, *Outline of the Counter-Terrorism Strategy for Syria and Iraq, with Particular Focus on Foreign Fighters*, Brussels, 16 January 2015, 5369/15, pp. 2–4.
62 Francois Duchêne, 'Europe's Role in World Peace', in Richard Mayne (ed.), *Europe Tomorrow: Sixteen Europeans Look Ahead* (London: Fontana, 1972), pp. 32–47; Christopher Hill, 'European Foreign Policy: Power Bloc, Civilian Model or Flop?', in Rudolph Rummel (ed.), *The Evolution of an International Actor: Western Europe's New Assertiveness* (Boulder, CO: Westview Press, 1990), pp. 31–55; Ian Manners, 'Normative power Europe: a contradiction in terms?', *Journal of Common Market Studies*, 40 (2002), 235–258; Jan Orbie, 'Civilian power Europe: review of the original and current debates', *Cooperation and Conflict*, 41:1 (2006), 123–128.
63 See Ian J. Manners and Richard G. Whitman, 'The "difference engine": constructing and representing the international identity of the European Union', *Journal of European Public Policy*, 10:3 (2003), 380–404.
64 European Parliament, *Report on the EU Counter-Terrorism Policy: Main Achievements and Future Challenges (2010/2311(INI))*, Committee on Civil Liberties, Justice and Home Affairs, Brussels, 20 July 2011, p. 16.
65 Henrik Larsen, 'The EU: a global military actor?' *Cooperation and Conflict*, 37:3 (2002), 298.
66 Richard Jackson, *Writing the War on Terrorism: Language, Politics and Counter-Terrorism* (Manchester: Manchester University Press, 2005); Richard Jackson, 'An analysis of EU counterterrorism policy discourse', *Cambridge Review of International Affairs*, 20:2 (2007), 233–247.

67 Jackson, 'An analysis of EU counterterrorism policy discourse', 234–235.

68 Claudia Aradau and Rens van Munster, 'Governing terrorism through risk: taking precautions, (un)knowing the future', *European Journal of International Relations*, 13:1 (2007), 89–115; Louise Amoore and Marieke de Goede (eds), *Risk and the War on Terror* (Abingdon: Routledge, 2008); Marieke de Goede, 'European Security Culture: Preemption and Precaution in European Security', University of Amsterdam Inaugural Lecture (Vossiuspers UvA: Amsterdam University Press, 2011).

69 Geoffrey Edwards and Christoph O. Meyer, 'Introduction: charting a contested transformation', *Journal of Common Market Studies*, 46:1 (2008), 10.

70 Council of the European Union, *Anti-Terrorism Roadmap*, Brussels, 26 September 2001, SN 4019/01.

71 Raphael Bossong, 'The Action Plan on Combating Terrorism', *Journal of Common Market Studies*, 46:1 (2008), 27–48.

72 Ben Hayes and Chris Jones, 'Report on How the EU Assesses the Impact, Legitimacy and Effectiveness of Its Counterterrorism Laws', *SECILE – Securing Europe through Counter-Terrorism: Impact Legitimacy and Effectiveness* (SECILE Consortium, 2013), p. 4.

73 Ibid.

74 See David Spence (ed.), *The European Union and Terrorism* (London: John Harper Publishing, 2007), pp. 12–14.

75 Walter B. Gallie, 'Essentially Contested Concepts', in *Proceedings of the Aristotelian Society* (London: Harrison & Sons, Ltd, 1955). By 'essentially contested' Gallie meant concepts 'the proper use of which inevitably involves endless disputes about their proper uses on the part of their users', p. 169.

76 Alex P. Schmid and Albert J. Jongman, *Political Terrorism: A New Guide to Actors, Authors, Concepts, Data-Bases, Theories and Literature*, 2nd edn (Amsterdam: Swidok, 1988), p. 1.

77 Bruce Hoffman, *Inside Terrorism*, 2nd edn (New York: Columbia University Press, 2006), p. 3.

78 Louise Richardson, *What Terrorists Want: Understanding the Terrorist Threat* (London: John Murray, 2006).

79 Examples of academic texts that articulate the 'new' terrorism thesis include Hoffman, *Inside Terrorism*; Dan Benjamin and Steven Simon, *The Age of Sacred Terror: Radical Islam's War against America* (New York: Random House, 2003); Walter Laqueur, *The New Terrorism: Fanaticism and the Arms of Mass Destruction* (New York: Oxford University Press, 1999); Ian O. Lesser, *Countering the New Terrorism* (Santa Monica, CA: Rand Corporation, 1999).

80 Lesser, *Countering the New Terrorism*, p. 2.

81 Martha Crenshaw, ' "New" vs. "Old" Terrorism: A Critical Appraisal', in Rik Coolsaet (ed.), *Jihadi Terrorism and the Radicalisation Challenge in Europe* (Aldershot: Ashgate, 2008).

82 Ibid., p. 27; and Alexander Spencer, 'Questioning the concept of "new terrorism" ', *Peace, Conflict and Development*, 8 (2006), 18.

83 Spencer, 'Questioning the concept of "new terrorism"', 19. Spencer identifies the use of chemical weapons by the PKK, who poisoned water tanks of the Turkish Air Force with a lethal dose of cyanide in 1992, as well as by the Tamil Tigers, who attacked a Sri Lankan military camp in 1990 with chlorine gas.

84 Crenshaw, ' "New" vs. "Old" Terrorism', p. 31.

85 Council, *EU Strategy against Proliferation of Weapons of Mass Destruction*, pp. 1–4.

86 Sonja Kittelsen, 'Conceptualizing biorisk: dread risk and the threat of bioterrorism in Europe', *Security Dialogue*, 40:1 (2009), 51–71.

87 Heather Rosoff and Detlof von Winterfeldt, 'A risk and economic analysis of dirty bomb attacks on the ports of Los Angeles and Long Beach', *Risk Analysis*, 27:3 (2007), 533–546.

88 Michael Stohl, *The Politics of Terrorism* (New York: Marcel Dekker, 1988), pp. 11–13; Michael Stohl, 'Old myths, new fantasies and the enduring realities of terrorism', *Critical Studies on Terrorism*, 1:1 (2008), 5–16.

89 Charles Townshend, *Terrorism: A Very Short Introduction* (New York: Oxford University Press, 2002).

90 See, for example, Tamara Makarenko, 'The crime–terror continuum: tracing the interplay between transnational organised crime and terrorism', *Global Crime*, 6:1 (February 2004), 129–145; John T. Picarelli, 'The turbulent nexus of transnational organised crime and terrorism: a theory of malevolent International Relations', *Global Crime*, 7:1 (2006), 1–24; Chester G. Oehme III, 'Terrorists, insurgents, and criminals: growing nexus?', *Studies in Conflict and Terrorism*, 31:1 (2008), 80–93.

91 Alex P. Schmid, 'Links between Terrorism and Drug Trafficking: A Case of "Narco-terrorism"?', paper presented at the 'International Summit on Democracy, Terrorism and Security', Madrid, 8–11 March 2005.

92 John Rollins and Liana Sun Wyler, 'International Terrorism and Transnational Crime: Security Threats, U.S. Policy, and Considerations for Congress', *Congressional Research Service*, R41004 (2009), p. 13.

93 Wyn Rees, 'Linking organised crime and terrorism', *ECPR Standing Group on Organised Crime*, E-Newsletter, 5:2 (May 2006).

94 Ibid., 9.

95 Jackson, 'An analysis of EU counterterrorism policy discourse'.

96 Ibid., 236.

97 Ibid., 242.

98 Stohl, 'Old myths, new fantasies', see p. 6.

99 Jackson, 'An analysis of EU counterterrorism policy discourse'.

100 Crenshaw, ' "New" vs. "Old" Terrorism', p. 35.

101 Ibid.

102 Council, *European Security Strategy*.

103 Jackson, 'An analysis of EU counterterrorism policy discourse', 243.

104 Anastassia Tsoukala, 'Defining the Terrorist Threat in the Post-September 11 Era', in Didier Bigo and Anastassia Tsoukala (eds), *Terror, Insecurity and Liberty: Illiberal Practices of Liberal Regimes after 9/11* (Abingdon: Routledge, 2008), p. 75.

105 Ibid., p. 75.
106 Council, *The European Union Counter-Terrorism Strategy*, p. 12.
107 Hayes and Jones, 'Report on How the EU Assesses the Impact', p. 26.
108 Ibid., p. 26.
109 Amnesty International, *Open Secret: Mounting Evidence of Europe's Complicity in Rendition and Secret Detention* (London: Amnesty International Publications, 2010), available online at: www.therenditionproject.org.uk/documents/RDI/101100-AI-Open_Secret.pdf (accessed June 2015).
110 European Parliament, *Report on the Alleged Use of European Countries by the CIA for the Transportation and Illegal Detention of Prisoners*, Temporary Committee on the Alleged Use of European Countries by the CIA for the Transportation and Illegal Detention of Prisoners, Brussels, 30 January 2007, A6-0020/2007 FINAL.
111 Parliament, *Report on the EU Counter-Terrorism Policy*, p. 13.
112 Nicolas Berger, 'European Governments Must Provide Justice for Victims of CIA Programmes', press release, Amnesty International, 2010, available online at: www.amnesty.eu/en/news/press-releases/eu/human-rights-in-the-eu/0470-0470 (accessed June 2015).
113 Nathalie van Raemdonck, 'Vested Interest or Moral Indecisiveness? Explaining the EU's Silence on the US Targeted Killing Policy in Pakistan', *IAI Working Papers*, 12 (March 2012).
114 Philip Alston, *Report of the Special Rapporteur on Extrajudicial, Summary or Arbitrary Executions*, United Nations, Human Rights Council, 2010, A/HRC/14/24/Add.6.
115 Ibid., p. 14.

4

Constructing the 'migrant' other: globalisation, securitisation and control

Introduction

This chapter explores the strand of the 'fight against terrorism' discourse that constructs the 'openness' of European Union (EU) society as an environment that terrorists seek to take advantage of, demonstrating how issues regarding migration and border control have come to occupy a key dimension of the EU counter-terrorism response. In the period before the events of 11 September 2001, migration was an important subject on the agenda of the EU in relation to the formulation of its internal security programme. The events of 11 September 2001 reinforced a perception amongst EU policy-makers that migration control should form a central part of EU counter-terrorism policy, impacting upon the framing of the debate over migration in the EU. This chapter focuses on how the EU's 'fight against terrorism' discourse constructs the 'migrant' other as a potential and an implicit terrorist threat through the linking of counter-terrorism to migration and border control policies. The chapter does this by identifying three intertwined themes that are prevalent within the 'fight against terrorism' discourse. First, the idea that the EU's 'globalised' or 'open' society represents a potential source of terrorist threat.[1] Second, a discourse of 'surveillance' and 'control', which operates to justify and legitimise the counter-response to the threat. Third, the construction of the figure of the 'returning foreign fighter', a 'new' and 'evolving' threat that necessitates further migration controls.

The first half of the chapter begins by mapping the three strands of the discourse, showing how each is constructed. I argue that, taken together, the representation of the 'openness' of EU society as threatening, the perceived necessity of border 'control' and 'surveillance' of border crossers, as well as the emergence and identification of the figure of the 'returning foreign fighter', all help to conflate the threat of terrorism with the issue of migration. The second half of the chapter analyses the functioning of the discourse, showing how the EU has invoked the terrorist threat in order to legitimise increasingly sophisticated policies, practices and measures aimed at the 'control' of the 'migrant' other.[2] The chapter considers the contested nature of various aspects of the discourse, including the extent to which a clear and identifiable external threat to the EU actually exists. The main argument that I put forward is that the discourse represents another site where the logic of extending the control of the movement of people, trans-nationally, be they migrant, refugee, asylum-seeker, potential terrorist or other border crosser, is articulated and strengthened. Adopting an under-standing of securitisation in line with the approach outlined in Chapter 1, I argue that the discourse reflects and contributes to wider securitisation processes within the EU. The chapter concludes by analysing how the emer-gence of the figure of the 'returning foreign fighter' has further strengthened the perception that border control must remain a central element of the EU's counter-terrorism response.

Terrorism and the threat posed by 'globalisation' or an 'open' society

At the outset of the analysis of this strand of the discourse, it is important to note that the 'fight against terrorism' does not construct the 'migrant' other as a potential terrorist threat in an explicit or obvious way. By this I mean that the discourse does not directly link the concept of 'terrorism' to the terms 'migrant', 'migration', 'immigrant', 'immigration', 'asylum-seeker' or 'refugee'. Instead, the perceived threat of the 'migrant' other is articulated in a more subtle way. It is expressed primarily through a number of impli-cit references to the problems associated with 'globalisation' or an 'open' society that has 'open' borders, which is at various points in the evolution of the discourse linked to the external dimension of the terrorist threat. This threat is then invoked to legitimise a perceived need for 'border control' and the 'surveillance' of border crossers in order to 'protect' against terror-ism.[3] This first section will therefore focus on the way in which the 'migrant' other has been implicitly constructed as a potential terrorist threat through numerous references to the threat posed by an 'open' society. Indeed, within the counter-terrorism discourse it is striking how many references there are that explicitly link the threat posed by 'terrorism' to the problems associated with 'globalisation' and to an 'open' society.

In the pre-September 11 period, the construction of the 'migrant' other as a potential threat to European society was a central theme of the EU's internal security policy. The *Tampere Milestones*, released in November 1999, set out a series of policy priorities that would be central to the com-pletion of the EU's Area of Freedom, Security and Justice (AFSJ). Drawing upon and reaffirming the identity of the EU, the document stated that

'European integration ... [is] rooted in ... a shared commitment to freedom based on human rights, democratic institutions and the rule of law',
as well as 'common values', 'securing peace' and 'developing prosperity'.[4]
With specific reference to migration, the document claimed that the very
existence of the EU acted as 'a draw to many others world-wide who cannot
enjoy the freedom union citizens take for granted' and argued that it would
go against European traditions 'to deny such freedoms to those whose circumstances lead them justifiably to seek access to our territory'.[5] The document described the main aim of the *Tampere Milestones* as 'an open and
secure European Union, fully committed to the obligations of the Geneva
Refugee Convention and other relevant human rights instruments, and able
to respond to humanitarian needs on the basis of solidarity'.[6] However, the
structure of the document also implied that migration could potentially
represent a significant risk to the security of the EU and its citizens. The
document focused primarily on the threat posed by 'serious organised and
transnational crime' and the challenge represented by 'illegal immigration'
as interlinked 'internal' and 'external' security problems for the EU, thereby
securitising the issue. In this period therefore it was the perceived threat of
'transnational crime' and the challenge posed by 'illegal immigration', not
terrorism, that played a significant role in the reinforcement of the idea that
the 'openness' of European society represented a significant security challenge to the EU and its developing role in the provision of security for its
citizens.

The discursive construction of the 'openness' of European society as a
potential security threat was strengthened in the period following the events
of 11 September 2001. As I explained in Chapter 2, it was the threat of
terrorism that was invoked to support this idea that the 'openness' of the
EU area was problematic rather than the threat of crime or the problem
of immigration. For example, the *Conclusions and Plan of Action of the
Extraordinary Meeting* of the European Council, from 21 September 2001,
defined the attacks as 'an assault on our open, democratic, tolerant and
multicultural societies'.[7] The EU promised to 'cooperate with the United
States in bringing to justice and punishing the perpetrators, sponsors and
accomplices of such barbaric acts' whilst simultaneously respecting 'the
fundamental freedoms which form the basis of our civilization'.[8] In this initial phase the attacks were interpreted through the prism of identity as an
attack on all countries with similar values of openness, democracy, tolerance and respect for all cultures.

The document also contributed to the construction of the threat from 'the
scourge of terrorism' as an external threat. It did this by focusing on the need
to engage in 'in-depth political dialogue with those countries and regions of
the world in which terrorism comes into being', as well as re-evaluating the

EU's relationship with third countries 'in light of the support which those countries might give to terrorism'.[9] The implicit assumption contained in such phrases helped to construct the contemporary terrorist threat as a phenomenon whose origins were (and to a certain extent remain) external to the EU. By constructing the threat of terrorism as an external threat, the 'fight against terrorism' discourse strengthened the perception that a 'globalised' or 'open' society could potentially fall victim to further acts of terrorism. Furthermore, this externalisation of the terrorist threat was also important in legitimising the introduction of security concerns into EU migration policy and migration concerns into EU security policy.

The *European Security Strategy* of 2003 built on this strand of the discourse by stating that the international environment in which the EU operated was 'one of increasingly open borders in which the internal and external aspects of security are indissolubly linked', stating that those who sought to engage in acts of terrorism aimed 'to undermine the openness and tolerance of our societies'.[10] Globalisation was presented as both an opportunity and a threat to Europe, in that 'flows of trade and investment, the development of technology and the spread of democracy have brought freedom and prosperity to many people'. However, the discourse also identified a negative side in that 'others have perceived globalisation as a cause of injustice'.[11] Drawing on the perceived terrorist threat represented by non-state actors, the document claimed that the process of globalisation had 'increased European dependence – and so vulnerability – on an interconnected infrastructure in transport, energy, information and other fields', again contributing to the construction of the 'openness' of European society as a threat to security.[12] In the post-Madrid period, although no longer the primary focus the external dimension of the threat was perceived as still retaining importance. In March 2004 the EU released its *Declaration on Combating Terrorism*, which focused on targeting external relations at priority 'third countries' where 'counter terrorist capacity or commitment to combating terrorism needs to be enhanced'.[13]

The *EU Counter-Terrorism Strategy*, from November 2005, maintained this process of defining terrorism through the prism of identity, by constructing terrorism as a threat to 'the values' of the EU's 'democratic societies' and to 'the rights and freedoms' of its citizens.[14] It reinforced the construction of the 'openness' of the EU area as an environment that terrorists could potentially use in order to pursue their objectives, with the opening preamble rearticulating this strand of the discourse by stating that 'The European Union is an area of increasing openness, in which the internal and external aspects of security are intimately linked. It is an area of increasing interdependence, allowing for free movement of people, ideas, technology and resources. This is an environment which terrorists abuse to pursue their objectives.'[15] The strategy went on to list a series of measures under the Protect and Pursue work themes that were suggested as essential for reducing the 'vulnerability' of the EU's 'open' society. Whilst the EU had by November 2005 begun to focus on terrorism as primarily an internal threat to European society, through a focus on 'home-grown' terrorist groups, the EU had also continued to construct the threat of terrorism as part of a wider external threat to European society. The EU *Counter-Terrorism Strategy* stated quite clearly that not only does 'much of the terrorist threat to Europe originate outside the EU', but 'the current international terrorist threat affects and has its roots in many parts of the world beyond the EU'.[16] It suggested that this threat could only be responded to through 'co-operation with and the provision of assistance to priority third countries – including in North Africa, the Middle East and South East Asia'.[17] The impact of this has been to continue to reinforce the implicit interlinking of terrorism with migration: the 'terrorist' other, as an individual or a group, abusing a 'globalised' and interdependent society in which people, including potential or actual terrorists, could migrate from all regions of the world into the EU area.

The 2008 *Report on the Implementation of the European Security Strategy* reinforced the construction of globalisation as both an opportunity and a threat to Europe. It emphasised that whilst 'globalisation' had 'brought new opportunities' it had 'also made threats more complex and interconnected'.[18] Using a biological 'life' metaphor, the document stated that the 'arteries of our society' were increasingly 'vulnerable' to the threat of terrorism and identified a need for increased cooperation in order to 'protect' against that threat.[19] Globalisation in particular was constructed as impacting upon identity in that it was 'accelerating shifts in power' and 'exposing differences in values'.[20] Similarly, although the *Stockholm Programme* of 2009 did not make any explicit links between the 'openness' of European society and terrorism, the debate over 'access to Europe in a globalised world' remained a central concern.[21] The document acknowledged that while access to EU territory for those with a legitimate interest should be made more effective and efficient, the EU should also 'guarantee security for its citizens'; an objective it argued could be achieved through 'integrated border management and visa policies'.[22] The construction of an external dimension to the threat of terrorism remained central to the discourse, with the document continuing to advocate cooperation with third countries in order to more effectively combat terrorism.

The 2010 EU *Internal Security Strategy* also contributed to the discursive construction of the openness of EU society as both a threat and an opportunity.[23] The document claimed that 'technological advances' had meant that 'not only our borders, but also our societies have opened up', making the EU an attractive destination for the 'migrant' other.[24] Framing this opportunity through the affirmation of EU identity, the document stated that 'through unity in diversity, this free and prosperous Europe continues to facilitate and enrich people's lives'.[25] However, this positive aspect of EU society was also thought to be threatened by 'crime-related risks and threats facing Europe today, such as terrorism' that could potentially 'undermine the values and prosperity of our open societies'.[26] It is clear therefore that throughout the evolution of the EU's counter-terrorism discourse the perceived threat of a 'globalised' and 'open' society, which as a result of this 'openness' is particularly 'vulnerable' to acts of terrorism, has come to occupy one of the central elements upon which the formulation of EU counter-terrorism policy has been based.

A discourse of 'surveillance' and 'control'

The assumption that there is a potential threat posed by terrorists seeking to take advantage of the migratory system of the 'globalised' or 'open' society of the EU is inextricably linked to another strand of the 'fight against terrorism' discourse. The identification of this potential 'vulnerability' within EU society is accompanied by a discourse strand that articulates a need for improved 'control' of the EU border and increased 'surveillance' of border crossers. I argue that this discourse of 'surveillance and control' has three main characteristics. First, it constructs 'control' of EU borders as a necessity in 'protecting' against the perceived threat of terrorism. Second, the 'migrant' or 'immigrant' other is implicitly constructed as a potential terrorist threat through the discursive fusing of migration policies with counter-terrorism policies, which serve to reconstruct instruments designed for migration control as instruments that can assist the EU's counter-terrorism response.[27] This is viewed as the discursive aspect of the securitisation process and of the securitisation of migration in the EU. Finally, the discourse strand plays a central role in the construction of a whole range of new surveillance technologies and biometric measures, used primarily at EU borders, as key elements in the EU's 'fight against terrorism'. It is argued that this is the performative aspect of the securitisation process in the sense that practices of migration control are made possible through the language of the 'fight against terrorism'.

The response to the events of 11 September 2001 by the key policy-making institutions of the EU made the first clear discursive links between the threat of terrorism and policy issues related to migration, asylum and border control. The *Conclusions Adopted by the Council (JHA)*, which were released on 20 September 2001, focused on the 'seriousness of events' as reasons for 'speeding up' the process of creating the AFSJ.[28] The document itself focused on seven key 'measures at borders'. The language played an important role in the discursive construction of the 'migrant' other as an implicit

security threat. In response to the terrorist threat, the document put forward measures designed to 'strengthen controls at external borders', as well
as 'strengthen immediately the surveillance measures' provided for in the
Schengen Agreement. The document focused on improving the exchange of
information between member states in order to 'combat terrorism', including through: 'Controls at airports, cross-border controls, controls at express
roads, controls at the external borders of the European Union.'[29] The document called on national authorities to 'exercise the utmost vigilance when
issuing identity documents' and suggested that EU member states 'examine
urgently the relationship between safeguarding internal security and com-
plying with international protection obligations and instruments'.[30]

The post-Madrid *Declaration on Combating Terrorism*, 2004, strengthened this strand of the discourse by linking counter-terrorism to migration
and border control.[31] There was an assertion within the policy document that
'improved border controls and document security play an important role in
combating terrorism'. The document offered a series of measures designed to
'ensure effective systems of border control', which included the establishment
of 'a European Borders Agency', 'incorporation of biometric features into
passports and visas' and the development of a common EU approach to 'the
use of passenger data for border and aviation security', including for 'other
law enforcement purposes'.[32] The discursive construction of measures of control at borders gained ever more traction in the post-Madrid environment.

The *Hague Programme*, released in December 2004, continued to reinforce the logic that the regulation of 'migration flows' and the 'control' of
'external borders' were essential if the EU were to 'repress the threat of terrorism'.[33] The document itself contained three sections, 'strengthening freedom', 'strengthening security' and 'strengthening justice', with the section
on freedom the longest and seemingly attributed the most importance. The
document clearly stated that 'Freedom, justice, control at the external borders, internal security and the prevention of terrorism should henceforth be
considered indivisible within the Union as a whole'.[34] The document interpreted the intrinsic EU value of 'freedom' as something best served through
restrictive immigration practices. Every measure proposed under the
'strengthening freedom' section of the *Hague Programme* related to immigration policy, border control and security, with the implicit assumption that
these measures would provide protection against the possibility of further
terrorist attacks. It was also interesting to note that the potential security
implications represented by advances in biotechnology were introduced for
the first time. The document called on the Council, the Commission and the
member states to 'integrate biometric identifiers in travel documents, visa,
residence permits, EU citizens' passports and information systems without delay and to prepare for the development of minimum standards for

national identity cards' as essential measures 'for the prevention and control of crime, in particular terrorism'.[35]

Similarly, migration and border control were dealt with under the Protect objective of the 2005 EU *Counter-Terrorism Strategy*. The document contributed to the continued construction of 'border control' as one of the most appropriate responses to the terrorist threat. It stated that, 'While member states have the primary responsibility for improving the protection of key targets, the interdependency of border security, transport and other cross-border infrastructures require effective EU collective action.' It focused on a 'need to enhance protection of our borders to make it harder for known or suspected terrorists to enter or operate within the EU'.[36] Simultaneously, it reinforced the link between a series of measures designed to enforce migration and asylum control with the desired policy response to terrorism. The use of new technologies, already advocated in earlier policy documents, was constructed as indispensable to the 'fight against terrorism'. For example, 'the capture and exchange of passenger data' and the 'inclusion of biometric information in identity and travel documents', it was argued, should play a role in improving 'the effectiveness of our border controls and provide greater assurance to our citizens'.[37] Migration control continued to be linked to counter-terrorism and constructed as a security problem, with the assertion that 'the European Borders Agency (Frontex) will have a role in providing risk assessment as part of the effort to strengthen controls and surveillance at the EU's external border'.[38] Like the concept of 'freedom' the notion of 'protection' was linked to the creation of border controls designed to restrict the movement into the EU area of the 'migrant' other.

Since the release of the *Counter-Terrorism Strategy* in 2005 the discourse of surveillance and control has come to form a central element of the counter-terrorism response. The various reports compiled by the EU Counter-Terrorism Coordinator (EU CTC) on the implementation of the EU *Counter-Terrorist Strategy* between 2005 and 2014 confirmed this. The report from November 2008 contained a specific section on 'border security', which continued to reinforce the link between counter-terrorism objectives and migration control.[39] It stated that the EU shall seek 'to protect citizens and infrastructure and reduce our vulnerability to attack, inter alia through improved security of borders, transport and critical infrastructure'.[40] The document also linked the Schengen Information System (SIS) to terrorism through a proposal to establish 'a system for early detection of persons suspected of activities related to terrorism or organised crime, with the help of SIS alerts'.[41] Similarly, the November 2009 report identified the introduction of legislation related to the Visa Information System (VIS) as a key part of the Protect objective of the *Counter-Terrorism Strategy*. The EU CTC report emphasised the importance of this database as a counter-terrorism tool through the assertion that access to the VIS was to be granted to 'the designated authorities of the Member States and to Europol for the purposes of the prevention, detection and investigation of terrorist offences and of other serious criminal offences'.[42]

Although the *Stockholm Programme*, 2009, did not explicitly link terrorism to border control policy, it continued to articulate the importance of 'surveillance' and 'control' through an assertion that technology could 'play a key role in improving and reinforcing the system of external border controls'.[43] The document explained that 'the entry into operation of the SIS II and the roll-out of the VIS system therefore remains a key objective' in terms of border management. The document also continued to advocate the development of an external border surveillance database that would be administered through Frontex. Within the document itself, the threat of terrorism remained in the background as an ancillary reason for the development of these policies. Likewise, the 2010 EU *Internal Security Strategy* continued to advocate the need for 'integrated border management' between EU member states. It argued that new technologies for border management would be important moving forward, given that 'they improve security by allowing for the necessary controls to be put in place so that borders are not crossed by people or goods which pose a risk to the Union'.[44] Again, the 'global reach' of the threat of terrorism and the 'devastating consequences' of acts of terrorism were invoked to legitimise the response.

Interestingly, since 2012 the perceived 'evolution' of the terrorist threat has meant that this discourse of surveillance and control has taken on more significance. For example, the EU CTC discussion paper, *Preventing Lone Actor Terrorism: Food for Thought*, noted that 'lone actor' terrorists had travelled abroad, therefore requiring more to be done at EU level in order 'to detect and follow people who travel to conflict zones'.[45] Similarly, the November 2014 EU CTC report stated that 'border management' and 'the exchange of information at external border controls' remained 'essential in the fight against terrorism'.[46] In particular, it drew attention to the 'new' and 'evolving' threat from 'returning foreign fighters', explicitly linking the response to this threat to border control with a specific aim to 'dissuade, detect and disrupt suspicious travel and investigate and prosecute foreign fighters'.[47] This threat has come to form the main focus of the EU counter-terrorism response in the post-Breivik period.

The threat of the 'returning foreign fighter'

In the post-Breivik period the EU has switched the focus of its counter-terrorism response to the perceived threat from 'returning foreign fighters' and 'lone actor' terrorism. By the phrase 'returning foreign fighter' the EU is referring to the threat posed by citizens of EU member states who have travelled to foreign conflict zones and may return and launch a terrorist attack against their country of origin. The 'returning foreign fighter' is unique in the sense that they traverse the distinction between the internal and external dimensions of the terrorist threat. I argue that this new strand of the discourse is extremely significant in relation to the ongoing securitisation of the 'migrant' other. In particular, it helps to strengthen the notion that the 'open' or 'globalised' society of the EU is 'vulnerable' to acts of terrorism, as well as confirming the logic that increased border control and the development of new technologies of surveillance for 'border crossers' should be essential elements of the EU counter-terrorism response. The discourse focuses specifically on policies designed to 'disrupt' and 'detect' any form of 'suspicious travel'.

The emergence of the figure of the 'returning foreign fighter' has to be understood in the context of the external dimension of the terrorist threat. As I have argued, since the events of 11 September 2001, whilst the EU has been preoccupied with the development of an internal security response to terrorism, it has still retained a focus on other parts of the world beyond the EU where terrorism was also thought to originate. The 2005 EU *Counter-Terrorism Strategy* and the *Strategy for the External Dimension of JHA* both highlighted a need on the part of the EU 'to engage more closely with [the] wider world, such as counter-terrorism with North Africa, the Middle East, Gulf countries and South East Asia'.[48] The identification of 'priority third countries' with whom closer cooperation should be sought has figured prominently within the discourse ever since. The war in Iraq and the growth of so-called 'conflict zones' directed Europol, in 2007, to begin developing a terrorist threat assessment picture of the 'situation outside the EU'.[49] North Africa, the Sahel region, Somalia, Yemen, Afghanistan and Pakistan were all named as areas that might represent a source of terrorist threat. Indeed, Europol was the first agency of the EU, before the main policy-making institutions, to identify the threat from 'foreign fighters'.

The 2008 TE-SAT report made specific reference to 'more than 90 suspected foreign Islamist insurgents' who were 'reported captured or killed' in Somalia during 2007, with a small number of EU citizens, 'five Swedish and five British nationals', reported to be amongst their number.[50] The identification of this threat led the EU CTC, in a discussion paper submitted to the Council from November 2010, to identify 'terrorist travel' as an important challenge in the 'fight against terrorism'.[51] The document stated quite clearly that 'The threat of Europeans travelling to conflict areas or attending terrorist training camps elsewhere and then returning home has become even more apparent.'[52] Tapping into other strands of the 'fight against terrorism' discourse, the report went on to claim that the 'majority of plots detected over the last few years' in the EU area had links to 'foreign fighters', and furthermore that individuals returning from 'conflict zones' also represented 'a radicalisation threat' who might potentially 'attract new recruits to the terrorist cause'.[53]

In the post-Breivik period, this new strand of the 'fight against terrorism' discourse developed quickly. The 2012 EU CTC discussion paper, *Preventing Lone Actor Terrorism*, included a section on 'foreign fighters and returnees' that again highlighted the main fear driving this aspect of the EU counter-terrorism response.[54] It stated that, 'On return, these people may use their newly-acquired experience and skills for terrorist actions and spread their radical ideas or give guidance to others to follow them on their path of violence. The majority of plots detected over the last few years have involved such "foreign fighters".'[55] Significantly, this threat was invoked to justify a counter-response focused primarily on the strengthening of 'border control' measures. It suggested that visa and Passenger Name Record (PNR) information could be used to detect 'travel patterns', and also called for 'improvement of documents checks and documents security, an enhanced exchange of information and a better international cooperation'.[56] The document put forward thirteen proposals to combat the threat from 'returning foreign fighters', eight of which were directly linked to border control, including the use of the SIS. A further EU CTC report in May 2014 on *Foreign Fighters and Returnees* continued this pattern of thought, highlighting the conflict in Syria as a particular draw to 'foreign fighters'.[57] The document put forward multiple policy proposals for the purpose of 'identification and detection of travel', promoting the benefits of using the SIS for law-enforcement purposes and again calling for the creation of an EU PNR, to collate all 'data on intra EU flights', which was henceforth to be 'considered a priority'.[58]

The emergence of Islamic State in Iraq and Syria in July 2014 added a new dimension to this issue and led to a further flurry of activity from the EU CTC who suggested a range of policy recommendations to combat the problem of 'returning foreign fighters'. The key document here was a working paper from November 2014 that aimed to 'take stock' of the steps taken to implement a series of measures agreed upon at the European Council JHA meeting in October 2014.[59] Invoking the 'threat posed by ISIL and other terrorist groups in Iraq and Syria', the document highlighted four main work areas: 'prevention', 'detection of travel', 'criminal justice response' and 'cooperation with third countries'.[60] The second section on the 'detection of travel' identified ten measures linked to 'border control' that the EU should seek to adopt, again advocating the development of an EU PNR database and the use of the various EU databases that were already operational (such as the SIS and VIS). The section on 'cooperation with third countries' also called for cooperation with priority third countries for the purpose of 'border control and border management'.[61]

In 2015, the European Council followed the lead of the EU CTC by releasing two strategies designed to guide the response to this threat, the *Counter-Terrorism Strategy for Syria and Iraq* and the EU *Regional Strategy for Syria and Iraq*.[62] Adopting a similar logic to that which had been advocated by the EU CTC, the documents outlined a guiding strategy designed to reduce 'the risks to Europe and European interests, and the threat to regional stability, from terrorism emanating from Syria and Iraq'.[63] The *Regional Strategy for Syria and Iraq* was particularly revealing in that it directly linked the prevention of 'foreign fighters' to 'border control'. The document identified 'regional spill over and border security' as priority objectives for the EU in the region.[64] As well as this, it suggested that the provision of 'technical assistance' and the development of 'integrated border management' for priority neighbouring countries such as Turkey would also be essential if the threat were to be contained.[65] The emergence of the figure of the 'returning foreign fighter' can be viewed therefore as having played a key role in strengthening this discourse of 'surveillance' and 'control', with the discursive construction of 'border control', 'border security' and 'border management' as important security responses to this threat contributing to the securitisation of 'border crossers', 'travel' and the 'migrant' other.

Analysing the functioning of the discourse

The previous section dealt with how the discursive interlinking of the threat of terrorism with the 'openness' of EU society, the need for border 'control' and 'surveillance' of border crossers, as well as the emergence of the figure of the 'returning foreign fighter', help to conflate terrorism with migration and contribute to the construction of the 'migrant' other as a potential security threat. This section deals with the ways in which these elements of the discourse relate to the practice of counter-terrorism policy by offering a critical analysis of how the discourse functions. It does this in three ways: first, by considering the ways in which the different strands of the discourse structure the logic and counter-terrorism policy response to the implicit threat of the 'migrant' other, as well as highlighting the ways in which practices of migration and border 'control' are legitimised; second, by revealing the contested nature of the knowledge that these ideas are based upon; and third, by reflecting on the wider political and societal implications of the operationalization of the policy discourse.

Structuring the policy response, legitimising security practice

It is important to recognise that the development of external migration control as a common policy area for cooperation between member states pre-dated the events of 11 September 2001. The creation of common EU regulations on migration has been a significant feature of EU policy since the Maastricht Treaty came into force in 1993. In the EU the steps taken towards removing internal barriers to freedom of movement for citizens of EU member states have been accompanied by similar moves to strengthen external immigration and border control measures, leading some scholars to argue that the EU has been in the process of creating a 'fortress Europe'.[66]

At risk of simplification it can be argued that the goal of creating a common market has given rise to two competing discourses on the implications of migration for the EU. The first is a discourse that emphasises the positive aspects of migration for European society, constructing external migration as an opportunity that can bring important economic benefits to the EU and its member states. By way of contrast, the second is a discourse that constructs migration, or more specifically 'irregular migration', as a potential threat to public order, domestic stability and the 'cultural composition of the nation'.[67] Christina Boswell has argued that the framing of 'irregular migration' in the period before 11 September 2001 was characterised by three themes.[68] The first focused on uncontrolled entry and the notion of 'hordes' of illegal migrants entering the European territory from the early 1980s onwards. The second concerned the economic and social impact of irregular migration, abuse of the welfare system and undercutting of the domestic labour force. The third pattern concerned the trafficking of people by international criminal networks engaged in forced labour, drugs and armament smuggling. For Boswell, what united these three patterns of framing was their 'emphasis on exclusion as the preferred solution'.[69]

The identification of these pre-existing discourses associated with the fear of the 'migrant' other helps to provide the context within which the EU's assumption that terrorists might potentially seek to take advantage of the EU migratory system was made possible. As Carl Levy explains, in reality the securitisation of migration began long before the events of 11 September 2001 and can be viewed as a consequence of the fraught EU policy of promoting the freedom of movement whilst simultaneously seeking to create a harmonised system of asylum and refugee policy based on 'restrictionist' first principles.[70] Mapping the various strands of the 'fight against terrorism' discourse is revealing in the sense that it helps to show how the EU counter-terrorism response has been structured on the basis of, as well as contributing to the continued articulation of, discourses associated with a deep-rooted fear or an implicit suspicion of the 'migrant' other as a possible security threat. To these different representations of the 'migrant' other, be it the hordes of immigrants, the welfare scrounger or the 'criminal', due to the necessary illegality of the irregular migrant's travel, has since the events of 11 September been added the label of 'potential terrorist'. It is also revealing in that it directly challenges Boswell's assertion that the issue of 'migration control' was not securitised by the EU after 11 September 2001.[71] Boswell's argument can in part be explained by her adoption of a Copenhagen School understanding of securitisation that is based on an analysis of media reporting and speeches by important European politicians on the issue of migration. From this perspective her point holds validity, the EU has not explicitly invoked the threat of terrorism in order to force through special measures on migration control.

However, by accepting a post-Copenhagen understanding of securitisation, and as the mapping of the discourse above demonstrates, it becomes clear that the EU counter-terrorism and security policy documents contain multiple instances of the discursive linking of counter-terrorism to migration control. This is an assessment agreed with by Andrew Neal, who has argued that in the early stages of the formulation of EU counter-terrorism policy, i.e. the post-September 11 period, the EU adopted a securitising language that demonstrated 'An assumption that the human rights and asylum regime is being abused or taken advantage of by actual or potential terrorists, and is an immediate externalisation of threat which is by implication foreign.'[72] As I have shown, the assumption that the EU migratory system might potentially be abused by terrorists has remained constant throughout the evolution of the 'fight against terrorism' discourse. In this context, what is important about the 'fight against terrorism' discourse is the way in which it strengthens the notion of 'fortress Europe' through the implicit construction of the 'migrant' other as a potential security threat, as well as the way in which it has helped to legitimise security practices of migration 'control' and 'surveillance' of border crossers that had already been put forward as policy proposal before the renewed focus on the threat of terrorism in the post-September 11 period.

In essence, the concept of identity has played a key role in the formulation of this dimension of the EU's 'fight against terrorism'. The blurring of the threat of the 'terrorist' other with responses to migration – and the 'migrant' other – has helped to reconstruct a series of border control measures as vital to the EU's counter-terrorism policy. The invocation of this threat has helped to legitimise and justify, for example: proposals for the use of the 'surveillance measures' contained within the 'Schengen Agreement' (SIS) for counter-terrorism purposes; the capture and exchange of passenger travel data, in particular the EU–US PNR agreement, the introduction of biometric identifiers into travel documents, the establishment of the VIS, the continued development of a second-generation Schengen Information System (SIS II) and the creation of a counter-terrorism role for Frontex.[73]

In the post-Breivik period, the formulation of a response structured around border control has continued to be strengthened as a result of the emergence of the figure of the 'returning foreign fighter'. EU policies created during this period have continued to advocate, for counter-terrorism purposes, the use of migration control technologies already at the disposal of the EU, including the VIS and the SIS. Identity is central here in that the potential terrorist threat represented by the 'migrant' other has led to the securitisation of EU values such as 'protection' and 'freedom'. For example, as Didier Bigo points out in relation to his analysis of the *Hague Programme*, the aim of 'strengthening freedom' in the document was infiltrated by the aim of 'strengthening security'. In the *Hague Programme*, 'freedom' is understood by the EU as a series of restrictive migration controls designed to 'protect' EU citizens. Similarly, this criticism is applicable to the EU's *Counter-Terrorism Strategy* in the sense that the section on protection from terrorism is also understood in the same way. For the EU, to 'protect' citizens is to take a series of border control measures developed for the purposes of managing migration and to reapply them in a counter-terrorism context.[74] The suggestion here then is that EU citizens need 'protection' from the potential security threat of the 'migrant' other.

Contested nature of the discourse

A highly contested aspect of the discourse concerns the extent to which the perception that there is a major external terrorist threat to the security of the EU can be viewed as accurate. This perception is understandable given the identity of those who committed the acts of terrorism in New York in 2001. The attacks on 11 September, which inspired the creation of an EU counter-terrorism policy, were committed by foreign migrants who had entered the US legally on regular visas and had typically overstayed their visa permits. They had also arrived from countries with large Muslim populations. As Mario Zucconi points out, these facts about the people behind the attacks of 11 September 2011 have resulted in it becoming more 'commonplace to establish a relationship between that new sort of international terrorism and globalisation, and especially the greatly intensified movement of people across borders'.[75] The growth of so-called 'conflict zones' in areas such as North Africa, the Sahel region, Somalia, Yemen, Afghanistan and Pakistan, as well as the growing instability that has characterised Iraq and Syria since 2011, has helped to confirm this perception that there is a potential terrorist threat to the EU from beyond its borders. Yet even a cursory glance at the list of terrorist attacks in the EU area since 2001 reveals that the majority of the attacks have been conducted by citizens of EU member states against their country of origin.[76] This suggests that the articulation of an external threat is based more upon the future-oriented fear of what could happen rather than an objective analysis of the likelihood of externally based terrorist groups or organisations launching attacks from outside the EU.

Indeed, the suggestion that the 'openness' of the EU's 'globalised' society makes it inherently susceptible to the threat of terrorism can be challenged on the basis that many of the 'terrorist' groups or organisations in the areas identified within the discourse are motivated not by hatred of the West but rather by local political grievances and issues.[77] There simply is not the political will on the part of these actors to attack the EU or its member states. For example, with respect to the conflicts in Mali and the Sahel region, which the EU has identified as a potential source of terrorist threat, Caitriona Dowd and Clionadh Raleigh have argued that they are driven by 'distinct domestic contexts and issues' and that these dynamics have been obscured by the 'totalizing narrative of global Islamic extremism'.[78] Similarly, a study by Arianna Robbins of so-called 'Al-Qaida affiliate groups' (AQAs) demonstrated that over 96 per cent of attacks by these groups occurred in a civil war setting and furthermore that affiliation to Al-Qaida did not make a 'terrorist' group or organisation more likely to attack the Western 'far enemy'.[79] As Richard Jackson points out, 'in-depth qualitative studies suggest that terrorism is always local; that is, it is driven by identifiable political grievances and issues specific to particular societies and locales'.[80] This sentiment is shared by Adrian Guelke, who has argued that the process of globalisation and its influence has been greatly over-exaggerated. He has noted that human beings continue to live in societies that are relatively independent of one another, and that consequently most sub-state political actors, including sub-state actors engaged in terrorism or political violence, seek primarily to influence events at that level. The construction of terrorism as an external threat to a political community is not new. As Guelke points out, 'the attribution of responsibility for acts of violence to outsiders is to be found throughout the history of violence'.[81]

What the suggestion of a major external threat from terrorism does in this context is to provide a simple threat narrative that can provide the basis for a coordinated EU policy response. However, this simplistic threat narrative obscures the complex nature of political conflict in those regions identified as potential sources of threat. Further to this, the EU 'fight against terrorism' discourse is also characterised by silence on, and a lack of recognition of, the role Western governments have played in the creation of the 'migrant' other as a potential 'security problem' through their foreign policies. EU

member states have been involved in conflicts in Iraq in 2003 (the UK) and
Libya in 2011 (the UK and France); as well as this there has been little in the
way of criticism of the role US policies have played in the creation of these
so-called 'conflict zones' in the Middle East and North Africa. This is an
argument supported by Frances Webber, who highlights the lack of responsibility taken by Western governments for the refugees created by the wars in
the Middle East, the resources wars in Africa, the fall-out wars from the 'per-
verse' boundaries of colonialism or the proxy wars against communism.[82]
According to Webber, it is the 'migrant' other and not the 'Western policies
and actions creating or contributing to their displacement' that are seen by
'European politicians and popular media as the problem'.[83] Regardless, the
formulation of certain dimensions of the EU counter-terrorism response has
continued to be based upon the perception that there remains an external
threat from third countries that requires enhanced border controls.

In particular, the conflict in Syria and Iraq and the emergence of the figure of the 'returning foreign fighter' has, it would seem, confirmed the worst
fears of the EU by providing the link between the internal and external
dimension of the perceived threat from terrorism. A number of citizens of
EU member states have travelled to and returned from the 'conflict zones'
identified within the discourse, 'abusing' the EU's migratory system in the
process, and, according to the logic of the discourse, may as a result of these
experiences potentially represent a source of terrorist threat. The first issue
that arises with the EU conceptualisation of the 'returning foreign fighter'
is that in all of the documents analysed a clear definition of the term 'foreign fighter' was not offered by the EU. Instead, the understanding of 'foreign fighter' that has guided the EU response is one that views the figure
of the 'foreign fighter' as a homogenised, singular 'terrorist' threat linked
to 'conflict zones' and in particular the emergence of Islamic State in Iraq
and Syria. Furthermore, the focus of the discourse has concentrated on the
'foreign fighter' as a 'returnee' and a citizen of an EU member state, thereby
constructing the threat as predominantly an internal threat. This understanding of what constitutes a 'foreign fighter' is a rather narrow one that
assumes that there is already a clearly definable category in place.[84]

It is important to recognise, therefore, that the concept of 'foreign fighters' is not a universally applicable category and is in fact a contested concept within the literature on this subject. Cerwyn Moore has argued that
the 'contested definitional parameters' of academic scholarship on 'foreign
fighters' can be traced across three phases, with each body of work reflecting differences over the constitutive elements that make up the figure of
the 'foreign fighter'.[85] Indeed, this criticism becomes more apparent when
analysing one of the earliest academic definitions of a 'foreign fighter'.
Moore and Paul Tumelty have defined foreign fighters as 'Non-indigenous,

non-territorialized combatants who, motivated by religion, kinship, and/or ideology rather than pecuniary reward, enter a conflict zone to participate in hostilities.'[86] The first thing that one notices about this definition is that the term terrorism is absent. Indeed, what this definition suggests is that the term 'foreign fighter' can be applicable to a range of activities that go beyond terrorist action. By constructing the threat of the 'foreign fighter' as part of its counter-terrorism strategy, and failing to offer a clear definition, the EU has implicitly constructed all 'foreign fighters' as potential terrorists. For example, there appears to be a worrying trend at EU level towards labelling all foreign fighters as 'foreign terrorist fighters', mirroring policy developments made at the United Nations.[87]

As Moore suggests, not only is the definitional issue contested but in fact many questions arise as to the different types of situation that the concept of 'foreign fighters' can be applied in; for example, should it include forms of volunteerism, ranging from 'training' to active combat? Do pre-existing networks need to be in place in order for mobilisation to occur? What other factors influence the scale of mobilisation? How can disengagement be effectively managed, and what influence do external actors have on local conflict dynamics?[88] In the period since the emergence of Islamic State this type of nuanced discussion of the phenomenon of 'foreign fighters' has been missing from the formulation of the EU's counter-response. Instead, the focus has been on the perception of an immediate and extreme threat from 'returning foreign fighters' to the EU and its member states. Yet, whilst it is true that some type of threat may possibly exist, it is argued here that this threat has been greatly over-exaggerated. For example, a study by Thomas Hegghammer found that in relation to the threat from 'foreign fighters', who had left one country to fight in another, the data indicated 'that no more than one in nine foreign fighters returned to perpetrate attacks in the West'.[89] However, he also offered the caveat that the data also pointed to a 'veteran effect' that makes 'returning foreign fighters' considerably more effective operatives. This research raises questions over the assertion by senior EU officials that a terrorist attack on mainland Europe by 'returning foreign fighters' is 'almost inevitable' and 'pre-programmed'.[90] It also raises questions about the effectiveness and legitimacy of border control measures as an element of the counter-terrorism response.

The most significant EU initiative for preventing 'returning foreign fighter' terrorism has been to try to revive the EU PNR agreement as part of a wider move to reinforce the EU border for counter-terrorism purposes.[91] The EU PNR was originally proposed by the European Commission in 2007 as a counter-terrorism and organised crime measure.[92] According to Evelien Brouwer, the EU's own Fundamental Rights Agency (FRA) found that the PNR proposal lacked essential guarantees on fundamental rights and contained open-ended, imprecise formulations that were based upon insufficient evidence that the collection and use of PNR data for law-enforcement purposes was either necessary or added value to the fight against terrorism.[93] Furthermore, according to Brouwer, there remains the added danger that the data collated through the PNR could be used for the investigation of other types of criminal activity including the prevention of irregular migration, which its development was not intended for.

What this clearly demonstrates is another example where the threat of terrorism, in this case the threat from 'returning foreign fighters', has been invoked by the main policy-making institutions of the EU to push through stalled measures that have rather tenuous links to the prevention of terrorism. The collation of all travel data on EU flights for the purpose of counter-terrorism can be questioned on the basis that it is an overreaction to what is a minor threat. There is a wider point here also about the effectiveness of border control measures for counter-terrorism in general. Sarah Leonard has pointed out that in this context gauging the effectiveness of border control measures is particularly challenging given that the evidence for success lies in the absence of a terrorist attack.[94] However, conclusively proving that a terrorist attack did not take place because of a certain border control measure is extremely difficult due to the fact that this information is either rare or does not exist. Leonard goes on to explain that border control has played a limited role in the 'fight against terrorism', with this trend set to continue in the future. What is certain is that this aspect of the EU counter-terrorism response prompts reflection on the wider political and societal implication of this strand of the 'fight against terrorism' discourse.

Political and societal implications

An important implication of the construction of the 'migrant' other as a potential terrorist threat is that it has securitised migration through making possible and further strengthening restrictive migration control practices, which are contributing to the normalisation of a deep-rooted suspicion of foreigners within European societies. The UN 'International Migration Report' of 2006 offered support to this line of argument by noting that 'concern about clandestine entry of foreigners has grown in the aftermath of the terrorist attacks of 11 September 2001 and the bombings in Bali, Casablanca, Madrid and London', and have led Western governments to introduce more 'stringent requirements for granting visas' or to 'impose visa requirements for nationals of countries that consistently produce unauthorized migrants'.[95] This perception has continued to be strengthened with the emergence of Islamic State in Iraq and Syria and the threat of the 'returning foreign fighter'.

According to Leonard, the linking of migration and terrorism has made travel into the EU area 'more difficult for *bona fide* travellers' that have no connection to terrorism, with the securitisation of migration having a real impact on migrants themselves.[96] For example, Robert Dover has shown in his research on migration between Sub-Saharan Africa (SSA) and the EU that fewer controls on the flow of people would have a positive impact on the individual migrants themselves, as well as bring increased economic benefits for African and European economies.[97] Dover argues that despite the fact there is 'very little evidence that migrants from SSA present a terrorist threat to the EU … the changes to how migrants enter the EU have been informed by these beliefs and the counter-terror agenda', and furthermore that 'the racial profiling that typifies these procedures constitutes a form of unacknowledged and systemic racism throughout the European policy sphere'.[98] For Dover, the securitisation of migration policy has been counter-productive for the EU and the migrants affected by it.[99] This view is supported by Didier Bigo and Elspeth Guild, who have analysed the impact of EU cooperation on visa systems on the securitisation of migrants.[100] As well as this, Leonard makes the more general point that the linking of counter-terrorism to asylum and migration control could 'have a harmful effect on the relations between various ethnic groups in multicultural societies' by presenting the 'migrant' other as someone 'particularly likely to engage in terrorist activities'.[101]

It should be noted that what is occurring here is a much more subtle form of securitisation that traverses the distinction between the two types of securitisation outlined in Chapter 1, exceptional measures on the one hand and the more mundane, everyday practices of security on the other. In essence, the securitisation of migration is representative of what Bigo has called a 'governmentality of unease'.[102] What Bigo means by this phrase is that there exists in Europe a solidly constituted transnational field of security professionals, both public and private, who are concerned with and have political authority over the management of security issues. In order to legitimise this role, extend their reach and justify the continued expansion of their remit as security actors, these 'security professionals' tap into or rearticulate a disparate array of 'internal security discourses', such as the 'threat' from organised crime, terrorism, drug trafficking and irregular migration, which are reconstructed as interlinked security issues requiring some type of counter-response. The strand of the discourse which links counter-terrorism to migration and border control therefore represents another site where the logic of extending the control of the movement of people, transnationally, be they migrant, refugee, asylum-seeker, potential terrorist or other border crosser, is articulated and strengthened. According to Bigo, the political and societal implications of such a discourse is that it makes possible and contributes to the legitimisation of new technologies of surveillance and control that have been created at the EU level, which are having a transformative impact upon the nature of policing in European societies.[103] In this instance, regulation of society goes beyond the parameters of conventional control measures and policing of foreigners to include persons deemed at 'risk', who are put under surveillance because they correspond to an identity or behaviour more likely to make them predisposed to that risk. In this case then, a precautionary security response to the 'migrant' other as a possible terrorist threat.

Central to the securitisation of migration has been the development of biometric measures for the purpose of border control. Juliet Lodge has drawn attention to this by arguing that the creation of an EU 'homeland security agenda' and the introduction of biometric instruments are not only representative of an increasing securitisation of social and political life within the EU more generally, they also challenge the EU's commitment to the principles of 'freedom, security and justice'.[104] For Lodge, the linking of migration control to counter-terrorism priorities has implications for civil liberties and fundamental rights such as the right to privacy and data protection. She argues that the use of biometric data to service immigration and 'internal security' concerns has been 'couched in', or legitimised through, 'the language of counter-terrorism' and instead may 'compromise rather than strengthen EU legitimacy'.[105] As Leonard points out, a growing amount of personal data, including biometric data, is already being collected from migrants entering the EU and stored in increasingly sophisticated databases, with the EU demonstrating 'a tendency to give ... increasingly wide access to such data to law enforcement authorities, including data that is not related to a specific crime and had originally been collected for other purposes'.[106]

This is a similar point to one made by Ben Hayes, who explains that EU moves towards ensuring the introduction of biometric identifiers (in this case fingerprints and digitised photos) into all passports, residence permits and visas issued by member states marks a fundamental shift in the European approach to privacy and civil liberties.[107] Hayes argues that whilst these technologies can have a role to play if adequately regulated, certain technologies such as CCTV or DNA profiling have 'generally been made available to the police with inadequate controls or regard for individual human rights'. As well as this, he argues that EU legislation on the introduction of biometric measures into passports and travel documents has come at 'the expense of democratic debate'. Hayes also points out that although technology can undoubtedly assist in police investigations, there is little evidence to suggest that it can actually prevent 'terrorism or crime' since 'technology can do nothing to address the multifaceted "root causes" of these social problems'.[108]

These developments have led Tony Bunyan to warn that the EU and its member states are set on a path that could potentially turn it 'into the most surveilled, monitored region in the world'.[109] Similarly, the European Civil Liberties Network (ECLN) has also concluded that EU security policy has taken 'a dangerously authoritarian turn', which has been reflected in EU moves towards 'militarised borders, mandatory proactive surveillance regimes and an increasingly aggressive external security and defence policy'.[110] The EU is therefore at the centre of a paradigm shift, with the 'fight against terrorism' providing a discursive legitimacy for this shift, in 'the way that Europe and the world beyond will be policed'.[111] The ECLN concludes that in effect these developments represent the 'militarisation of security' and the 'securitisation of everything', the result of which is 'an increasingly security-militarist approach to protracted social and economic problems'.[112] For the 'migrant' other, the political and social implications of these developments are that, in practice, they come to be the focus of restrictive border control policies reinforced for the purpose of responding to perceived threats to security.

Conclusion

This chapter has sought to demonstrate the role that the 'fight against terrorism' has played in the securitisation of migration at the EU level. It has been argued that the discursive construction of the 'migrant' other as a potential security threat has been achieved through the articulation of three interlinked strands of the 'fight against terrorism' discourse. First, through the consistent rearticulation of a claim that actual or potential terrorists are seeking to take advantage of the 'open' or 'globalised' environment provided by the EU migratory system. Second, through an assertion that the 'openness' of European society requires adequate 'border controls' and 'surveillance' of border crossers in order to 'protect' against any further terrorist attacks. Third, through the identification of the figure of the 'returning foreign fighter', an individuals who abuses the EU migratory system and who represents a 'new' and 'evolving' potential terrorist threat to the EU and its member states. Taken together, these interlinked representations help to conflate the 'terrorist' other with the 'migrant' other and form a powerful image of the terrorist threat against which the identity of the EU is once again reproduced.

In particular, the discourse has played a key role in the legitimisation of new policies and practices of security at the EU border, helping to normalise the use of new measures (biometrics) and instruments of 'control' (IT systems and databases), which are advocated by the EU as central to the counter-terrorism response. In this instance, securitising practices are made possible by the language of the EU's 'fight against terrorism'. Yet, the type of securitisation identified is not one concerned with existential threats but rather the more mundane threat represented by the everyday risk of the migrant traveller. As Bigo points out, migration and the terrorist threat become combined as a problem 'not because there is a threat to the survival of society' but because 'scenes from everyday life are politicized, because day-to-day living is securitised'.[113] It has also been argued that the threat of terrorism has led to a fundamental change in how the EU perceives concepts such as 'freedom' and 'protection'. In the 'fight against terrorism', freedom is conflated with security and redefined as protection from certain threats that discourses of insecurity tell 'us' we are prey to. Within this discursive environment biometrics, information systems and border controls represent a first step towards a much broader form of social control, which is concerned not just with migrants but citizens as well. As such, it is argued that the discourse of a 'fight against terrorism' plays a central role in the legitimisation of these policies and represents another site where the securitisation of social and political life within Europe continues to be made possible. Having explored the various ways in which the 'migrant' other has been securitised, the next chapter turns to an analysis of how the EU counter-terrorism discourse helps to construct the 'Muslim' other as potential terrorist threat.

Notes

1 I use the phrase 'European society' to refer to the 'globalised' or 'open' society that the EU views as under threat.
2 'Migration control' consists of numerous policies that are designed to exclude irregular migrants and other unwanted foreign nationals through restrictions on entry, border controls, detention and deportation.
3 The 'Protect' dimension of the *EU Counter-Terrorism Strategy* focuses specifically on migration control policies to 'protect' against terrorism. See Council of the European Union, *The European Union Counter-Terrorism Strategy*, Brussels, 30 November 2005, 14469/4/05.
4 European Council, 'Presidency Conclusions', Tampere European Council, 15–16 October 1999, 200/1/99, Article 1.
5 Ibid., Article 3.
6 Ibid., Article 4.
7 Council of the European Union, *Conclusions and Plan of Action of the Extraordinary European Council Meeting on 21 September 2001*, 2001, SN140/01.
8 Ibid., p. 1.

9 Ibid., p. 3.
10 Council of the European Union, *A Secure Europe in a Better World: European Security Strategy*, Brussels, 12 December 2003.
11 Ibid., p. 3.
12 Ibid., p. 3.
13 Council of the European Union, *Declaration on Combating Terrorism*, Brussels, 25 March 2004, 7906/04, pp. 9–12.
14 Council, *The European Union Counter-Terrorism Strategy*, p. 6.
15 Ibid.
16 Ibid., see pp. 7, 14.
17 Ibid., p. 7.
18 Council of the European Union, *Report on the Implementation of the European Security Strategy: Providing Security in a Changing World*, Brussels, 11 December 2008, S407/08, p. 1.
19 Ibid., p. 4.
20 Ibid., p. 1.
21 Council of the European Union, *The Stockholm Programme: An Open and Secure Europe Serving and Protecting Citizens*, Brussels, 2 December 2009, 17024/09.
22 Ibid., p. 4.
23 Council of the European Union, *Draft Internal Security Strategy for the European Union: Towards a European Security Model*, Brussels, 8 March 2010, 7120/10.
24 Ibid., p. 2.
25 Ibid.
26 Ibid.
27 These instruments of 'control' refer specifically to a series of EU databases that have been developed since the Treaty on European Union, 1992. They include: the Schengen Information System (SIS & SIS II), European Dactyloscopy (Eurodac) and the EU Visa Information System (VIS). The SIS is a large-scale information system that supports external border control and law enforcement cooperation in the Schengen area. It has been in operation since 1995. Eurodac is a biometric database that has been in operation since 2003. It stores the fingerprints of asylum seekers at their point of entry into the EU. The VIS is a database that allows for the sharing of visa information between Schengen states. It has been in operation since 2001 and stores the biometric information of third country nationals (digital facial images and digital fingerprints) over the age of 12 who have applied for a visa to enter an EU member state. Although originally developed for purposes of border control, the EU has sought to remodel these databases for the purposes of counter-terrorism. Similarly, the EU has developed a counter-terrorism role for its external border agency (Frontex), which since 2013 has operated an external border surveillance system (Eurosur) the development of which has been justified through linking to counter-terrorism objectives.
28 Council of the European Union, *Conclusions Adopted by the Council (Justice and Home Affairs)*, Brussels, 20 September 2001, SN3926/6/01 Rev 6.

29 Ibid., p. 7, Article 16.
30 Ibid., see pp. 8–9, Articles 24–30.
31 European Council, *Declaration on Combating Terrorism*.
32 Ibid., pp. 7–8.
33 Council of the European Union, *The Hague Programme: Strengthening Freedom, Security and Justice in the European Union*, Brussels, 13 December 2004, 16054/04.
34 Ibid., p. 4, para. 2.
35 Ibid., pp. 16–17.
36 Council, *The European Union Counter-Terrorism Strategy*, p. 10.
37 Ibid.
38 Ibid.
39 Council of the European Union, *Implementation of the Strategy and Action Plan to Combat Terrorism*, Brussels, 19 November 2008, 15912/08.
40 Ibid., p. 6.
41 Ibid.
42 Council of the European Union, *EU Action Plan on Combating Terrorism*, Brussels, 26 November 2009, 15358/09, p. 7.
43 Council, *The Stockholm Programme*, p. 57.
44 Council, *Draft Internal Security Strategy*, p. 15. For example, one suggestion was the development of a 'European Passenger Names Record (PNR)' database 'for the purpose of preventing, detecting, investigating and prosecuting terrorist offences and serious crime'; see p. 12.
45 Council of the European Union, *Preventing Lone Actor Terrorism: Food for Thought*, Brussels, 23 April 2012, 9090/12, p. 8.
46 Council of the European Union, *Report on the Implementation of the EU Counter-Terrorism Strategy*, Brussels, 24 November 2014, 15799/14, p. 18.
47 Ibid., p. 6.
48 Council of the European Union, *A Strategy for the External Dimension of JHA: Global Freedom, Security and Justice*, Brussels, 30 November 2005, 14366/3/05, p. 9.
49 Europol, *TE-SAT 2007: EU Terrorism Situation and Trends Report* (The Hague, 2007), p. 23. First instances of the phrase 'conflict zones' can be found in the 2008 revised 'counter-radicalisation' strategy and in the 2009 TE-SAT report; see Council of the European Union, *Revised EU Strategy for Combating Radicalisation and Recruitment to Terrorism*, Brussels, 14 November 2008, 15175/08, p. 4; Europol, *TE-SAT 2009: EU Terrorism Situation and Trends Report* (The Hague, 2009), p. 7.
50 Europol, *TE-SAT 2008: EU Terrorism Situation and Trends Report* (The Hague, 2008), pp. 27–28.
51 Council of the European Union, *EU Counter-Terrorism Strategy: Discussion Paper*, Brussels, 29 November 2010, 15894/1/10, Rev 1.
52 Ibid., p. 3.
53 Ibid.
54 Council, *Preventing Lone Actor Terrorism*, p. 8.

55 Ibid.

56 Ibid.

57 Council of the European Union, *Foreign Fighters and Returnees from a Counter-Terrorism Perspective*, Brussels, 5 May 2014, 9280/14.

58 Ibid., p. 7.

59 Council of the European Union, *Foreign Fighters and Returnees: Implementation of the Measures Decided by the JHA Council on 9–10 October 2014*, Brussels, 24 November 2014, 16002/14, p. 2.

60 Ibid., pp. 2–20.

61 Ibid., pp. 14–18.

62 Council of the European Union, *Outline of the Counter-Terrorism Strategy for Syria and Iraq, with Particular Focus on Foreign Fighters*, Brussels, 16 January 2015, 5369/15; Council of the European Union, *Council Conclusions on the EU Regional Strategy for Syria and Iraq as well as the ISIL/Da'esh Threat*, Brussels, 16 March 2015, 7267/15.

63 Council, *Counter-Terrorism Strategy for Syria and Iraq*, p. 2.

64 Council, *EU Regional Strategy for Syria and Iraq*, p. 35.

65 Ibid., p. 21.

66 Patrick R. Ireland, 'Facing the true "Fortress Europe": immigrants and politics in the EC', *Journal of Common Market Studies*, 29:5 (1991), 457–480.

67 Jef Huysmans, 'The European Union and the securitization of migration', *Journal of Common Market Studies*, 38:5 (2000), 756.

68 Christina Boswell, 'Migration control in Europe after 9/11: explaining the absence of securitization', *Journal of Common Market Studies*, 45:3 (2007), 589–610.

69 Ibid., 595.

70 Carl Levy, 'The European Union after 9/11: the demise of a liberal democratic asylum regime?', *Government and Opposition*, 40:1 (2005), 28.

71 On the 'non-securitisation of migration control', see Boswell, 'Migration control in Europe after 9/11', 596–600.

72 Andrew Neal, 'Securitization and risk at the EU border: the origins of Frontex', *Journal of Common Market Studies*, 47:2 (2009), 339.

73 Council, *Conclusions Adopted by the Council (Justice and Home Affairs)*, p. 8; see also Council, *The European Union Counter-Terrorism Strategy*.

74 Didier Bigo, 'Liberty, Whose Liberty? The Hague Programme and the Conception of Freedom', in Thierry Balzacq and Sergio Carrera (eds), *Security versus Freedom? A Challenge for Europe's Future* (Aldershot: Ashgate, 2006), p. 35.

75 Mario Zucconi, 'Migration and Security as an Issue in US–European Relations', in John Tirman (ed.), *The Maze of Fear: Security and Migration after 9/11* (New York: The New Press, 2004), p. 143.

76 See the Europol TE-SAT reports.

77 Adrian Guelke, *Terrorism and Global Disorder* (London: I.B. Tauris, 2006).

78 Caitriona Dowd and Clionadh Raleigh, 'The myth of global Islamic terrorism and local conflict in Mali and the Sahel', *African Affairs*, 112:148 (2013), 1–12, see p. 1.

79 Arianna J. Robbins, 'All terrorism is local? A quantitative analysis of Al Qaeda affiliation and rebel group behavior', *The Eagle Feather*, 11 (2014), available online at: http://eaglefeather.honors.unt.edu/2014/article/324#.VWV_RJXbLIW (accessed May 2015).

80 Richard Jackson, 'Constructing enemies: "Islamic terrorism" in political and academic discourse', *Government and Opposition*, 42:3 (2007), 394–426, see p. 418.

81 Guelke, *Terrorism and Global Disorder*, p. 15.

82 Frances Webber, 'Border wars and asylum crimes', *Statewatch* (2006), available online at: www.statewatch.org/analyses/border-wars-and-asylum-crimes.pdf (accessed May 2015).

83 Ibid., 3.

84 Cerwyn Moore, 'Introductory comments to Foreign Fighters Research: special mini-series', *Terrorism and Political Violence*, 27:3 (2015), 393–394.

85 Cerwyn Moore, 'Foreign bodies: transnational activism, the insurgency in the North Caucasus and "beyond"', *Terrorism and Political Violence*, 27:3 (2015), 395–415.

86 Cerwyn Moore and Paul Tumelty, 'Foreign fighters and the case of Chechnya: a critical assessment', *Studies in Conflict & Terrorism*, 31:5 (2008), 412–433.

87 See Council, *EU Regional Strategy for Syria and Iraq*, which contains four references to the phrase 'foreign terrorist fighters'.

88 Moore, 'Introductory comments', 393–394.

89 Thomas Hegghammer, 'Should I stay or should I go? Explaining variation in Western jihadists' choice between domestic and foreign fighting', *American Political Science Review*, 107:1 (2013), 10.

90 Ian Traynor, 'Major Terrorist Attack Is "Inevitable" as Isis Fighters Return, Say EU Officials', *Guardian* (25 September 2014), available online at: www.theguardian.com/world/2014/sep/25/major-terrorist-attack-inevitable-isis-eu (accessed 27 March 2014).

91 The EU PNR directive will make it a legal requirement that air carriers collect passenger travel data on flights between member states and between member states and non-EU countries, with the data to be used for border control or law-enforcement purposes.

92 See European Commission, *Proposal for a Council Framework Decision on the Use of Passenger Name Record (PNR) for Law Enforcement Purposes*, COM (2007) 654.

93 Evelien Brouwer, 'The EU Passenger Name Record (PNR) System and Human Rights: Transferring Passenger Data or Passenger Freedom?', *CEPS Working Document No. 320* (Brussels: Centre for European Policy Studies, 2009), p. 13.

94 Sarah Leonard, 'Border controls as a dimension of the European Union's counter-terrorism policy: a critical assessment', *Intelligence and National Security*, 30:2–3 (2015), 306–332.

95 United Nations, 'International Migration Report 2006: A Global Assessment', United Nations Department of Economic and Social Affairs/Population Division, available online at: www.un.org/esa/population/publications/2006_MigrationRep/part_one.pdf (accessed May 2015).

96 Ibid., p. 330.
97 Robert Dover, 'Towards a common EU immigration policy: a securitization too far', *Journal of European Integration*, 30:1 (2008), 113–130.
98 Ibid., 127.
99 He acknowledges that some benefits have been accrued in relation to certain unspecified wealth-creation models.
100 Didier Bigo and Elspeth Guild, 'Policing at Distance: Schengen Visa Policies', in Didier Bigo and Elspeth Guild (eds), *Controlling Frontiers: Free Movement into and within Europe* (Aldershot: Ashgate, 2005).
101 Leonard, 'Border controls', 331.
102 Didier Bigo, 'Globalized (In)Security: The Field and the Ban-Opticon', in Didier Bigo and Anastassia Tsoukala (eds), *Terror, Insecurity and Liberty: Illiberal Practices of Liberal Regimes after 9/11* (Abingdon: Routledge, 2008), pp. 10–48.
103 By this Bigo means the ever-closer merging of policing, intelligence and military activities for the purposes of surveillance of a small number of people predefined as potential security threats (i.e. third country nationals migrating into the EU).
104 Juliet Lodge, 'EU homeland security: citizens or suspects?', *European Integration*, 26:3 (2004), 257.
105 Ibid., 254.
106 Leonard, 'Border controls', 331.
107 Ben Hayes, 'Arming Big Brother: the EU's Security Research Programme', *Statewatch and the Transnational Institute* (2006), p. 30, available online at: www.statewatch.org/analyses/bigbrother.pdf (accessed June 2015).
108 Ibid., 39.
109 Tony Bunyan, 'Just over the horizon: the surveillance society and the state in the EU', *Race & Class*, 51:3 (2010), 7.
110 European Civil Liberties Network, 'Statement on the Stockholm Programme' (April 2009), p. 1, available online at: www.ecln.org/ECLN-statement-on-Stockholm-Programme-April-2009-eng.pdf (accessed January 2015).
111 Ibid., p. 3.
112 Ibid.
113 Didier Bigo, 'The Mobius Ribbon of Internal and External Security(ies)', in Mathias Albert, David Jacobson and Yosef Lapid (eds), *Identities, Borders, Orders: Rethinking International Relations Theory* (Minneapolis: University of Minnesota Press, 2001).

5

Constructing the 'Muslim' other: preventing 'radicalisation', 'violent extremism' and 'terrorism'

Introduction

This chapter explores the strand of the 'fight against terrorism' discourse that connects the threat of terrorism to 'violent religious extremism'. The chapter focuses specifically on an EU belief that preventing terrorism is best achieved through the development of policies designed to combat the process of 'radicalisation'. The chapter considers the emergence and evolution of the EU's counter-radicalisation discourse. It shows how the 'radicalisation' strand of the discourse was initially constructed on the basis of an assumption that members of the 'Muslim communities' of Europe were more susceptible to 'radicalisation' into 'violent religious extremism' and terrorism. I argue that by adopting a belief in the notion of 'radicalisation' as a central aspect of the counter-terrorism response, the discourse implicitly constructs the Muslim 'other' as a potential terrorist threat. Identity is central to this strand of the discourse in that the use of terms or labels such as 'Muslim community', the 'Muslim world', the 'Islamic world' or the 'Arab and Muslim world' help to construct an 'other', the 'Muslim' other, who represents the primary target of the counter-radicalisation policies of the EU and its member states. I argue that the discourse delineates a separate group identity, the 'Muslim community', against which the identity of the EU is differentiated, noting that within the logic of the discourse the 'Muslim' other is thought to represent a member of a community that must be 'engaged' if terrorism is to be defeated.

The first half of the chapter begins by mapping this strand of the discourse, highlighting the ways in which it has developed since the events of 11 September 2001. I suggest that although the EU has consistently stated that it rejects any equation of Islam and the 'Muslim world' with terrorism, it has contradicted this position and done so anyway. I show how, in its initial phase, the language of the EU's policy to combat 'radicalisation and recruitment' into terrorism contained numerous references to Islam and Muslims. I argue that this language helped to construct 'radicalisation' as a process that occurred primarily within 'Muslim communities', playing a key role in the representation of the 'Muslim' other as a potential terrorist threat. The analysis demonstrates how, since 2004, when preventing 'radicalisation' was first discussed by the European Commission, the EU has undertaken a process of 'discursive learning' that has led to a transformation in the discourse and a move away from the framing of 'radicalisation' as a problem inherently linked to Islam or 'violent religious extremism'. It shows how by 2008 the EU understanding of 'radicalisation' had been expanded to include all forms of terrorism, not just those inspired by a 'distorted version of Islam'. I argue that by 2015 a broader conceptualisation of 'radicalisation' had emerged that centred on 'violent extremism', rather than solely religion, as the motivation for contemporary terrorist threats.

The second half of the chapter critiques the concept of 'radicalisation', highlighting the social and political implications of this strand of the discourse. I show how the 'conventional wisdom' on this issue has retained an understanding of 'radicalisation' as a process more likely to occur within certain suspect communities. It is argued that the more general public discourse on 'radicalisation' retains an implicit link to the threat of 'Islamist-inspired' forms of terrorism, suggesting that attempts by the EU to broaden and disassociate 'radicalisation' from the implicit threat of the 'Muslim' other will prove unsuccessful. I contend that in the minds of politicians, policy-makers, the media or the general public, when 'radicalisation' is spoken of it is always taken to mean the 'radicalisation' of Muslims into extremism and terrorism. I argue therefore that the 'radicalisation' discourse contains an *inherent racial bias* against Muslims. I go on to consider the ways in which 'front-line' professionals, such as teachers, health workers and prison officers, have been co-opted to deliver the counter-radicalisation strategies of EU member states, arguing that counter-radicalisation policy, in essence, represents a step towards the securitisation of civil society in Europe. The chapter concludes by suggesting that the notion of 'radicalisation' helps to provide legitimacy for the development of a complex mode of governance, which extends out from the European level and cuts across national and local boundaries.

The emergence of the EU's discourse on 'violent religious extremism'

On 21 September 2001, in the immediate aftermath of the terrorist attacks in New York, the European Council set out the initial EU position on the threat posed by terrorism.[1] The *Conclusions and Action Plan of the Extraordinary Council Meeting* clearly stated that whilst 'the fight against terrorism will, more than ever, be a priority objective of the European Union', the EU 'categorically rejects any equation of groups of fanatical terrorists with the Arab and Muslim world'.[2] This initial perception of the threat posed by terrorism, as a threat that needed to be disassociated from Islam, has since come to form one of the main elements of the EU's 'fight against terrorism' discourse.[3] The action plan went on to state that the EU should play a key role in the establishment of 'the broadest possible global coalition against terrorism', designed to defend 'our common values' and including 'our Arab and Muslim partners' or 'any other country ready to defend our common values'.[4] The document also stated that the 'fight against terrorism' would require the EU to play 'a greater part in the efforts of the international community to prevent and stabilise regional conflicts'.[5] The document suggested that in order to meet this objective the EU would have to work with the United States (US), Russia and its 'partners in the Arab and Muslim world', claiming that it would 'make every endeavour to bring the parties to the Middle East conflict to a lasting understanding on the basis of the relevant United Nations resolutions'.[6] At this early stage there was a tacit acceptance that, whilst it was important not to link terrorism to Islam or the 'Arab and Muslim world', the context within which the September 11 terrorist attacks had occurred would require some sort of resolution to the Arab–Israeli conflict if the EU were to be successful in reducing the threat from terrorism.

In the initial post-September 11 phase of the formulation of EU counter-terrorism policy, it was the Europol Terrorism Situation and Trend reports (TE-SAT) that first introduced the notion of 'Islamic extremist terrorism' into the EU lexicon.[7] Although the first two TE-SAT reports were careful to outline a number of different types of terrorist threat to the EU and its member states, including separatist, anarchist, left-wing and right-wing terrorism, the potential threat posed by 'Islamic extremist terrorism' was considered to be the most concerning. The second report from October 2003 drew an implicit relationship between terrorism and the 'Muslim community' by highlighting the importance of the United States' war against Iraq in creating a sense of 'mounting frustration within Muslim communities', which by October 2003 had as yet not led to a terrorist attack.[8] Indeed, the report was quick to highlight that 'bio terrorism and use of Weapons of Mass Destruction' (WMDs) should still be perceived as a 'major threat most often linked to Islamic related terrorism and al Qaeda'.[9] Tapping into the various discourse strands outlined in the previous chapters about the nature and causes of the so-called 'new terrorism', the first TE-SAT reports played a central role in framing the EU's interpretation of the terrorist threat and, in particular, drawing a link between Islam, terrorism and the threat posed by Al-Qaida.

The next important step in the framing of the terrorist threat to the EU came with the release in December 2003 of the *European Security Strategy*.[10] Again, the strategy employed a reconciliatory language towards the 'Muslim world' in that, although it did not explicitly link this policy goal to prevention of terrorism in Europe, the strategy once again emphasised a need for 'resolution of the Arab/Israeli conflict'.[11] Under the headline goal of 'building security in our neighbourhood', the resolution of this conflict was defined as 'a strategic priority for Europe', without which it was argued 'there will be little chance of dealing with other problems in the Middle East'.[12] It also reinforced the need for cooperation and engagement with Muslim countries, stating that 'broader engagement with the Arab world should also be considered'.[13]

Importantly, the document introduced the concept of 'violent religious extremism' into the EU lexicon, stating that 'The most recent wave of terrorism is global in scope and is linked to violent religious extremism. It arises out of complex causes. These include the pressures of modernisation, cultural, social and political crisis, and the alienation of young people living in foreign societies.'[14] As explained in the previous chapters, until this point, the threat of terrorism had been interpreted as a threat emanating primarily from sources external to the EU. Building on the recognition of a relationship between 'Islamic extremist terrorism' and the 'mounting frustration within Muslim communities', identified in the TE-SAT report from October 2003, the *European Security Strategy* put forward for the first time an acknowledgement of an internal, 'home-grown', dimension to the terrorist threat.[15] The strategy identified Europe as 'both a target and a base' for terrorism inspired by 'violent religious extremism' and suggested that 'this phenomenon is also a part of our own society'.[16]

Again, although the EU was quick to recognise the diverse nature of the threat facing Europe, the TE-SAT reports continued to emphasise the potential threat from 'radical Islamic movements', 'Islamic radical fundamentalism' and 'radical Islamist movements', which were identified as the most prevalent threats.[17] The growing EU concern with the threat posed by 'Islamic extremist terrorism' was thought to be confirmed by the terrorist attacks that took place in Madrid, on 11 March 2004. The attacks prompted the release of the *Declaration on Combating Terrorism*.[18] The document was significant because it was the first occasion on which the EU spoke of tackling or combating 'recruitment' into terrorism. Objective six of the renewed Action Plan for combating terrorism highlighted a perceived need to 'address the factors which contribute to support for, and recruitment into, terrorism', part of which included a focus on 'the links between extreme religious or political beliefs, as well as socio-economic and other factors, and support for terrorism'.[19] This was followed by a statement later that year in the *Hague Programme*, released in December 2004, which called on the European Council to 'by the end of 2005, develop a long-term strategy to address the factors which contribute to radicalisation and recruitment for terrorist activities'.[20]

In the initial phase of the formulation of EU counter-terrorism policy, between September 2001 and the start of the post-Madrid period, an inherent tension within the 'fight against terrorism' emerged. Although the EU made every effort during this period to avoid explicitly linking Islam to terrorism, the introduction and use of terms like 'Islamic extremist terrorism' by Europol, as well as the arguments put forward by the European Council about the threat from 'violent religious extremism', had the opposite effect. It was this perception of a religious dimension to the terrorist threat that encouraged the EU to highlight the need for a separation of terrorism from Islam; but was simultaneously the reason why the threat of terrorism was constructed as a threat implicitly linked to Islam and the place of the 'Muslim' other in European societies. As I demonstrate below, during the post-Madrid period the EU continued to formulate its counter-terrorism policy on the basis of an assumption that the terrorist threat to the EU should be understood as a phenomenon linked to Islam.

The threat of 'radicalisation' and the 'Muslim' other

From 2005 onwards, the EU really began to push the idea that if it were to be truly effective in 'preventing' terrorism, then it must 'address the root causes of terrorism'.[21] Identifying the so-called *process* of 'radicalisation' into terrorism as one of the foremost concerns of EU counter-terrorism policy, the European Council tasked the European Commission with developing a counter-strategy. In September 2005, the Commission submitted to the Council a report entitled: *Terrorist Recruitment: Addressing the Factors Contributing to Violent Radicalisation.*[22] With reference made to the terrorist attacks in London, in July 2005, as well as the attacks in Madrid a year earlier, the Commission argued that 'addressing violent radicalisation' would form part of a comprehensive EU approach to terrorism. The document defined 'violent radicalisation' as 'The phenomenon of people embracing opinions, views and ideas which could lead to acts of terrorism.'[23] The Commission explained that although Europe had experienced 'different types of terrorism in its history', the main threat to the EU 'comes from terrorism that is underlined by an abusive interpretation of Islam'; however, it was also noted that 'Many of the motivational factors for violent radicalisation and the remedies dealt with by this Communication are equally valid for all violent radicalisation, whether of a nationalistic, anarchic, separatist, extreme left or extreme right kind.'[24] Although the EU made a clear statement that 'violent radicalisation' should not be seen as a process restricted to an 'abusive interpretation of Islam', the document chose to focus primarily on this issue. It advocated the promotion of 'inter-cultural' and 'inter-religious' understanding between Europe and third countries, 'in particular those in which Islam is the predominant religion', as well as focusing on the need to engage with 'some young people from Muslim immigrant families', all put forward as ways in which to combat 'violent radicalisation'.[25] What this reveals then is that from the outset this strand of the discourse was based on an implicit assumption that 'radicalisation' was somehow linked to Islam and the place of Muslims within European society.

The Commission communication paved the way for the *EU Strategy for Combating Radicalisation and Recruitment to Terrorism*, which has since come to form the basis of the preventative dimension of the EU's *Counter-Terrorism Strategy*.[26] The *Strategy for Combating Radicalisation* was quick to state that the EU should work to 'correct unfair or inaccurate perceptions of Islam and Muslims' as well as seek to 'develop a non-emotive lexicon for discussing the issues in order to avoid linking Islam to terrorism', reflecting the direction taken in earlier policy documents.[27] Yet, although the EU suggested that 'radicalisation and recruitment' to terrorism should not be viewed as 'confined to one belief system or political persuasion', and that Europe has experienced other forms of terrorism throughout its history, it explained that 'the terrorism perpetrated by Al-Qaida and extremists inspired by Al-Qaida has become the main terrorist threat to the Union'.[28] This statement was followed by a particularly revealing line, which clarified that 'While other types of terrorism continue to pose a serious threat to EU citizens, the Union's response to radicalisation and recruitment focuses on this type of terrorism.'[29] Once more the document emphasised the considered nature of the EU response to terrorism through phrases that claimed the EU would 'engage in dialogue', 'not undermine respect for fundamental rights' and develop 'the right legal framework' to combat terrorism. However, the problem of terrorism in Europe was again constructed as primarily a problem linked to the 'Muslim community'.

This implicit construction of the 'Muslim' other as a potential threat occurred through three clearly identifiable discursive practices. First, the document articulated an assumption that the only way to defeat 'Al-Qaida and those inspired by them' would be through 'engagement of the public, and especially Muslims, in Europe and beyond'.[30] It also stated that the EU welcomed 'the strong stance that the people of Europe and beyond, including Muslims, have taken to reject terrorism and urges them not to relent in their condemnation'. Second, it outlined what the main provisions of the policy would consist of. It explained that the central element of the policy was the need to 'empower moderate voices by engaging with Muslim organisations and faith groups', 'reject the distorted version of Islam put forward by Al-Qaida and others', 'encourage the emergence of European imams and enhance language and other training for foreign imams in Europe' and 'enhance our efforts to change the perceptions of European and Western policies particularly among Muslim communities'.[31] Third, there was the suggestion of a potentially all-encompassing threat, with the statement that 'Radicalisation of certain Muslim individuals in Europe is a relatively recent phenomenon. Even those areas of Europe where radicalisation is not a major issue at present, or where large Muslim communities do not exist, could become targets for extremists.'[32]

Indeed, the use of terms and phrases such as 'Muslims', 'Muslim immigrant communities' and 'Muslim communities', whilst not necessarily creating a radically threatening other, certainly highlight a process of othering that differentiates members of that community from other citizens of the EU. It can therefore be argued that in its first iteration, at the very least, the EU counter-radicalisation strategy was originally based on an assumption that the process of 'radicalisation' was a phenomenon more likely to occur within 'Muslim communities' in Europe. The suggestion that 'Muslim communities' must be engaged if terrorism is to be prevented only serves to further strengthen the implicit construction of the 'Muslim' other as a potential terrorist threat. Moreover, statements alluding to the need for Muslims to continue to reject violence insinuated that not only was this a problem with 'Muslim communities' in Europe, but also that it was their job to fix it.

The evolution of the EU's 'radicalisation' discourse

As the idea of 'radicalisation' took hold in the imagination of EU policy-makers, the EU began to demonstrate a more nuanced understanding of the role of language in relation to the causes of terrorism and its own counter-terrorism response. The EU started to speak of the importance of countering the 'narrative' of 'extremists', which was thought to lead individuals to consider and justify acts of terrorism and political violence. One of the first instances of the use of the term 'narrative' was by the EU Counter-Terrorism Coordinator (EU CTC) in a report that highlighted Commission proposals for a series of studies into the factors that trigger 'radicalisation among youths, narratives used by extremists, and the methods through which terrorists find new recruits'.[33] Whilst this focus on the 'narrative' propagated by 'extremists' still reflected an inherent bias towards identifying the process of 'radicalisation' as a phenomenon linked to Islam, an accompanying change occurred as the EU began an explicit transformation of its own 'radicalisation' discourse. In November 2008 the European Council released a *Revised Strategy for Combating Radicalisation and Recruitment to Terrorism*.[34] This document was significant in that it removed all but one reference to Islam and stated that the new counter-radicalisation

strategy 'must reflect Europe's desire to combat all forms of terrorism, who-
ever the perpetrators may be'.[35] However, although only one explicit reference was made to Islam, many of the policies in the new strategy remained
the same. The policy rearticulated the suggestion that there was an 'extremist world view' that 'distorts perceptions of Western policies', which must
be countered if further terrorist threats were to be prevented. The document
suggested similar proposals to 'empower mainstream voices', 'promote inter-
cultural dialogue' and to 'ensure that voices of mainstream opinion prevail
over those of extremism', as measures that might be effective in response.
Although the EU counter-radicalisation policy no longer drew an explicit
link between Islam and 'radicalisation', the language of the proposals suggested that Muslims would remain the primary target of such policies.

The removal of all references to Islam and Muslims from the
counter-radicalisation strategy did, however, indicate the start of a transformation in the EU discourse on 'radicalisation'. In part this process of
what I term here 'discursive learning' can be attributed to the EU's desire
to embrace 'evidence-based' academic research.[36] In September 2005, the
European Commission put forward proposals for the creation of a 'network
of experts' on 'violent radicalisation'.[37] These proposals led to the creation
of the Expert Group on Violent Radicalisation in April 2006 (EGVR).[38] The
group was set up to investigate 'factors contributing to violent radicalisation'
and, as a result, four major studies into processes leading to 'violent radicalisation' were prescribed by the European Commission.[39] These reports
were significant in relation to their impact on the continued evolution of
the counter-radicalisation strand of the 'fight against terrorism' discourse.
Investigating issues such as factors leading to 'recruitment and mobilisation
for the Islamist militant movement in Europe', the 'beliefs, ideologies and
narratives' thought to underpin 'violent radicalisation' and 'radicalisation
processes leading to acts of terrorism', three of the four studies were characterised by an exclusive focus on the relationship between these issues and
Islam and contained no mention of other forms of 'radicalisation'.

The one report that took a broader view on the process of 'radicalisation'
was the report by the EGVR, which investigated *Radicalisation Processes
Leading to Acts of Terrorism*. Importantly, the report took issue with the
idea of 'violent radicalisation', noting that the process did not necessarily
have to involve violence, as well as explaining that there are 'remarkable
parallels between radicalisation to current jihadist terrorism and radicalisation to left-wing, right-wing or nationalist separatist terrorism'.[40] This language directly mirrored the line of argument taken by the Council in the
revised counter-radicalisation strategy, suggesting that the EU was prepared
to learn from the research that it had commissioned. Yet, as I have highlighted, although it was possible to identify a process of 'discursive learning'

in terms of the EU's move to frame 'radicalisation' as an issue not solely associated with Islam, the overall direction of the 'radicalisation' discourse continued to be implicitly aimed at 'Muslim communities' in Europe.

During the post-Madrid period, between January 2005 and December 2008, the strand of the discourse concerned with 'violent religious extremism' witnessed an important evolution. Initially, in the post-September 11 period, the EU had identified 'Islamic extremist terrorism' and 'violent religious extremism' as the main terrorist threat to its member states. In this second period, the focus switched to the role of 'radicalisation' in leading individuals or groups to engage in terrorist activities. The *Strategy for Combating Radicalisation and Recruitment to Terrorism* was significant because it constructed 'radicalisation' as *a process* most likely to occur in 'Muslim communities', with the suggested responses to 'radicalisation' emphasising this point. However, the EU continued to underscore its belief that terrorism should not be associated with Islam or Muslims. The studies commissioned by the EU during this period reflected this inconsistent position by focusing on 'radicalisation' as a phenomenon most associated with the Muslim community (and an underlying cause of terrorism), revealing potentially one source of the inherent contradiction in the EU statements about not associating Islam with terrorism yet implicitly doing so anyway. By December 2008 the EU had released a new strategy on combating 'radicalisation', which moving forward promised a broader focus on other forms of 'radicalisation' and its role in leading people to engage in other types of terrorism.

The expansion of the EU's 'radicalisation' discourse

Since the end of 2008, the 'radicalisation' strand of the 'fight against terrorism' discourse has been broadened to incorporate all other forms of terrorism, with the EU moving to adopt the term 'violent extremism' rather than 'violent religious extremism'. The EU's third internal security programme, the *Stockholm Programme*, again identified combating 'radicalisation' as a priority concern.[41] It put forward proposals that included: the development of 'prevention mechanisms, in particular to allow the early detection of signs of "radicalisation" or threats, including threats from violent, militant extremism'; initiatives 'to counter radicalisation in all vulnerable populations on the basis of an evaluation of the effectiveness of national policies'; and the incorporation of strategies to combat 'radicalisation' into bilateral relations with third countries.[42] Alongside this the EU *Internal Security Strategy* also prioritised counter-radicalisation policies.[43] The document spoke of addressing radicalisation from a broader perspective, arguing that the central objective of counter-radicalisation policy should be to 'empower' communities to respond to the threat. In the post-Breivik period, 'radicalisation' has also been linked to the threat from 'lone actor' terrorism and the threat from 'foreign fighters and returnees'.[44] In 2012, the EU CTC proposed that the focus of counter-radicalisation would have to be expanded out to consider not just those individuals who form part of a network but also those individuals who exist 'on the periphery' as 'lone actors'.[45] The EU suggested that an effective counter-radicalisation policy must contain measures to 'identify' and 'detect' processes of 'radicalisation'. In order to do this, it proposed that the counter-radicalisation policies of EU member states should engage and make use of 'frontline workers', such as 'health care workers' and 'medical professionals', in the delivery of these programmes.[46] Furthermore, to support the broadened objectives of its counter-radicalisation discourse, the EU recommended the creation of the Radicalisation Awareness Network (RAN).[47]

Building on the previous experiences of the EGVR and the European Network of Experts on Radicalisation (ENER), the RAN has been promoted by the EU as a new forum through which to combat terrorism and 'violent extremism'. The RAN consists of eight working groups, each focusing on a topic thought to be linked to the 'radicalisation' process. The different working groups focus on: police and law enforcement (RAN POL); voices of victims of terrorism (RAN VVT); Internet and social media (RAN @); prevention (RAN PREVENT); de-radicalisation (RAN DERAD); prison and probation (RAN P&P); health (RAN HEALTH); and the internal and external dimension of radicalisation policies (RAN INT/EXT). The RAN aims to connect first-line practitioners, field experts, social workers, teachers, non-governmental and civil society organisations, victims' groups, local authorities, law enforcement, academics and others, all for the purpose of combating potential pathways into violence.

The rationality for the expansion of the counter-radicalisation policies of the EU and its member states was captured succinctly in a speech by Cecilia Malmström, EU Commissioner for Home Affairs, in the run-up to the RAN's first major conference, held on 29 January 2013, in which she stated: 'Violent extremism represents one of the greatest threats to EU citizens' security. It is an ever-growing and increasing internal security concern. The terrorist threat has in part shifted away from organised groups to individuals, who are harder to detect, and whose actions are harder to predict.'[48] I argue that this broadening is significant for three reasons. First, not only do 'violent extremism' and the 'radicalisation' process continue to be perceived as the key contributory factors that lead people to engage in acts of terrorism, but they are also perceived to be 'one of the greatest threats to the security of EU citizens'. The 'radicalisation' discourse therefore represents an extension of the terrorism as extreme threat discourse, which I outlined in Chapter 2. Second, whilst the EU moved away from explicitly linking 'radicalisation' to one specific religion, a cursory analysis of the various RAN working group programmes reveals a continued focus on 'radicalisation' as an issue implicitly linked to Islam and the place of Muslims in European societies. Third, the extension of the focus of counter-radicalisation to include a role for teachers, prison staff and health professionals represents another step towards the securitisation of social and political life within Europe akin to the securitisation of migration outlined in the previous chapter.

In May 2014, the EU released the third iteration of its *Strategy for Combating Radicalisation and Recruitment to Terrorism*.[49] By this point the EU spoke solely of the need to prevent 'radicalisation' leading to 'terrorism' and 'violent extremism', with no reference made to 'Islam', 'Muslims' or any other term that might create an unintended link between terrorism, 'violent extremism' and the 'Muslim community'. The main objective set out by the strategy was to 'Prevent people from becoming radicalised, being radicalised and being recruited to terrorism and to prevent a new generation of terrorists from emerging.'[50] The document highlighted ten areas of counter-radicalisation cooperation that EU member states should focus upon. The language used in the document was very similar to the previous strategy released in 2008, with suggestions that the EU should work towards 'promoting inter-cultural dialogue', ensuring 'voices of mainstream opinion prevail over those of extremism' and developing a 'counter-narrative' to that propagated by the 'extremists', with the addition of new areas such as the training and engagement of 'first line practitioners across sectors' in techniques for 'detecting' and 'identifying' those most 'at risk' from being 'drawn into terrorist related activity'.[51] In particular, the strategy identified 'teachers, social and health care workers, religious leaders, community police officers, and prison and probation staff', as 'front-line' workers who should be given counter-radicalisation training.[52] The strategy also contributed to a broadening of the 'radicalisation' threat to consider not just internal but external sources of 'radicalisation', calling for an alignment of 'internal and external counter radicalisation work'.[53] The document highlighted the threat of radicalised 'foreign fighters' and the role of 'ideology developed in third countries and messages broadcast or sent into Europe', as areas that would need to be addressed.[54]

The period from January 2009 to March 2015 was characterised by further evolution in the 'radicalisation' strand of the 'fight against terrorism' discourse. The EU began to embrace a broader understanding of the 'radicalisation' process, noting that 'radicalisation' should not be seen as a process limited to just one form of terrorist threat. The removal of all references to 'Islamic' or 'Islamist terrorism' during this period represented a step forward in relation to the EU's stated aim of disassociating Islam from terrorism. By March 2015 the language of the EU discourse spoke solely of 'countering violent extremism'. However, as I will argue, this refining and broadening of the counter-radicalisation discourse does not mean that it was no longer of consequence for the 'Muslim' other, as the various work streams of the RAN implicitly indicate. The most concerning development that occurred during this period, though, can be attributed to the policy proposals themselves. The idea that front-line professionals working in the public sector (including teachers, social workers and health professionals), and in civil society more generally, needed to be trained in 'radicalisation awareness' techniques can be interpreted as a new and potentially troubling development in terms of the counter-radicalisation discourse. This will be considered in more detail in the next section.

Analysing the functioning of the discourse

The previous section dealt with how the strand of the 'fight against terrorism' discourse that linked the threat of terrorism to 'violent religious extremism', 'radicalisation' and the 'Muslim' other has evolved since it first emerged in 2002. It argued that in its first iteration the EU's counter-radicalisation strategy contained an implicit assumption that 'radicalisation' was something more prevalent within the 'Muslim communities' of Europe and that, as a result, the EU's aim of not associating terrorism with Islam was contradictory in the sense that an implicit link was made anyway. By 2009 it was argued that the EU discourse on 'radicalisation' had moved away from a focus on 'violent religious extremism' and by 2015 the policy discourse had instead switched to centre on 'countering violent extremism'. This section explores the relationship between the 'counter-radicalisation' discourse and the practice of counter-terrorism policy by offering a critical analysis of how the discourse functions. It does this in three ways: first, by considering the ways in which this strand of the discourse structures the logic of the EU counter-terrorism response, as well as highlighting the ways in which securitising practices linked to counter-radicalisation are legitimised; second, by revealing the contested nature of the knowledge that ideas about 'radicalisation' are based upon; and third, by reflecting on the wider political and societal implications of the operationalisation of the policy discourse.

Structuring the policy response, legitimising security practice

As I have argued throughout, the EU has structured its counter-terrorism response through particular representations of identity. In Chapter 3

I showed how the identity of the EU has been constituted in relation to the figure of the 'terrorist' other; an 'other' that is viewed as radically different and a threat to the EU and its member states. However, it is important to recognise that this is not the way in which the identity of the 'Muslim' other has been represented in the formulation of EU counter-terrorism policy. Indeed, the EU has demonstrated a degree of restraint in its use of language, in comparison to, say, the US 'war on terror' discourse, with regard to the question of Islam and terrorism. The focus of EU counter-terrorism policy on developing a 'non-emotive lexicon' for discussing such issues is supported by the fact that the European Council and the European Commission did not at any point use phrases such as 'Islamic terrorism', 'Islamic fundamentalism', 'Islamofascism' or any of the other pejorative terms that have found their way into social discourse through usage in the media or by politicians in the public sphere.[55] The closest the policy documents came to drawing an explicit link between Islam and terrorism was in the first iteration of the EU's counter-radicalisation strategy, where it was claimed that 'the terrorism perpetrated by Al-Qaida and extremists inspired by Al-Qaida' is based on a 'distorted version of Islam' or in a report from the EU CTC that claimed the EU must seek to combat 'recruitment and mobilisation for the Islamist militant movement in Europe'.[56]

However, identities do not necessarily have to be constructed through juxtaposition to a radically different and threatening 'other', as the previous chapter on the threat of the 'migrant' other made clear.[57] In the initial phase of the formulation of the EU's counter-terrorism and counter-radicalisation policy, separate group identities from that of the EU were constructed through reference to 'the Arab and Muslim world' or the 'Muslim community'. Importantly, the first *EU Strategy for Combating Radicalisation and Recruitment to Terrorism* defined the terrorist threat as one predominantly represented by Al-Qaida and those inspired by Al-Qaida, asserting that this threat could only be defeated through the 'engagement of the public, and especially Muslims, in Europe and beyond'.[58] It emphasised the need for policies designed to 'empower moderate voices by engaging with Muslim organisations and faith groups', 'reject the distorted version of Islam put forward by Al-Qaida and others' and 'enhance our efforts to change the perceptions of European and Western policies particularly among Muslim communities', concluding that 'even those areas of Europe where radicalisation is not a major issue at present, or where large Muslim communities do not exist, could become targets for extremists'. By introducing these groups as targets for counter-terrorism policy and by constructing 'engagement' and 'dialogue' with the 'Islamic' or 'Muslim world' as an essential aspect of the 'fight against terrorism', the structure of the policy placed the 'Muslim community' at the centre of counter-radicalisation policies and an implicit link between Islam and terrorism was made. What underpinned all of these assumptions was an initial belief that 'radicalisation' was a phenomenon primarily linked to Islam and the Muslim community, reflecting a tension at the heart of EU counter-terrorism policy in terms of stating that there was a need to disassociate terrorism from Islam but then doing so implicitly. It is surely contradictory to state at once that terrorism and Islam are not inter-linked, and yet to defeat terrorism it is essential to engage with the 'Muslim community'.

In the second phase of EU counter-radicalisation, from 2008 onwards the EU sought to move away from this type of language, reflecting a process of what I have termed 'discursive learning'. As was noted above, the EU created working groups such as the ENER and commissioned a series of academic studies that it actively sought to learn from in terms of the cre-ation of knowledge about 'terrorism' and 'radicalisation', which later fil-tered through into the EU's 'fight against terrorism' discourse. For example, a European Parliament report, from 2011, on the main achievements of EU counter-terrorism policy contained a suggestion that 'It is a mistake to label as "Islamist terrorism" what should rather be described as "radical Jihadist terrorism"; consider[ing] that making generalisations that discredit the whole of a legitimate religious belief is neither just nor proper.'[59] This sug-gestion mirrored academic research in this area, most notably Rik Coolsaet's edited collection on *Jihadi Terrorism and the Radicalisation Challenge in Europe*.[60] Reflecting on 'today's main terrorist threat' to Europe, Coolsaet observed that because *Al-Salafiyya al-Jihadiyya* is 'the closest denomination to describe the terrorists' discourse and ideology', it is more appropriate to call them 'jihadis' and their type of terrorism 'jihadi terrorism', thereby emphasising that 'we are not confronted with a clash between the West and Islam, but with a common threat and challenge for Western and Muslim countries alike'.[61]

Indeed, this process of 'discursive learning' was most evident in the Europol TE-SAT reports where on the recommendation of the European Economic and Social Committee, since 2012, Europol has dropped all references to 'Islamic' or 'Islamist Terrorism' in the TE-SAT reports.[62] However, the reports have continued to use phrases such as 'violent jihad-ist terrorist groups' and 'violent jihadist terrorism', as well as referring to 'radical Muslim groups' and 'Muslim extremists'. Significantly though, the European Council and European Commission have dropped all references to these terms, including since 2015 the use of the term 'jihadi' to describe certain terrorist groups or individuals. For example, the guiding strategy for EU foreign policy in Iraq and Syria, the *Council Conclusions on the EU Regional Strategy for Syria and Iraq*, from March 2015 made multiple ref-erences to 'violent extremism' and no references to 'Islam', 'Muslims' or 'jihad', suggesting that the EU response would be from that point onward structured around 'countering violent extremism'.[63]

In terms of the types of practice legitimised by the 'radicalisation' strand of the EU counter-terrorism discourse, there are three points to be made. First, as I noted above, the EU's focus on 'radicalisation' represents an extension of the terrorism as extreme threat discourse. The language clearly constructs the threat of 'violent extremism' and 'radicalisation' as a major threat to the security of EU citizens, with 'radicalisation' viewed as process that always precedes terrorism. The creation of this threat discourse is important in a more general sense in that like the 'fight against terrorism' discourse itself, and the threat of the 'terrorist' other, the threat of 'radicalisation' represents another discourse strand that policy-makers and politicians can tap into in order to justify and legitimise certain courses of policy action. Second, as Jörg Monar explains, the EU represents an arena where national concerns can be uploaded and objectives agreed at the European level can be pushed through at the domestic level on the basis of a 'European consensus'.[64] This appears to be the case with the EU's counter-radicalisation policy in the sense that the need for a deeper understanding of 'radicalisation' was first put forward by the Dutch intelligence service (AIVD) in 2002.[65]

Since then a number of the member states most invested in the idea of preventing 'radicalisation' have taken the lead in developing policies that might be used by all member states, with the United Kingdom (UK) focusing on the role of media and communication in countering 'extremist narratives', Sweden, on the role of community policing in recognising and countering 'radicalisation', Spain on the training of imams, the Netherlands on the role of local authorities and Denmark on preventing radicalisation amongst young people.[66] Although formal competence for counter-radicalisation remains with national actors, the EU's 'radicalisation' discourse is significant in the sense that it represents another site where the discourse is articulated and reinforced, helping to legitimise and provide impetus for initiatives developed by the member states.[67] Third, developing policies for the purpose of preventing 'radicalisation' into terrorism represents an activity where the EU can actually contribute to counter-terrorism cooperation without much controversy. Oldrich Bures has extensively detailed the issues that the EU has had in terms of developing and implementing effective counter-terrorism measures, which can in part be attributed to the sensitive nature of counter-terrorism policy as an area so closely linked to the sovereignty of member states.[68] Similarly, Björn Müller-Wille has drawn attention to the problems that have occurred at the European level in terms of intelligence cooperation between member states and European agencies, such as Europol, on counter-terrorism issues.[69] It can be argued therefore that the focus of counter-radicalisation policies on issues linked to social policy, multiculturalism and community cohesion helps to make counter-radicalisation more amenable to cooperation at the European level.

Contested nature of the discourse

There is little doubt that the concept of 'radicalisation' has come to form the central preoccupation of EU efforts to prevent terrorism. Since the term first emerged in European policy circles in 2002 a clear consensus has arisen that 'radicalisation' constitutes a major threat to the member states of the EU. This consensus has given way to 'a torrent of research on the issue ... funded both by the Commission and by member states', which has, rather unsurprisingly, helped to confirm the view that 'radicalisation' does indeed pose a major threat.[70] According to Jonathan Githens-Mazer, as of early 2011 there were 107 books, journal articles, government papers and documents, working papers, think-tank reports and publicly available postgraduate theses that were of direct relevance to the study of 'radicalisation'.[71] Yet, for all the literature that has been produced, the debate over what is meant by the term 'radicalisation' has been characterised by a substantial degree of conceptual confusion.

In terms of policy formulation, in the first iteration of its counter-radicalisation strategy the EU focused on the notion of 'violent radicalisation', which it defined as 'the phenomenon of people embracing opinions, views and ideas which could lead to acts of terrorism'.[72] This understanding of 'radicalisation' was quite different from that of the Danish government, who defined it as 'the process in which a person gradually accepts the ideas and methods of extremism and, possibly, joins its organised groups'.[73] The difference in these two definitions cuts to the heart of the debate on 'radicalisation': Does 'radicalisation' lead to violence or not? Is there really a linear path that exists between holding views that governments consider to be 'extreme' and an individual committing an act of violence? And what role should governments or institutions such as the EU play in regulating what are basically the private beliefs of its citizens? Similarly, in academic debate, these issues have also been highlighted. At risk of simplification, there are currently two academic positions on the utility of the concept of 'radicalisation'. The first position views 'radicalisation' as an important concept that can provide policy-makers with a tool to prevent terrorism; the second position is much more sceptical of the concept, drawing attention to its weaknesses and the problems that arise from its usage.

The majority of research in this area has been in support of the notion of 'radicalisation'. Key authors who have contributed to the development of this concept include Walter Lacquer, Marc Sageman and Quintan Wiktorowicz. Lacquer, writing in 2004, was quick to frame 'radicalisation' as a phenomenon most likely to occur within 'Muslim communities' in Europe, offering an explanation that based support for terrorism on a failure to integrate, the embrace of religious extremism, a sense of resentment towards their country of residence and hostility to Western values.[74] Sageman has offered a sophisticated explanation for 'radicalisation' that focuses on the importance of 'social networks', yet like Lacquer his analysis has focused solely on one form of terrorism, what he calls 'the global Islamist social movement'.[75] Similarly, Wiktorowicz has offered a social-psychological account of recruitment by 'radical Islamist groups' in the UK that is based upon the role of religious beliefs and group dynamics.[76]

A more nuanced argument, which moves away from a focus on the role of Islam and religion, in support of the notion of 'radicalisation' has been offered by Peter Neumann.[77] He argues that those who deny 'radicalisation' exists, the 'radicalisation deniers' as he calls them, are 'missing the point'. For Neumann 'radicalisation' is not a myth but rather its meaning is ambiguous, and it is as a result of this ambiguity that all of the controversies about 'radicalisation' stem. He contends that the conceptual confusion that characterises the debate on 'radicalisation' can be attributed to the differences between explanations of 'radicalisation' that emphasise 'extremist beliefs', what he calls 'cognitive radicalisation', and 'extremist behaviour', what is referred to as 'behavioural radicalisation'.[78] Neumann argues that studying 'cognitive radicalisation' is extremely important in that, in his opinion, it always precedes an individual's decision to commit a terrorist offence, which he views as the end-point of 'behavioural radicalisation'. According to Neumann, understanding 'cognitive radicalisation' is essential in that it provides a framework for exploring the role of political and ideological beliefs in an individual's decision to commit an act of terrorism. As the analysis of the 'radicalisation' discourse strand above reveals, the EU has adopted a counter-radicalisation strategy informed by this type of thinking and that embraces the need to respond to both 'cognitive' and 'behavioural radicalisation'.

By way of contrast, there is an emerging body of literature that views the 'radicalisation' process as a highly suspect contention. As Charlotte Heath-Kelly, Lee Jarvis and I suggest, the notion of 'radicalisation' has in the post-September 11 era been constructed into being. As we argue: 'It does not matter whether people experience a process of radicalisation or not, because the discursive apparatus of academia, media and state have already decided that radicalisation [exists and that it] always precedes violence.'[79] Furthermore, we contend that the idea of a 'radicalisation process' is inherently problematic on the basis that the logic of 'radicalisation' is reductive and overly simplistic. 'Radicalisation' focuses on explanations that link terrorist violence to ideology, extremism and religion, obscuring other factors that might include but are not limited to poverty, social and political injustice or Western foreign policy.[80] It is important to note that in the third iteration of its counter-radicalisation strategy the EU offered a more nuanced understanding of terrorism that took account of social issues in the 'radicalisation' process, such as inequality, marginalisation and social exclusion.

However, throughout all three counter-radicalisation strategies there was no reference to foreign policy as a motivating factor in the 'radicalisation' process, beyond a claim that it is the 'extremist world view' that 'distorts perceptions of Western policies'.[81] The suggestion here being that it is not foreign policies that are the problem but rather a misperception of those policies. As Heath-Kelly et al. explain, even more problematically, the focus of the 'radicalisation' discourse on 'extremist' ideology or religion has led to the attribution of 'vulnerability' to certain groups or individuals identified by the apparatus of the state as more 'susceptible' to 'extremism'.[82] The EU counter-radicalisation strategy remains centred on understanding 'radicalisation' in this way. For example, the third strategy makes numerous references to the need to identify 'individuals at risk' and the 'need to reach those most vulnerable' to 'radicalising messages'.[83] Indeed, it is not foreign policy or a genuine sense of political grievance that explains terrorist violence but the 'susceptibility' and 'vulnerability' of certain communities identified as suspect that is the problem. In this way, the implicit construction of the 'Muslim' other as potential terrorist threat continues.

The one certainty about the concept of 'radicalisation', as Arun Kundnani points out, is that it has been utilised by governments in order to provide a 'vehicle for policy-makers to explore the process by which a terrorist is made', as well as to offer a logic for 'preventive strategies that [go] beyond the threat of violence or detention'.[84] However, for Kundnani, the fact that research on 'radicalisation' was from the very start directed by government meant that the concept was oriented towards the demands of security professionals and counter-terrorism policy-makers, rather than operating as an objective attempt to study how terrorism comes into being.[85] As a result, regardless of EU attempts to broaden 'radicalisation' to all forms of terrorism, the notion of 'radicalisation' remains inextricably linked to an assumption that those most likely to engage in terrorism come from the 'Muslim community' in Europe and are drawn from 'a larger pool of extremist sympathisers who share an Islamic theology that inspires their actions'.[86]

Jonathan Githens-Mazer and Robert Lambert build on this criticism by pointing out that one of the main problems with the 'radicalisation narrative' is that it has now come to form the 'conventional wisdom' for both the media and policy-makers to explain how individuals come to engage in acts of terrorism, with its primary focus on the role of Islam.[87] They argue that this pathway approach provides a simplistic explanation or an easy story about 'How an individual departed from point a to arrive at point b'; for example, 'how a "good Muslim boy" (or "a good Asian boy") became a suicide bomber'.[88] The issue here then is that when the term 'radicalisation' is used in public discourse, it is almost always to refer to the 'radicalisation' of Muslims.[89] In Githens-Mazer's study, he found that of the 107 sources on 'radicalisation' that he examined, 78 (73 per cent) referred exclusively to 'radicalisation' with reference to Muslims or Islam, or both.[90] Yet, even if we were to accept the highly problematic suggestion that 'radicalisation' is a phenomenon more prevalent in 'Muslim communities', the figures demonstrate that the threat from so-called 'Islamist-inspired' forms of terrorism is relatively insignificant. As Githens-Mazer suggests, by taking all 210 arrests for terrorist offences in the EU area in 2010, which were categorised by Europol as examples of 'Islamist terrorism', and dividing by the number of Muslims living in Europe, 58 million, we discover that the perceived threat of 'radicalisation' within these communities is based on a threat that emanates from 0.0004 per cent of the entire European Muslim population.

It is quite clear then that, whilst 'radicalisation' has come to form the 'conventional wisdom' for explaining the process of how an individual becomes involved in terrorism, the knowledge upon which it is based is highly contested and open to criticism. The contested nature of knowledge about 'radicalisation' therefore raises a number of important political and societal implications in relation to the 'radicalisation' strand of the 'fight against terrorism' discourse. In particular, given the explicit focus of the more general public discourse on 'radicalisation' as a phenomenon most likely to affect and have its roots in the 'Muslim communities' in Europe, it raises implications for those minority communities identified by the apparatus of the state, academia and the media as communities that should be targeted by counter-radicalisation initiatives.

Political and societal implications

The first significant implication of the 'radicalisation' strand of the 'fight against terrorism' discourse is that it undoubtedly contributes to the ongoing securitisation, both discursively and in practice, of Europe's 'Muslim communities'. Although the EU has sought to move understandings of 'radicalisation' away from explanations centred on religion, the way in which 'radicalisation' first emerged has meant that it has been unable to shed the intrinsic association it has with the perception of the 'Muslim' other as a potential terrorist threat. A conference report from 2007, prepared by the Centre for the Study of 'Radicalisation' and Contemporary Political Violence, highlights this problem.[91] The report argues that the use of the term 'radicalisation' as understood in contemporary public discourse: first, assumes simplistic or mono-causal explanations of political violence based on notions of extremist 'infection' or 'radicalisation pathways'; second, constructs everyday Muslim practices, Islamically inspired political activism and the broader Muslim community as 'suspect'; third, restricts the scope of legitimate debate about foreign policy and divisive political domestic issues; and fourth, is counter-productive, inconsistent and highly negative in terms of government goals of preventing further terrorist violence. The report concluded by stating that the use of the term 'radicalisation' needs to be opposed or resisted by leaders, scholars, activists and concerned individuals because of the impact that the term is having on Muslims.

Whilst the EU's attempts to rearticulate a more nuanced understanding of the notion of 'radicalisation' based around 'countering violent extremism' can be viewed as a significant step towards changing the 'conventional wisdom' on 'radicalisation', the concept remains tainted by its original association with so-called 'Islamist inspired terrorism'. When the term is used in public discourse, it is primarily associated with this 'type' of terrorism. For example, Maura Conway has shown how the notion of 'radicalisation' has been used by the press in the UK to frame the activities of 'British jihadis', i.e. British Muslims involved in terrorism, whilst the 'terrorist' activities of dissident Irish Republicans were framed with no reference to this concept.[92] Likewise, debate on the act of terrorism by Anders Breivik in Norway in July 2011 has been most conspicuous by the lack of discussion of 'radicalisation' as a factor in the attack.[93] For example, the EU CTC report on *Preventing Lone Actor Terrorism*, from 2012, was interesting in that it was quick to discuss the case of Mohammed Merah, a French citizen of Algerian descent whose act of terror was described in the 2013 TE-SAT report as 'religiously inspired', as an instance of 'lone actor' terrorism where the perpetrator was radicalised.[94] Yet, the same document contained no discussion of the 'radicalisation' of Breivik. As such, the main problem with the 'radicalisation' discourse is that it remains wedded to Western beliefs about the potential threat posed by Islam and Muslims in general. For as long as the EU continues to promote the idea of 'counter-radicalisation', regardless of its intentions to the contrary, the ongoing implication for the 'Muslim' other in Europe will be their continued implicit construction as a potential terrorist threat.

A second implication of the EU discourse on 'radicalisation' arises from its focus on the creation of measures that allow for the 'detection' and 'identification' of those individuals or sections of a particular community thought to be most 'vulnerable' to the message of 'extremism'. Heath-Kelly has argued that this understanding of vulnerability is problematic in the sense that those individuals identified as 'at risk' of 'radicalisation' are thought to have an inclination towards violence that in essence means 'that they are *always already rendered as dangerous*'.[95] Not only does this notion of 'vulnerability' lead to a disproportionate targeting of 'Muslim communities', as the potential source of terrorist threat, it also creates a policing role for 'front-line' workers in helping to identify and report to the relevant authorities those individuals who are thought to be most at risk of 'radicalisation'. Significantly, by enlisting civil society workers, such as 'teachers, social and health care workers, religious leaders, community police officers, and prison and probation staff', in the EU's efforts to combat 'radicalisation', the discourse has made possible an embedding of 'expert knowledge' on 'radicalisation' that helps to securitise the role of those professions identified by the apparatus of the state as essential partners in the 'fight against terrorism'.[96] As Marieke de Goede and Stephanie Simon explain, in this 'expansive spatial imaginary' attempts to prevent 'radicalisation' should by the logic of the discourse be 'imminent' or central 'to the unfolding of the average school day, parole meeting, or youth football practice'.[97] In this way, counter-radicalisation represents a perfect example of the securitisation of social and political life within Europe.

Importantly, they argue that these types of securitising practice are made possible through the use of a language of 'care and protection', which produces a more palatable form of intervention than the more punitive or coercive aspects of counter-terrorism policy. The discourse employs a 'viral' metaphor whereby individuals are constructed as in need of 'support', 'at risk' from or 'vulnerable' to the contagious 'extremist narrative' of the 'radicaliser'.[98] Not only does this language reflect a 'care based language of individual dislocation', it implies its own exclusions. According to de Goede and Simon, the discourse reduces the impetus for extremism to factors like 'social dislocation', in effect reorienting explanations for extremism or terrorism away from genuine political motivations, such as societal disenfranchisement or disagreements on the direction of foreign policy, thereby preventing a serious engagement with 'potentially explosive political agendas'.[99] Furthermore, the understanding of 'radicalisation' enacted by the discourse is one that is directed at the identified 'vulnerable' individual before they are suspected of a crime or have committed a criminal act.[100] This is inherently problematic in the sense that interventions to prevent 'radicalisation' are based upon an imagined anticipatory knowledge of the future, which is itself located within and produced by an imperfect society with all its social and racial biases. Regardless, then, of attempts to disassociate particular communities from 'radicalisation', it becomes apparent that this type of logic makes possible practices that implicitly criminalise those 'others' whose behaviour does not conform to governmental interpretations of that which is thought to be 'normal'.

A third implication of the 'radicalisation' strand of the EU's 'fight against terrorism' discourse is that it helps to legitimise and justify a complex mode of governance that extends out across local, national and European borders, drawing in an array of public and private actors, for the purposes of responding pre-emptively to the perceived threat from 'violent extremism' or 'terrorism'. In this way, the concept of 'radicalisation' can be understood as more than simply a tool used against 'Muslim communities', and instead interpreted as a 'technique of governance' that operates through discourses of 'risk' and 'the unknown'.[101] Although it retains an implicit link with Islam, the idea of 'radicalisation' as a 'technique of governance' gives us a clue as to the future implications of the EU's continued commitment to counter-radicalisation.

The creation of the RAN has been significant in that it has continued a trend towards the production of knowledge about 'radicalisation' in order to make the phenomenon 'governable'.[102] To give one example of how this line of thinking is developing, take the policy recommendation from the report by the Prevent working group of the RAN.[103] Although the views of the working group should not as yet be taken to represent the views of the EU, the working group has recommended that the EU develop policies designed around the idea of 'early intervention'. This involves the development of programmes designed 'to challenge ideas and attitudes at the earliest possible stage in schools/ youth groups/ community settings', which might provide individuals with 'pathways' into 'radicalisation' or 'extremism'.[104] Likewise, the RAN working group for health has extended this interventionist logic towards a role for health professionals in identifying those most 'at risk' of 'radicalisation'. It contends that there is a 'need for the health sector across EU member states to ensure that they have systems and processes in place to reduce the risk of radicalisation by empowering and equipping their frontline healthcare staff with knowledge, (training) tools and guidelines of the risks of radicalisation'.[105] By advocating a crucial role for 'teachers, youth workers, community workers' and 'health workers' alike in both identifying and challenging those types of attitudes and behaviours that might lead individuals to engage in acts of 'violent extremism', the role of these professionals will continue to be securitised and this system of pre-emptive governance further legitimised.

Conclusion

This chapter has focused on the strand of the discourse that connects 'radicalisation' and 'extremism' to terrorism. The first section of the chapter mapped how this strand of the discourse has been constructed and how it has evolved. It was argued that initially the EU identified 'Islamic' or 'Islamist-inspired' terrorism as the most prevalent terrorist threat facing the EU, leading it to assume that 'radicalisation' was a process more likely to affect 'Muslim communities' in Europe. Implicitly linked to Islam through the counter-radicalisation policies it advocated, it was argued that the 'radicalisation' strand of the discourse played a key role in framing the 'Muslim' other as a potential terrorist threat. This, it was noted, occurred despite the EU consistently stating that counter-terrorism policy should not associate Islam or Muslims with terrorism. In the second stage the discourse was characterised by an extension and broadening of 'radicalisation' beyond a sole focus on counter-radicalisation policies targeted at the 'Muslim community' in Europe. Demonstrating a degree of what was termed 'discursive learning', the EU commissioned a series of studies into the phenomenon of 'violent radicalisation', as well as embracing the recommendations of wider academic research in this area, which has since led the EU to focus on the broader notion of 'violent extremism' rather than a more specific focus on 'violent religious extremism'.

The second section of the chapter offered a series of observations on the way in which the 'radicalisation' strand of the 'fight against terrorism' discourse functions. First, it was argued that the concept of 'radicalisation' has played a key role in the construction of an 'other', the 'Muslim' other, through which the EU's own identity is constituted, differentiated and reinforced. Second, it highlighted the inherent contradiction that existed between the EU's stated policy goal of avoiding associating Islam or Muslims with terrorism but then doing so anyway through its counter-radicalisation policies. Third, it demonstrated how the idea of 'radicalisation' has become the 'conventional wisdom' for policy-makers, politicians and the media by providing simplistic and easy to understand notions of 'radicalisation' pathways into terrorism. In particular, it drew attention to the contested nature of knowledge about 'radicalisation', arguing that the way in which the concept first emerged, as a process assumed to occur primarily within a particular suspect community, has meant that the term retains an inherent racial bias against the 'Muslim community' from which it has struggled to disassociate itself. The second section concluded by questioning the broadening of the 'conventional wisdom' on 'radicalisation', suggesting that the EU move to extend counter-radicalisation policies into new areas of public life, through the creation of a policing role for 'front-line' professionals such as teachers, health workers, social workers and prison and probation staff, should be interpreted as highly problematic given the securitising effect this will undoubtedly have on European civil society.

I contend that the threat of an emerging 'radicalised' or 'radicalising' other, like the threat of the 'terrorist' other, provides the EU with another self-justifying or legitimising security discourse, which EU policy-makers and politicians invoke in order to support further integration in the fields of internal security and external security. In this way, the perception of 'radicalisation' as one of the 'greatest threats' to the security of the EU and its citizens represents a further extension of the 'terrorism as extreme threat' discourse discussed in Chapter 2. Yet, as I have suggested above, the notion of 'radicalisation' is extremely problematic for many reasons. In particular, exactly who should be the target of the policy is unclear. It is extremely difficult to identify the dividing line between those who espouse extreme political views and those who are willing to go on and act upon those views. Furthermore, who defines what is considered 'extreme'? If it is the government of a state, then there is the very real fear that counter-radicalisation could be used as a cover to suppress legitimate forms of protest and dissent.

Similarly, the general aims of EU counter-radicalisation are very broad; the EU spoke of targeting 'inequalities and discrimination', promoting 'inter-cultural dialogue', 'long-term integration', 'good governance', 'human rights', 'democracy', as well as 'education and economic prosperity', all of which are admirable aims but have little to do with directly combating terrorism. By moving responses to these issues into a security framework, the EU is contributing to a securitisation of policies designed to promote community cohesion and multiculturalism. I want to conclude by suggesting that the notion of 'radicalisation' fails for two main reasons. First, pathways into terrorism are so complex that in truth anyone can become 'radicalised'. The simplistic and reductive logic of 'radicalisation' lacks the capacity to account for that complexity. Second, 'radicalisation' continues to retain an inherent racial bias against Muslims that renders the EU's continued commitment to – and reinforcement of – the concept of 'radicalisation' highly problematic. Regardless, events in the post-Breivik period, including the emergence of so-called Islamic State in the summer of 2014 and the terrorist attack on *Charlie Hebdo* in Paris in January 2015, promise that the EU focus on 'radicalisation' will continue for the foreseeable future, irrespective of the concerns outlined above.

Notes

1 Council of the European Union, *Conclusions and Plan of Action of the Extraordinary European Council Meeting on 21 September*, 2001, SN 140/01.
2 Ibid., p. 1.
3 Across the time period and in the documents analysed, the EU consistently made statements that the threat from terrorism should not be conflated with Islam.
4 Council, *Conclusions and Plan of Action*.

5 Ibid., p. 3.

6 Ibid.

7 Europol, *Terrorist Activity in the European Union: Situation and Trend Report*, The Hague, October 2001–October 2002; Europol, *Terrorist Activity in the European Union: Situation and Trends Report*, The Hague, October 2002–October 2003.

8 Europol, *Terrorist Activity in the EU*, October 2003, p. 5.

9 Ibid., p. 19. The report also noted that the finding of traces of ricin in at least one terrorism incident reported by a member state confirmed the will of terrorists to obtain and make use of WMDs.

10 Council of the European Union, *A Secure Europe in a Better World: European Security Strategy*, Brussels, 12 December 2003.

11 Ibid., p. 7.

12 Ibid., p. 9.

13 Ibid.

14 Ibid., p. 4.

15 Europol, *Terrorist Activity in the EU*, October 2003, p. 5.

16 Council, *European Security Strategy*, p. 4. The *European Security Strategy* tied this notion of home-grown terrorism into other strands of the 'fight against terrorism' discourse concerning the idea of 'new' terrorism, including the suggestion that the 'terrorist' other is willing 'to use unlimited violence to cause massive casualties' and potentially through the use of WMDs.

17 It is important to note that whilst the TE-SAT focused on the threat posed by radical Islam, it also highlighted other forms of 'radical' terrorist threat, including in Italy the 'radicalism of the whole anarchist movement' and in Sweden 'numerous national radical groups on the extreme right and left'; see Europol, *Terrorist Activity in the EU*, October 2003. This language was also used in the TE-SAT reports from 2004 and 2005.

18 Council of the European Union, *Declaration on Combating Terrorism*, Brussels, 25 March 2004, 7906/04.

19 Ibid., p. 16.

20 Council of the European Union, *The Hague Programme: Strengthening Freedom, Security and Justice in the European Union*, Brussels, 13 December 2004, 16054/04.

21 Council of the European Union, *Presidency Conclusions*, Brussels, 1 February 2005, 16238/1/04.

22 European Commission, *Communication Concerning Terrorist Recruitment: Addressing the Factors Contributing to Violent Radicalisation*, Brussels, 21 September 2005, COM (2005) 313 final.

23 Ibid., p. 2.

24 Ibid.

25 Ibid., p. 14.

26 Council of the European Union, *The Strategy for Combating Radicalisation and Recruitment to Terrorism*, 24 November 2005, 12781/1/05; Council of the European Union, *The European Union Counter-Terrorism Strategy*, Brussels, 30 November 2005, 14469/4/05.

27 Council, *The Strategy for Combating Radicalisation and Recruitment*, p. 4.

28 Ibid., p. 2.

29 Ibid.

30 Ibid.

31 Ibid., p. 4.

32 Ibid., p. 5.

33 Council of the European Union, *Implementation of the Strategy and Action Plan to Combat Terrorism*, Brussels, 15 November 2006, 15266/06, p. 5.

34 Council of the European Union, *Revised EU Strategy for Combating Radicalisation and Recruitment to Terrorism*, Brussels, 14 November 2008, 15175/08.

35 Ibid., p. 3.

36 By 'discursive learning' I mean the way in which EU policy in a particular area has developed as a result of adapting to and learning from both the research that the EU has itself commissioned and from broader academic research in that particular area.

37 Commission, *Communication Concerning Terrorist Recruitment*, p. 8.

38 The EU CTC report from June 2009 described the group as 'a network of leading experts on radicalisation from different academic disciplines who are renowned specialists in their field', their role being to focus on the processes of 'violent radicalisation and extremism that leads to acts of terrorism' through the production of studies and organisation of seminars, with the aim of 'deepening understanding of the violent radicalisation phenomenon in order to enhance counter-terrorism and preventive approaches being pursued at EU and Member State levels'. From 2008 until 2009 this expert group was known as the 'European Network of Experts on Radicalisation' (ENER). See Council of the European Union, *Implementation of the Strategy and Action Plan to Combat Terrorism*, Brussels, 2 June 2009, 9715/1/09, p. 2.

39 They were undertaken by King's College London, the Change Institute and the ENER, respectively. See King's College London, 'Recruitment and Mobilisation for the Islamist Militant Movement in Europe', International Centre for the Study of Radicalisation and Political Violence, December 2007; Change Institute, 'Studies into Violent Radicalisation: The Beliefs, Ideologies and Narratives', February 2008; Change Institute, 'Study on the Best Practices in Cooperation between Authorities and Civil Society with a View to the Prevention and Response to Violent Radicalisation', July 2008; European Network of Experts on Radicalisation, 'Radicalisation Processes Leading to Acts of Terrorism', 15 May 2008, available online at: www.clingendael.nl/publications/2008/20080500_cscp_report_vries.pdf (accessed June 2015).

40 EGVR, 'Radicalisation Processes Leading to Acts of Terrorism', p. 6.

41 Council of the European Union, *The Stockholm Programme: An Open and Secure Europe Serving and Protecting Citizens*, Brussels, 2 December 2009, 17024/09.

42 Ibid., pp. 51, 77.

43 European Commission, *The EU Internal Security Strategy in Action: Five Steps towards a More Secure Europe*, Brussels, 22 November 2010, COM (2010) 673 final.
44 Council of the European Union, *Preventing Lone Actor Terrorism: Food for Thought*, Brussels, 23 April 2012, 9090/12.
45 Ibid., p. 3.
46 Ibid., p. 6.
47 The RAN was officially launched on 9 September 2011. According to the European Commission website, the RAN is an umbrella network connecting people involved in preventing radicalisation and violent extremism throughout Europe. In the RAN, front-line professionals from different member states can meet, each in their area of expertise, in order to exchange ideas, knowledge and experiences on countering radicalisation and violent extremism.
48 European Commission, 'Sharpening Our Tools against Violent Extremism', press release, Brussels, 28 January 2013.
49 Council of the European Union, *Revised EU Strategy for Combating Radicalisation and Recruitment to Terrorism*, Brussels, 19 May 2014, 9956/14.
50 Ibid., p. 3.
51 Ibid., pp. 3–10.
52 Ibid., p. 10.
53 Ibid., p. 13.
54 Ibid.
55 Council, *The Strategy for Combating Radicalisation and Recruitment*, p. 4.
56 Ibid., p. 2; see also Council of the European Union, *Implementation of the Strategy and Action Plan to Combat Terrorism*, Brussels, 19 November 2008. The phrase 'recruitment and mobilisation for the Islamist militant movement in Europe' was lifted directly from the report into radicalisation processes by King's College London, 2007.
57 See Lene Hansen, *Security as Practice: Discourse Analysis and the Bosnian War* (London and New York: Routledge, 2006), p. 6.
58 Council, *The Strategy for Combating Radicalisation and Recruitment*, p. 5.
59 European Parliament, *Report on the EU Counter-Terrorism Policy: Main Achievements and Future Challenges*, Committee on Civil Liberties, Justice and Home Affairs, A7-0286/2011, 20 July 2011, p. 20.
60 Rik Coolsaet, *Jihadi Terrorism and the Radicalisation Challenge in Europe* (Aldershot: Ashgate, 2008).
61 Ibid., p. 2. Like almost all previous research in the field of (counter) radicalisation the focus of the book was on the radicalisation of Muslims and the relationship between terrorism and Islam.
62 European Economic and Social Council, 'Opinion of the Section for Employment, Social Affairs and Citizenship on the Communication from the Commission to the European Parliament and the Council: The EU Counter-Terrorism Policy – Main Achievements and Future Challenges', Brussels, 31 March 2011, SOC/388.
63 Council of the European Union, *Council Conclusions on the EU Regional Strategy for Syria and Iraq as well as the ISIL/Da'esh Threat*, Brussels, 16 March

2015, 7267/15. The document made multiple references to 'countering violent extremism'.

64 Jörg Monar, 'Common threat and common response? The European Union's counter-terrorism strategy and its problems', *Government and Opposition*, 42:3 (2007), 311.

65 Rik Coolsaet, 'EU counterterrorism strategy: value added or chimera?', *International Affairs*, 86:4 (2010), 868.

66 Ibid., 870.

67 Marieke de Goede and Stephanie Simon, 'Governing future radicals in Europe', *Antipode*, 45:2 (2013), 316.

68 Oldrich Bures, *EU Counterterrorism Policy: A Paper Tiger?* (Farnham: Ashgate, 2011).

69 Björn Müller-Wille, 'The effect of international terrorism on EU intelligence co-operation', *Journal of Common Market Studies*, 46:1 (2008), 49–73.

70 Coolsaet, 'EU counterterrorism strategy', 870.

71 Jonathan Githens-Mazer, 'The rhetoric and reality: radicalization and political discourse', *International Political Science Review*, 33:5 (2012), 556–567.

72 Commission, *Communication Concerning Terrorist Recruitment*, p. 2.

73 Danish Government, *A Common and Safe Future: An Action Plan to Prevent Extremist Views and Radicalisation among Young People* (2009), available online in English at: www.nyidanmark.dk/NR/rdonlyres/58D048E7-0482-4AE8-99EB-928753EFC1F8/0/a_common_and_safe_future_danish_action_plan_to_prevent_extremism.pdf (accessed June 2015).

74 Walter Laqueur, 'The terrorism to come', *Policy Review*, 126 (August–September 2004), 49–64.

75 Marc Sageman, *Leaderless Jihad: Terror Networks in the Twenty-First Century* (Philadelphia: University of Pennsylvania Press, 2008).

76 Quintan Wiktorowicz, *Radical Islam Rising: Muslim Extremism in the West* (Oxford: Rowman & Littlefield, 2005).

77 Peter Neumann, 'The trouble with radicalization', *International Affairs*, 89:4 (2013), 873–893.

78 Ibid., see 873–876. According to Neumann, 'cognitive radicalisation' refers to the process that culminates in the adoption of radically different ideas about society and governance, whilst 'behavioural radicalisation' refers to the use of violent or coercive actions, which directly result from those ideas.

79 Charlotte Heath-Kelly, Christopher Baker-Beall and Lee Jarvis, 'Introduction', in Christopher Baker-Beall, Charlotte Heath-Kelly and Lee Jarvis (eds), *Counter-Radicalisation: Critical Perspectives* (Abingdon: Routledge, 2015), p.1.

80 I view the socialisation processes by which a person becomes involved in terrorism as extremely complex and not reducible to simplistic or mono-causal explanations, and as potentially involving any or all of the factors outlined above (i.e. religion, extremism, injustice or foreign policy, etc.).

81 Council, *Revised EU Strategy for Combating Radicalisation* (2008), p. 4.

82 Heath-Kelly *et al.*, 'Introduction', pp. 1–2.

83 Council, *Revised EU Strategy for Combating Radicalisation* (2014), see pp. 8, 10.
84 Arun Kundnani, 'Radicalisation: The Journey of a Concept', in Christopher Baker-Beall, Charlotte Heath-Kelly and Lee Jarvis (eds), *Counter-Radicalisation: Critical Perspectives* (Abingdon: Routledge, 2015), p. 15.
85 Ibid.
86 Ibid.
87 Jonathan Githens-Mazer and Robert Lambert, 'Why conventional wisdom on radicalization fails: the persistence of a failed discourse', *International Affairs*, 86:4 (2010), 889–901.
88 Ibid., 889.
89 In this context I use the phrase 'public discourse' to refer to the general, dominant discourse on a particular topic within wider civil society in Europe.
90 Githens-Mazer, 'The rhetoric and reality', 558.
91 Centre for the Study of 'Radicalisation' and Contemporary Political Violence, *The Politics of Radicalisation: Reframing the Debate and Reclaiming the Language*, London Muslim Centre, Whitechapel, 18 October 2007, available online at: www.aber.ac.uk/en/media/departmental/interpol/csrv/radicalisation-reportjg2.pdf (accessed June 2015).
92 Maura Conway, 'Born or Made? Irish Republicans, British Jihadis, and the Diffusion of Radicalisation Discourse in the UK', paper presented at the International Studies Association (ISA) Annual Conference, San Francisco, CA, 3–6 April 2013.
93 For example, see Edwin Bakker and Beatrice de Graaf, 'Preventing lone wolf terrorism: some CT approaches addressed', *Perspectives on Terrorism*, 5–6 (2011), available online at: www.terrorismanalysts.com/pt/index.php/pot/article/view/preventing-lone-wolf/html (accessed June 2015).
94 Council, *Preventing Lone Actor Terrorism*.
95 Charlotte Heath-Kelly, 'Counter-terrorism and the counterfactual: producing the "radicalisation" discourse and the UK PREVENT strategy', *British Journal of Politics & International Relations*, 15:3 (2013), 15. Emphasis added.
96 Council, *Revised EU Strategy for Combating Radicalisation* (2014), p. 10.
97 De Goede and Simon, 'Governing future radicals in Europe', 326.
98 Council, *Revised EU Strategy for Combating Radicalisation* (2014).
99 De Goede and Simon, 'Governing future radicals in Europe', 326.
100 Ibid., 332.
101 Heath-Kelly, 'Counter-terrorism and the counterfactual'.
102 Ibid., 18.
103 RAN Prevent, 'Proposed Policy Recommendations for the High Level Conference', Radicalisation Awareness Network, Brussels, December 2012, available online at: http://ec.europa.eu/dgs/home-affairs/what-we-do/networks/radicalisation_awareness_network/ran-high-level-conference/docs/proposed_policy_recommendation_ran_prevent_en.pdf (accessed June 2015).
104 Ibid., p. 2.

105 RAN Health, 'Proposed Policy Recommendations for the High Level Conference', Radicalisation Awareness Network, Brussels, December 2012, available online at: http://ec.europa.eu/dgs/home-affairs/what-we-do/networks/radicalisation_awareness_network/about-ran/ran-health/index_en.htm (accessed June 2015).

Conclusion: the 'fight against terrorism' discourse and the EU's emerging role as a holistic security actor

Introduction

The reason that I undertook this study was to make the argument that an in-depth analysis of the language of European Union (EU) counter-terrorism policy, the 'fight against terrorism', is essential if we are to gain a more comprehensive understanding of the processes through which security practices at the European level are *made possible*. In doing so I have sought to draw attention to the important role that the concept of identity plays in the creation of security policies. The main argument that I put forward, which I have attempted to demonstrate throughout, is that the counter-terrorism policies of the EU are constituted through representations of identity, but it is also through the formulation of counter-terrorism policies that the identity of the EU is created and recreated. In drawing attention to the importance of identity I have sought to move beyond a sole focus on the external projection of the 'international identity' of the EU, which characterises much of the literature on EU foreign policy, to consider also the internal projection of what I have termed 'EU identity' through the formulation of its counter-terrorism and internal security policies.

I have argued that the 'fight against terrorism' discourse is based upon – and contributes to – the rearticulation of an 'accepted knowledge' about what terrorism is, who the terrorists are and what type of threat they represent, in the post-September 11 era, helping to strengthen a 'conventional wisdom' on how best to respond to that threat. In particular, I have sought to demonstrate how the discourse on terrorism that the EU articulates is one that rests upon a perception of terrorism as an extreme threat to society, which I have argued is to a great extent over-exaggerated. Significantly, I have suggested that in the minds of EU policy-makers this perception of the terrorist threat is confirmed with every new terrorist attack. The result of this has been for the EU to move towards the developments of policies that are designed to respond pre-emptively through the imagination and anticipation of the potential terrorist threats of the future. As such, I have argued that the 'fight against terrorism' is about more than just responding to terrorism but is also about a particular way of governing society; it is also about governance through precautionary responses to risk. Analysing the language of the 'fight against terrorism' therefore becomes crucial if we are to understand how the EU goes about legitimising and justifying this developing role in the field of counter-terrorism and security governance.

In this chapter, I aim to draw together the main threads from the arguments that I have made throughout the book. The first section outlines the key contribution that this research makes to the literature in this area, highlighting the important role that the identity of the EU has played in the creation of EU counter-terrorism policy. Significantly, I suggest that the study of 'others' is essential if we are to develop a comprehensive understanding of the EU's 'fight against terrorism'. The second section considers the role of the 'fight against terrorism' with a broader focus on its implications for the EU's emerging role as a holistic security actor. I argue that the 'fight against terrorism' discourse is helping to facilitate emerging security practices that challenge the separation of internal and external security, contributing to a blurring of the once-traditional distinction between the two domains. The third section highlights the emergence of a European security culture, understood as a system of governance, which is based upon a precautionary approach to security policy. I argue that an analysis of the language of the 'fight against terrorism' helps to reveal the logic that underpins this emerging system of governance. The fourth section reflects on the implications of the 'fight against terrorism' for human rights, as well as the extent to which the EU counter-terrorism response can be considered effective. The fifth section offers some discussion of future avenues for research, including some of the limitations of my interpretive approach.

The 'fight against terrorism': identity and the study of 'others'

The main argument I have put forward in this book is that the identity of the EU plays an intrinsic role in the formulation of counter-terrorism policy, representing an important site where the identity of the EU is articulated and rearticulated. In essence, what I have argued is that EU counter-terrorism policies rely on representations of EU identity, but it is also in the process of formulating counter-terrorism policy that the identity of the EU is created and recreated. As I explained in the Introduction, although the EU consists of a heterogeneous array of actors and processes, there is enough consistency within the 'fight against terrorism' discourse as articulated by the main policy-making institutions, the European Council and the European Commission, to identify specifically the collectively agreed view of the organisation on counter-terrorism issues and more generally an emerging EU security identity. Building on the research of Ian Manners and Richard Whitman, who have analysed the external projection of the 'international identity of the EU' (IIEU), I have argued for a reconceptualisation of the IIEU so that we instead speak simply of 'EU identity'. I suggest this for a particular purpose: to enable the broadening of research on EU security policies to consider not just the external projection of 'EU identity' but its internal projection as well.[1] In doing so, I have sought to respond to their call to identify and analyse the various 'others' with which differentiation occurs.[2] In this way, broadening the understanding of identity allows for a focus not just on external 'others' but on those internal 'others', including 'others' who traverse the internal/external divide, against which the identity of the EU is constituted, differentiated and (re)produced.

Following Lene Hansen's conceptualisation of identity as 'discursive, political, relational, and social', it has been argued that EU counter-terrorism policy always articulates a sense of self that is understood through differentiation from a series of 'others'.[3] The position that I took was a reflexive one, which recognises that identity is constituted through process of differentiation and linking that understand 'otherness' as more than just the articulation of radical difference. Indeed, I understand difference between 'self' and 'other' to be constituted through degrees of difference from the radically threatening to the less than radical or similar.[4] By applying an identity-focused discursive approach to my analysis of the 'fight against terrorism' I was able to reveal how the EU perceives itself as a particular type of actor in the field of security. Through the articulation of a set of values that the EU uses to describe itself, including 'open', 'democratic', 'tolerant', 'multicultural', 'prosperous', 'secure' and 'free', I argued that the EU constructs itself as a 'civilian' or 'normative' power within the international system. Furthermore, I suggested that these values ground the EU approach to counter-terrorism firmly within the framework of a criminal justice-based approach to terrorism. This was taken to represent a manifestation of the EU's perception of itself, of its identity, which shapes not only its external security policies but *all* of its security policies. Set against the identity of the EU is the radical threat of terrorism against which that identity has been affirmed and reaffirmed. Again, through the discursive approach that I adopted, I was able to reveal three prominent 'others' within the 'fight against terrorism' discourse, which I have argued are central to the formulation of EU counter-terrorism policy and the affirmation of the identity of the EU.

First, I identified the radically different, dangerous and threatening figure of the 'terrorist' other. I argued that the discourse constructs the 'terrorist' other in a variety of ways, as simultaneously a 'criminal' with links to 'organised crime', a 'new' and 'evolving' type of threat that has links to 'violent religious extremism', as well as a non-state actor, a member of a group or an individual, such as a 'lone actor' or a 'returning foreign fighter', who seeks to inflict 'massive casualties' against the EU and its member states. Within the discourse the threat of the 'terrorist' other was always constructed as a particularly acute or extreme threat to the EU. Moreover, the 'terrorist' other was presented as more than just a material threat to the EU but also as a threat to the values and ideals upon which the EU is itself founded. The 'terrorist' other, then, as a direct threat to the identity of the EU.

Second, I drew attention to the 'migrant' other, a less radically different 'other' than the 'terrorist' other, who was constructed within the discourse as a *potential* threat to the EU and its member states. I argued that unlike the explicitly threatening figure of the 'terrorist' other, the 'migrant' other was constructed as a threat implicitly through an assumption that the 'open' or 'globalised' environment of the EU migratory system is an environment that can be abused by terrorists. In this way the 'migrant' other may also be the 'terrorist' other. Third, I identified the 'Muslim' other who, like the 'migrant' other, was also constructed as a less radically different 'other' against which the identity of the EU is differentiated. I have shown how the discourse constructs and reinforces the concept of 'radicalisation', which, regardless of the EU's intentions to the contrary, retains an implicit racial bias against the 'Muslim community' that constructs the 'Muslim' other as a potential future source of terrorist threat.

I focused on the role of identity not to offer explanations for why the EU has developed particular counter-terrorism policies or why they might have been ineffective but instead to reveal how EU counter-terrorism policy has been *made possible* through the social construction of the threat of terrorism.[5] As I have noted above, the 'fight against terrorism' discourse functions through the constant (re)articulation of this 'accepted knowledge' about what terrorism is and who the terrorists are. In essence, it provides a dominant discursive framework through which contemporary terrorist threats are interpreted. However, as I have suggested throughout, the 'fight against terrorism' discourse goes beyond a mere focus on counter-terrorism. The threat of terrorism has also been invoked by the EU to legitimise a broader array of internal and external security policies adopted since 11 September 2001, including many measures that have tenuous links to counter-terrorism. In response to the explicit threat from the radical threat of the 'terrorist' other, the EU has pushed for and achieved: the creation of a European Arrest Warrant (EAW); increased bilateral cooperation with the United States (US), including the Passenger Name Record Agreement (PNR); the development of financial tracking instruments; and an expansion of responsibilities in matters of counter-terrorism for existing EU agencies such as Europol and

Eurojust. As well as this, the threat of terrorism has been invoked on numerous occasions to justify the continued development of the EU's broader internal security agenda. Similarly, in response to the potential threat of the 'migrant' or the 'Muslim' other, the EU has sought to strengthen and normalise a series of pre-existing border control measures, such as the use of biometric identifiers in travel documents, and instruments of 'migration control' including the various IT systems and databases that the EU has developed, as well as push forward the notion of 'counter-radicalisation' and its associated policies. I argue that identity is central to this process in that the 'terrorist', the 'migrant' and the 'Muslim' other represent the implicit and explicit targets of the various dimensions of EU counter-terrorism policy. Significantly, these developments are contributing to a developing role for the EU as a holistic security actor, which is blurring the once-clear distinction between internal and external security.[6]

The blurring of internal and external security

Throughout the historical evolution of the EU's 'fight against terrorism' discourse, the EU has consistently called for the creation of a coordinated response by EU member states to the threat of terrorism. The central aspect of this has been the assertion that to respond to this threat the EU should develop internal and external security policies. However, within this, the EU has called for the creation of internal policies that take account of the external dimension of the threat and vice versa. In this way the EU has sought to develop policies that traverse the distinction between internal and external security. This can in part be explained by the perception of the threat represented by the various 'others' that I have identified above.

As I demonstrated in Chapter 3, the 'terrorist' other is at once an internal and/or an external threat. The 'migrant' other, who represents an implicit source of potential terrorist threat, is also constructed as both an internal and/or external threat. Externally, think of the claim that 'much of the terrorist threat to Europe originates outside the EU', making the 'open society' of the EU particularly 'vulnerable'.[7] Likewise, internally, think of the 'returning foreign fighter', a citizen of an EU member state who goes to fight in a 'conflict zone' and returns to the EU potentially to carry out an act of terrorism. Similarly, the 'Muslim' other rests within the imagination of the EU as part of a community particularly susceptible to 'radicalisation' and therefore an implicit source of internal, or 'home-grown, terrorist threat. Yet, within the third iteration of the EU's counter-radicalisation strategy an external dimension to this threat is created with the suggestion that 'ideology developed in third countries and messages broadcast or sent into Europe may have an impact on radicalisation'.[8] The construction of terrorism as both an internal and/or external security threat is significant in that it helps to legitimise new and pre-existing security practices at the EU level, which are blurring the distinction between internal and external security and helping to carve out an emerging role for the EU as a holistic security actor.

Accompanying this is a discourse strand, within the overarching 'fight against terrorism' discourse, that constructs this blurring of internal and external security policy as a necessity. Within the documents, there are numerous instances of this across the period analysed. In the post-September 11 period, the *European Security Strategy*, released in December 2003, was one of the first EU security documents to make the claim that 'the post-Cold War environment is one … in which the internal and external aspects of security are indissolubly linked'.[9] Likewise, the EU's second multi-annual internal security programme, the *Hague Programme*, released a year later in December 2004, made a similar claim about the relationship between internal and external security policy. It stated that the need to tackle cross-border problems, such as terrorism, had meant that 'in the field of security, the coordination and coherence between the internal and the external dimension has been growing in importance and needs to continue to be vigorously pursued'.[10]

Again, the EU *Counter-Terrorism Strategy*, from November 2005, rearticulated this idea that 'the internal and external aspects of security are intimately linked'.[11] The *Stockholm Programme*, released in December 2009, offered the clearest example of how this strand of the discourse has come to structure the logic of EU counter-terrorism and security policy. As well as advocating a number of internal counter-terrorism measures, the document reasserted that counter-terrorism 'cooperation with third countries in general and within international organisations needs to be strengthened'.[12] The threat of terrorism was invoked, alongside other threats, to help push for the amalgamation and 'increased integration' of Area of Freedom Security and Justice (AFSJ) policies 'into the general policies of the European Union'.[13] The document constructed the external dimension of EU internal security policy as 'crucial to the successful implementation of the objectives of this programme' and explained that the policy should 'be fully coherent with all other aspects of EU foreign policy'.[14] Furthermore, it stated quite clearly that 'internal and external security' policy were now seen as 'inseparable' and that 'addressing threats, even far away from our continent, is essential to protecting Europe and its citizens'.[15] In the post-Breivik period, this commitment to a holistic approach to security issues was once again reaffirmed by the European Council in June 2014.[16] In the document, the EU stated that the answer to 'many of the challenges' in completing the AFSJ manifest themselves 'in relations with third countries, which calls for improving the link between the EU's internal and external policies'.[17]

It is clear then, in the 'fight against terrorism', the EU views the 'internal' and 'external' aspects of security policy as inextricably linked. The perceived threat of terrorism has played a central role in facilitating emerging security practices that challenge the separation of internal and external security. The need for these policies is in turn based on logic of a 'new' threat environment, i.e. terrorism as an internal and/or external threat, articulated repeatedly throughout the formulation of counter-terrorism policy. This merging of internal and external security is a process that Didier Bigo has referred to as the 'de-differentiation' of internal and external security, a process, it should be noted, that was already under way before the events of 11 September 2001.[18] He has argued that this tendency is particularly acute at the European level, where the idea of 'internal security' is now taken to refer to a holistic or hybridised security approach that reaches beyond the traditional boundaries of 'internal security'. This reach is viewed as both geographic, in terms of transatlantic cooperation between Europe and the US, and bureaucratic, reflected in an expansion of the 'role and duties of the various agencies of (in)security' that have been created at the European level.[19]

According to Bigo, it is the convergence of defence and 'internal security' into interconnected networks, blurring the distinction between internal and external issues, that lies at the heart of this transformation. For Bigo, this blurring is characterised on the one hand by the adoption of policing techniques in external, war-based situations, and the militarisation of domestic policing on the other. Derek Lutterbeck concurs with this assessment.[20] He argues that in Europe 'military forces are turning to internal security missions, and are adopting certain police features', whilst 'police forces have been taking on certain military characteristics, for example in the form of more proactive (or pre-emptive) styles of policing'.[21] He also notes that this has led to transformation at the technological level, where police forces' increasing resort to the use of military-style hardware or external military forces' use of non-lethal weapons is growing in importance.

Bigo argues that these developments have been legitimised through discourses that assert the necessity to 'globalize security', in response to a wide range of disparate threats that include the fight against terrorism, drugs, organised crime, cross-border criminality and illegal immigration.[22] Significantly, these issues are perceived as interlinked and representative of a 'new' and 'evolving' strategic threat environment. According to Bigo, it is precisely the reconceptualisation of these security concerns as 'international' problems requiring 'transnational' solutions that has meant that the distinction between internal and external security has become increasingly difficult to maintain.[23] At the discursive level, the analysis conducted in this book helps to add weight to Bigo's argument in two ways. First, by demonstrating how the language of the 'fight against terrorism' articulates this type of security logic acting as a site where the necessity of the blurring of internal and external security is reinforced. Second, by showing how the construction of the multidimensional, internal and/or external threat of terrorism makes the merging of internal and external security possible.

These developments are not without consequence and raise important implications for the EU as a security actor in relation to their securitising impact on social and political life within Europe. I have argued throughout that the 'fight against terrorism' discursively securitises issues by rearticulating those issues as part of a security framework. However, securitisation also occurs in practice through the implementation of those policies *made possible* by the discourse. Importantly, Lutterbeck's assertion that the EU has moved towards a 'preemptive' form of security practice can be viewed as a manifestation of the performative dimension of this securitising process. I argue below that this move to adopt a pre-emptive, anticipatory and holistic style of security governance is having a transformative impact upon the identity of the EU, reflecting what Marieke de Goede has referred to as an emerging 'European security culture'.

European security culture and the security identity of the EU

Following de Goede, I argue that at the European level the link between security discourse and security practice is best characterised by the notion of an 'emergent European security culture', a phrase that describes the dual concern with the discursive construction, or 'imagination', of security threats and the practice of security policies designed to combat those threats.[24] For de Goede, the EU security culture is based upon a particular style of governance that aims to imagine and anticipate security threats before they are realised. This, then, is the precautionary principle, where action is taken in order to respond to an issue in an environment characterised by uncertainty. The move to adopt a precautionary approach to security issues, such as terrorism, is underpinned by a 'rationality of catastrophic risk' that translates into policies that 'actively seek to prevent situations from becoming catastrophic at some indefinite point in the future'.[25]

As I have demonstrated, this is certainly the case with the EU's 'fight against terrorism', which throughout its historical evolution has conjured up various representations of *the risk* of potentially catastrophic terrorist events. For example, the *European Security Strategy* imagines a scenario where 'Taking these different elements together – terrorism committed to maximum violence, the availability of weapons of mass destruction, organised crime, the weakening of the state system and the privatisation of force – we could be confronted with a very radical threat indeed.'[26] As

Chapter 3 explained, this process of threat construction has been a consistent theme within the 'fight against terrorism' discourse, with the EU consistently drawing a clear link between the construction of the radically threatening figure of the 'terrorist' other and the development of various security and counter-terrorism measures. Think also of EU claims that terrorist organisations 'might eventually turn to unconventional weapons', in the form of chemical, biological, radiological and nuclear (CBRN) terrorism, 'potentially leading to a high number of casualties and causing huge socio-economic damage'.[27] This type of logic, what de Goede calls the 'threat imaginary', provides the legitimacy for the development of a system of precautionary security governance at the European level, with the threat of terrorism providing 'a powerful logic for post-national security cooperation'.[28] This then is the performative dimension of the securitisation process described in Chapter 1.

Yet, as de Goede suggests, identity continues to retain significance within this emergent EU security culture, with the field of security representing an important site through which 'the EU articulates its public legitimacy and contemporary identity'.[29] Indeed, the creation of security policies based around prevention, anticipation and early intervention are having a transformative impact upon the identity of the EU as a security actor. By adopting security policies based upon the prevention of security threats before they actualise, the EU's emerging security culture is one that displays a commitment to a 'banal' form of pre-emptive security.[30] As Brian Massumi points out, this pre-emptive security logic is problematic in that the security that 'preemption is explicitly meant to produce is predicated on its tacitly producing what it is meant to avoid'; in this way we can argue that the pre-emptive security policies that the EU has created are predicated upon 'a production of insecurity to which it itself contributes'.[31]

In essence, what this means is that success in responding to a threat is measured not by the prevention of actual instances of terrorism, but simply by the practice of taking precautionary action. Alongside the various representations of threat that help to legitimise this new style of security governance, the 'fight against terrorism' discourse is replete with references to the language of risk. For example, think of the arguments put forth by the EU about the 'vulnerability' of the 'arteries of our society', invoked to legitimise the broadening of border control policies.[32] Similarly, think of the suggestion in the first iteration of the EU *Strategy for Combating Radicalisation and Recruitment to Terrorism*, where the document spoke of 'areas of Europe where radicalisation is not a major issue at present' as areas that may eventually 'become targets for extremists'.[33] These are all risks that are extremely hard to verify, yet in their articulation necessitate some type of response on the part of the EU lest they were to actually occur.

This analysis of the language of EU counter-terrorism helps to support Claudia Aradau and Rens van Munster's assertion that in the contemporary security environment international actors view terrorism 'to some extent [as] a "risk beyond risk", of which [they] do not have, nor cannot have, the knowledge or the measure'.[34] As they explain, a precautionary logic towards governing terrorism has arisen out of the uncertainty and lack of clear and verifiable knowledge surrounding the extent of the contemporary terrorist threat. Remember, as Javier Solana suggested, the greatest worry for the EU and its member states is that 'terrorism can strike anywhere, anytime, anyone'.[35] As such, it is the imagination of the 'worst case scenario', based upon the already 'accepted knowledge' of the radically threatening figure of the 'terrorist' other, that is invoked in order to make the ungovernable threat of terrorism governable. In this environment, the EU has sought to develop a system of pre-emptive security governance that can help member states to predict and try to prevent the potential terrorist threats of the future.

This type of logic is reflected in the EU's counter-radicalisation strategies and in the technologies of border control, such as the various databases and PNR initiatives, which I have discussed above. These types of initiatives are presented not only as necessities if the security of EU citizens is to be ensured but also as policies that do not contradict the EU's stated goal of promoting a counter-terrorism policy that ensures the 'protection of human rights' and an effective 'criminal justice response to terrorism'.[36] In this way, as de Goede suggests, 'pre-crime and pre-conflict security practice has become the face of normative power Europe, offering an appealing security identity to the Union'.[37] However, as de Goede goes on to explain, whilst on the surface this type of security governance may appear banal, it still raises significant questions regarding 'human rights, civil liberties and democratic accountability'.[38] Moreover, it demands discussion of the place of the aforementioned implicit targets of these policies, the 'migrant' or 'Muslim' other, who are put under surveillance for corresponding to an identity or behaviour that is imagined to represent a potential source of terrorist threat.[39]

Civil liberties, human rights and the effectiveness of EU counter-terrorism policy

In drawing attention to this emerging system of security governance at the EU level, I have suggested that certain issues concerning civil liberties and human rights have adopted a new significance. In order to explore the issue of human rights further, I want to return to an argument I made in Chapter 3 about the way in which the identity of the EU has been constituted through references to these values. In particular, I suggested that although the EU had made reference to developing counter-terrorism policies in accordance with human rights, there had been little elaboration on how this would be achieved in practice. It is important to remember that, historically, this has been a theme throughout the formulation of EU counter-terrorism policy.

In the post-September 11 period, the strand of the discourse that constructed counter-terrorism as requiring measures that respect human rights was most notable by its absence from the 'fight against terrorism' discourse. Many of the key policy documents released during this period, such as the *Conclusions Adopted by the Council* for Justice and Home Affairs and the *European Security Strategy*, contained no references to developing policies in accordance with human rights. When human rights was discussed it was either to highlight the threat that terrorism posed to the identity of the EU or as a set of values that the EU sought to promote in all of its policy areas.[40] Similarly, the *Declaration on Combating Terrorism*, from December 2004, made no reference to 'human rights' as an intrinsic aspect of EU counter-terrorism policy. In the post-Madrid period, the first document that placed some emphasis on formulating security policies that would be developed with 'respect for the basic values of the European Union and fundamental human rights' was the *Hague Programme*.[41] The document spoke of incorporating the Charter of Fundamental Rights into the EU treaty base, as well as extending the mandate of the European Monitoring Centre on Racism and Xenophobia (EMCU) 'towards a Human Rights Agency'.[42] However, beyond these basic proposals, and the assertion that human rights must be incorporated into the security policies of the EU, there was little explanation of how this would be achieved.

It was not until the release of the European Commission's *Communication Concerning Terrorist Recruitment* and the EU *Counter-Terrorism Strategy* in late 2005 that the EU begun to speak of respect for human rights as a strategic commitment of, specifically, the EU counter-terrorism response.[43] However, beyond a call for counter-terrorism policies to continue 'to respect human rights and international law', there was once again no discussion of how this aspiration would be achieved through specific measures or policies.[44] This pattern has remained consistent in the time period since, from the post-Madrid period through to the post-Breivik period. For example, the EU *Internal Security Strategy*, from March 2010, or the third iteration of the EU *Strategy for Combating Radicalisation and Recruitment to Terrorism*, from May 2014, are representative of this trend, with both documents articulating a need to develop policies with 'respect for human rights' without actually explaining how this would be accomplished.[45]

The EU's third multi-annual internal security programme, the *Stockholm Programme*, from December 2009, remains the only document to explain how the discursive commitment to the protection of, or respect for, human

rights in the 'fight against terrorism', but also in security policy more generally, might be achieved in practice.[46] The document listed five key political
priorities, the first of which was 'promoting citizenship and fundamental
rights'. The second section on 'Promoting citizens' rights: a Europe of rights'
outlined in great detail an EU commitment to ensuring respect for human
rights in all 'legal initiatives', 'legislative processes' and the development of
all 'policies and legislation'.[47] Significantly, the European Council 'invited' the
European Commission to 'submit a proposal on the accession of the EU to
the European Convention on Human Rights as a matter of urgency' (ECHR),
as well as inviting all EU institutions 'to ensure that legal initiatives are and
remain consistent with fundamental rights throughout the legislative process
[through the] rigorous monitoring of compliance with the Convention and
the rights set out in the Charter of Fundamental Rights' and to make 'full use
of the expertise of the European Union Agency for Fundamental Rights'.[48]

However, even these concrete policy proposals for the amalgamation of
human rights concerns into the formulation of counter-terrorism and security policies are incredibly weak. The suggestion that the EU join the ECHR
has been in the pipeline since 1979. The proposal that the EU Agency for
Fundamental Rights be consulted on security matters appears promising until
we look below the surface. Like the EMCU and the European Network of
Independent Experts on Fundamental Rights that preceded it, the EU Agency
for Fundamental Rights is purely an advisory body that has no binding power
to ensure that the EU adopts its opinions or recommendations.[49] The agency
spreads its work across ten thematic areas, all of which are related to fundamental rights, but has no competence in relation to the evaluation of internal or
external security policy more generally, or counter-terrorism policy specifically.

Historically, the actions of the EU would suggest that the integration of
human rights into EU counter-terrorism policy is little more than an aspiration; a reflection of the EU's own identity and sense of self. This assertion is supported by the fact that human rights was not mentioned in the
initial phase of EU counter-terrorism policy. It appears that human rights
were merely tacked on in the post-Madrid period as an afterthought, with
responding to security concerns viewed by the EU as more important than
ensuring the principle of liberty. A cursory analysis of the 2010 review of
EU counter-terrorism policy by the European Commission supports this
line of argument.[50] Again, the document was quick to rearticulate that 'fundamental rights and the rule of law is at the heart of the EU's approach
to countering terrorism', yet the document contained no analysis of how
the policies created by the EU since 11 September 2001 met the stated goal
of developing policies in accordance with those rights.[51] Indeed, across the
entire period analysed, the 'fight against terrorism' always offered tangible
counter-measures in response to the threat of terrorism, yet offered nothing

more than a vague commitment to the idea that counter-terrorism measures should be developed with respect for 'fundamental/human rights'.

In addition to its failure to substantiate how commitments to human rights would be kept in practice, there has also been little reflection by the EU on the implications of adopting a precautionary approach to security. As de Goede explains, the measures enacted by this system of governance 'Entail a broad securitisation of societal spaces and mundane transactions. They target people who have not yet engaged in violence, and indeed may never do so. The precautionary logic prioritises disruption over prosecution, but often lacks accountability.'[52] If we take, for example, any of the three EU counter-radicalisation strategies as a specific representation of this broader trend towards precautionary security governance. It can be argued that the logic of precautionary security may eventually empower those agencies of the EU tasked with responding to the threat of 'radicalisation' with the right to decide on what constitutes an acceptable travel pattern or acceptable use of the Internet, the right to decide on what is an acceptable political view, even to go as far as deciding what constitutes the right type of behaviour in a particular setting, all in the name of the 'fight against terrorism'.[53]

As Anastassia Tsoukala points out, this type of logic rests upon an acceptance that security comes before liberty.[54] It is the obligation of the EU and its member states to protect the lives and properties of its citizens, which always comes before ensuring the protection of human rights. In adopting this type of approach to counter-terrorism the EU aspiration towards the development of counter-terrorism policy with respect for human rights is still possible, yet remains unfulfilled. Indeed, if the EU were genuinely serious about integrating 'human rights' and 'civil liberties' into its counter-terrorism policy, then it would offer concrete proposals that would ensure all future initiatives in the 'fight against terrorism' are developed in accordance with these values. Moving forward, there is little to suggest that the EU's prioritisation of security over liberty, in the 'fight against terrorism', will alter in the immediate future.

Alongside the issue of human rights and counter-terrorism rests the question of effectiveness. As Raphael Bossong has argued, it is important to acknowledge that evaluating or measuring the long-term effectiveness of any counter-terrorism strategy is extremely difficult.[55] In the academic literature there have been very few studies that try to assess the effectiveness of counter-terrorism.[56] This can in part be explained by the difficulty that exists in proving what would have happened in the event that a particular counter-terrorism policy had not been in place. Sarah Leonard's observation about the effectiveness of EU border control policies in preventing terrorism is particularly pertinent here and can be applied across the entire spectrum of the EU's counter-terrorism response.[57] Trying to gauge the effectiveness of counter-terrorism lies in the *absence* of an attack, with information on this either rare or non-existent. These types of issue with measuring effectiveness are even more pronounced with counter-radicalisation strategy, which aims to intervene *before* an individual has even thought of committing a crime. As such, there is little evidence to suggest that any of the counter-terrorism policies put forward by the EU actually do anything to help prevent terrorism.

The EU has at no point attempted to genuinely evaluate the effectiveness of the measures that it has put forward or prove that the policies are in any way useful. Indeed, a resolution by the European Parliament, in 2011, calling for the main policy-making institutions to conduct a review into the effectiveness of the entire 'framework of counter-terrorism measures', including the role of the various EU agencies and 'a full overview of the accumulated impact of counter-terrorism measures on civil liberties and fundamental rights', has yet to be addressed.[58] As Hayes and Jones argue, the EU is not without the capacity to 'provide for a competent if not comprehensive evaluation of the impact, legitimacy and effectiveness of all EU legislation' on counter-terrorism.[59] However, they contend that not only have those resources been underutilised but that the EU appears more concerned with exercising its authority than evaluating the effectiveness of its counter-terrorism policy. Indeed, this analysis of the 'fight against terrorism' discourse helps to support their argument that EU counter-terrorism policy has been driven by the European Council and the European Commission, with both institutions playing the key role in deciding and evaluating that policy.

Avenues for future research

Before offering some final concluding remarks I want to reflect briefly on the limitations of the research that I have conducted, as well as to suggest a number of avenues for future research in this area. I am aware that the discourse approach that I have adopted is based upon an intellectual tradition that attempts to destabilise 'truth' claims rather than to establish them.[60] I am also aware, therefore, that the interpretations of EU counter-terrorism that I have offered are wholly contingent on what I view as important and are therefore open to contestation. However, by offering a clear methodological framework explaining how I conducted this analysis, I hope that I have at least provided an opportunity for others to follow my process so that they can offer their own interpretations of the EU's 'fight against terrorism' discourse. In addition, I chose to focus on a specific set of discourse strands and a specific set of 'others' that I interpreted as significant. I also limited the analysis of the 'fight against terrorism' discourse to the policy documents produced by the main policy-making institutions of the EU, the European Council and the European Commission, since I argued that they represent the primary source of the 'fight against terrorism' discourse. As I elaborate below, these are all areas that could be further developed to offer an extended and even more comprehensive analysis of the discourse.

Within the 'fight against terrorism' discourse I limited the analysis to the various ways in which the identity of the EU was constituted, differentiated and (re)produced through articulations of the 'terrorist', the 'migrant' and the 'Muslim' other. Alongside these 'others' there are additional strands of the 'fight against terrorism' discourse that could provide the focus of future analysis. For example, as early as 2001, the European Commission was speaking of the need to combat 'cyber-terrorism', which has remained a theme throughout the period analysed.[61] Similarly, the EU *Counter-Terrorism Strategy* articulated a variety of issues linked to the 'fight against terrorism', which include the 'retention of telecommunication data', 'combating terrorist financing', 'research and development policy', 'critical infrastructure protection' and 'disaster response' management.[62] Each of these areas represents further strands of the 'fight against terrorism' that are constituted through reference to identity, including EU threat perception and the way in which the EU views itself as a particular type of security actor.

As well as this, it is also important to recognise that the EU counter-terrorism discourse is constituted at sites other than the European Council and the European Commission. This includes other institutions within the EU such as the European Parliament or the European Court of Justice, the speeches of European policy-makers and politicians and in the articulations of the myriad EU agencies, such as Europol or Frontex, tasked with responding to the threat of terrorism. Whilst I used these other sites at which the discourse is produced, where appropriate, to critically analyse the 'fight against terrorism' discourse, there is scope to take this analysis forward and develop a more complete understanding of EU counter-terrorism discourse with a further avenue of research to expand the analysis to include a focus on these other sites. This is especially the case with the European Parliament, which has acted as a site of resistance to the dominant discourse on terrorism as articulated by the European Council and European Commission.

Finally, there is scope to further explore the relationship between the US counter-terrorism discourse, the 'war on terror', and EU counter-terrorism discourse, the 'fight against terrorism'. As I have argued throughout, it is clear that the US has focused primarily on the external dimension of the threat posed by terrorism, emphasising an approach based on a military response, whilst the EU has focused primarily on the internal response to the threat of terrorism, emphasising an approach based on police, judicial and intelligence cooperation. These differences provide yet another 'other', the American 'other', through which the identity of the EU can be explored. Yet, as I have noted, difference is not always constituted through radical difference. As Wyn Rees has explained, whilst transatlantic security cooperation on counter-terrorism has been undermined as a result of difference over the external dimension of the counter-terrorism response, this contrast in threat perception has not prevented the development of significant cooperation in internal security matters between the US and EU.[63] Indeed, there remain strong similarities between the EU and the US discourse on terrorism, with both the EU and the US releasing a number of 'joint declarations' on terrorism across the period analysed.[64] As Richard Jackson points out, the core elements of the 'common language' of the present counter-terrorism discourse are not unique to the EU and the US. He argues that they also form the basis of counter-terrorism discourse in most states, especially those allied to the 'war on terrorism', and 'in all major international organizations such as the United Nations (UN), North Atlantic Treaty Organisation (NATO), Organization for Security and Co-operation in Europe (OSCE) and the like'.[65] Therefore, the relationship between the EU discourse on terrorism and that of the US, or other international organisations such as the UN, NATO and the OSCE, may all provide avenues for future research in this area.

Concluding remarks

The purpose of the analysis conducted in this book was to explore the discursive construction of the EU's 'fight against terrorism'. In doing so I sought to differentiate my approach to the study of this topic from traditional approaches to EU counter-terrorism policy, which have primarily focused on its historical and legal evolution or issues related to its implementation, legitimacy and the effectiveness of the EU as a counter-terrorism actor. I argued that these approaches are characterised by an inattentiveness to discourse and language that this book aimed to address. By adopting a discourse approach I was able to make the novel argument that the counter-terrorism policies of the EU are constituted through representations of identity, whilst it is also through the formulation of counter-terrorism policies that the identity of the EU is created and recreated. In this way, I was able to show how the practice of identity is central to the practice of counter-terrorism and vice versa. I have argued that in order to explore the role of EU identity in the formulation of EU counter-terrorism policy it is necessary to broaden our understanding of how EU identity is projected and to consider not just the external projection of EU identity but also its internal projection as well, so that we can understand how the EU constructs itself as a 'holistic' security actor. By analysing EU counter-terrorism in this way I was able to reveal a set of 'others' through which the identity of the EU has been constituted, differentiated and (re)produced: the 'terrorist' other, the 'migrant' other and the 'Muslim' other. I have shown throughout how these 'others' represent either the explicit or implicit target of the various counter-terrorism initiatives developed by the EU since the events of 11 September 2001.

In terms of the discourse itself, I have argued that the 'fight against terrorism' provides a language for talking about terrorism that helps to reinforce an 'accepted knowledge' or 'conventional wisdom' about *what terrorism is* and *who the terrorists are*. I have sought to show how this knowledge about terrorism conditions the type of policy responses that have been developed, making certain counter-terrorism practices possible whilst precluding others. Significantly, I contend that whilst terrorism does indeed represent a threat to the EU and its member states, the idea that it is an extreme or existential threat has been largely exaggerated. Indeed, the claims that terrorism somehow threatens the values upon which the EU itself is founded lend support to this argument. Terrorism is certainly a significant challenge for the EU and its member states, but the extent to which the EU can add value to the member states' own counter-terrorism responses remains open to question, especially given the sensitivity of counter-terrorism issues and its centrality to the sovereignty of the state.

Yet, I think that to concentrate on the extent to which the EU can be considered an effective counter-terrorism actor somewhat misses the point when it comes to the 'fight against terrorism'. Whilst I agree with the likes of Oldrich Bures that it is important to consider how problems over implementation of certain EU counter-terrorism measures have meant that the effectiveness of EU counter-terrorism policy can be called into question, I think it does not provide the full picture in relation to how the 'fight against terrorism' functions on a discursive level or in practice. Indeed, I claim that what is unique about the 'fight against terrorism', what is most effective about it, is the way in which the discourse has been invoked by EU institutions, politicians and policy-makers, on a consistent basis, in order to legitimise and to justify the development of a variety of EU internal and external security policies and furthermore to support the creation of a transnational and holistic system of EU security governance.

I have argued that whilst the EU's 'criminal justice-based approach' to counter-terrorism has meant that the EU has avoided some of the worst excesses that characterised the US war-based response to the threat of terrorism, the 'war on terror', it is not without consequence. The 'fight against terrorism' has played a key role in the creation of a new system of security governance that is blurring the once-clear distinction between internal and external security, with the discourse acting as a site where the necessity of a holistic EU approach to security is reinforced. Indeed, I have shown how this emerging system of security governance is providing the EU with a particular security identity, one that is based upon anticipatory, pre-emptive and precautionary responses to security threats such as terrorism, which raise significant concerns for human rights and civil liberties within Europe.

Within this emerging security framework, the 'fight against terrorism' discursively securitises a wide range of issues, from migration, travel and border control through to social policy, community cohesion and the role of public sector professionals. In the process of developing this system of security governance the EU has sought to empower a wide range of public and private actors to help to respond to the threat of terrorism. From this perspective success is measured not by how 'effective' the EU is in preventing actual instances of terrorism but by the success that it has in creating new policies and practices that limit the risk of, or potential for, terrorism to occur, without giving due consideration to what these types of practices might mean for human rights and civil liberties within Europe. The EU's 'fight against terrorism' discourse helps to *make possible* this new and emerging system of security governance, which is reflective of a turn towards an approach that prioritises security over liberty. With the EU actively seeking to develop and promote forms of counter-terrorism governance that allow for interventions before an individual has committed a crime, the 'fight against terrorism' will continue to provide a fruitful area for critically minded research in the coming years.

Notes

1 Ian J. Manners and Richard G. Whitman, 'The "difference engine": constructing and representing the international identity of the European Union', *Journal of European Public Policy*, 10:3 (2003), 380–404.
2 Ibid., 400.
3 See Lene Hansen, *Security as Practice: Discourse Analysis and the Bosnian War* (London and New York: Routledge, 2006), p. 6.
4 For an in-depth discussion of identity and difference, see ibid., pp. 33–49.
5 Roxanne Doty, 'Foreign policy as social construction: a post-positivist analysis of US counterinsurgency policy in the Philippines', *International Studies Quarterly*, 37:3 (1993), 297–320.
6 By holistic security actor I mean an actor that has competence in internal and external security, including areas that bridge and blur the gap between internal and external security. For an excellent analysis of the EU as a holistic security actor in the foreign policy arena, see Kamil Zwolski, 'The EU as an international security

actor after Lisbon: finally a green light for a holistic approach?', *Cooperation and Conflict*, 47:1 (2012), 68–87.

7 Council of the European Union, *The European Union Counter-Terrorism Strategy*, Brussels, 30 November 2005, 14469/4/05, see pp. 3, 14.

8 Council of the European Union, *Revised EU Strategy for Combating Radicalisation and Recruitment to Terrorism*, Brussels, 19 May 2014, 9956/14, p. 13.

9 Council of the European Union, *A Secure Europe in a Better World: European Security Strategy*, Brussels, 12 December 2003, p. 3.

10 Council of the European Union, *The Hague Programme: Strengthening Freedom, Security and Justice in the European Union*, Brussels, 13 December 2004, 16054/04, p. 3.

11 Council, *The European Union Counter-Terrorism Strategy*, p. 6.

12 Council of the European Union, *The Stockholm Programme: An Open and Secure Europe Serving and Protecting Citizens*, Brussels, 2 December 2009, 17024/09, p. 52.

13 Ibid., p. 73.

14 Ibid.

15 Ibid.

16 Council of the European Union, *European Council Conclusions 26/27 June 2014*, EUCO 79/14, Brussels, 27 June 2014.

17 Ibid., p. 2.

18 Didier Bigo, 'Globalized (In)Security: The Field and the Ban-Opticon', in Didier Bigo and Anastassia Tsoukala (eds), *Terror, Insecurity and Liberty: Illiberal Practices of Liberal Regimes after 9/11* (Abingdon: Routledge, 2008), p. 23.

19 Ibid., p. 18.

20 Derek Lutterbeck, 'Blurring the dividing line: the convergence of internal and external security in Western Europe', *European Security*, 14:2 (2005), 231–253.

21 Ibid., 231, 248.

22 Bigo, 'Globalized (In)Security', p. 19.

23 Didier Bigo, 'When Two Become One: Internal and External Securitisations in Europe', in Morten Kelstrup and Michael C. Williams (eds), *International Relations Theory and the Politics of European Integration, Power, Security and Community* (London: Routledge, 2000), pp. 171–205.

24 Marieke de Goede, 'European Security Culture: Preemption and Precaution in European Security', University of Amsterdam Inaugural Lecture (Vossiuspers UvA: Amsterdam University Press, 2011).

25 Claudia Aradau and Rens van Munster, 'Taming the Future: The Dispositif of Risk in the War on Terror', in Louise Amoore and Marieke de Goede (eds), *Risk and the War on Terror* (Abingdon: Routledge, 2008), p. 32.

26 Council, *European Security Strategy*, p. 6.

27 European Commission, 'Securing Dangerous Material', DG Migration and Home Affairs, available online at: http://ec.europa.eu/dgs/home-affairs/what-we-do/policies/crisis-and-terrorism/securing-dangerous-material/index_en.htm (accessed May 2015).

28 De Goede, 'European Security Culture', p. 7.

29 Ibid., p. 12.

30 Louise Amoore and Marieke de Goede, 'Transactions after 9/11: the banal face of the preemptive strike', *Transactions of the Institute of British Geographers*, 33:2 (2008), 173–185.

31 Brian Massumi, 'The Future Birth of the Affective Fact: The Political Ontology of Threat', in Greg Seigworth and Melissa Greg (eds), *The Affect Reader* (Durham, NC: Duke University Press, 2010).

32 Council of the European Union, *Report on the Implementation of the European Security Strategy: Providing Security in a Changing World*, Brussels, 11 December 2008, S407/08, p. 1.

33 Council of the European Union, *The Strategy for Combating Radicalisation and Recruitment to Terrorism*, 24 November 2005, 12781/1/05, p. 5.

34 Claudia Aradau and Rens van Munster, 'Governing terrorism through risk: taking precautions, (un)knowing the future', *European Journal of International Relations*, 13:1 (2007), 102.

35 Javier Solana, 'Protecting People and Infrastructure: Achievements, Failures and Future Tasks', The EastWest Institute, Second Annual Worldwide Security Conference (Brussels), 7 February 2005, available online at: www.eu-un.europa.eu/articles/fr/article_4320_fr.htm (accessed January 2015).

36 Council of the European Union, *EU Counter-Terrorism Strategy: Discussion Paper*, Brussels, 23 May 2012 9990/12, p. 11.

37 De Goede, 'European Security Culture', p. 16.

38 Ibid.

39 Bigo, 'Globalized (In)Security', p. 19.

40 For example, the 'Framework Decision on Combating Terrorism', from 2002, was clear in stating both that terrorism was a threat to the values of human rights upon which the EU was founded and that the definition of terrorism contained within the decision should not lead EU member states to compromise fundamental rights that were already contained within the treaty.

41 Council, *The Hague Programme*, p. 21.

42 Ibid., p. 5.

43 European Commission, *Communication Concerning Terrorist Recruitment: Addressing the Factors Contributing to Violent Radicalisation*, Brussels, 21 September 2005, COM (2005) 313 final; Council, *The European Union Counter-Terrorism Strategy*.

44 Council, *The European Union Counter-Terrorism Strategy*, p. 12.

45 Council of the European Union, *Draft Internal Security Strategy for the European Union: Towards a European Security Model*, Brussels, 8 March 2010, 7120/10; Council, *Revised EU Strategy for Combating Radicalisation and Recruitment to Terrorism* (2014).

46 Council, *The Stockholm Programme*.

47 Ibid., pp. 11–12.

48 Ibid., p. 12.

49 Ben Hayes and Chris Jones, 'Report on How the EU Assesses the Impact, Legitimacy and Effectiveness of Its Counterterrorism Laws', *SECILE – Securing Europe through Counter-Terrorism: Impact Legitimacy and Effectiveness* (SECILE Consortium, 2013), p. 24.

50 European Commission, *The EU Counter-Terrorism Policy: Main Achievements and Future Challenges*, Brussels, 20 July 2010, COM (2010) 386 final.

51 Ibid., p. 11.

52 De Goede, 'European Security Culture', p. 17.

53 See Marieke de Goede, 'The politics of preemption and the war on terror in Europe', *European Journal of International Relations*, 14:1 (2008), 161–185.

54 Anastassia Tsoukala, 'Defining the Terrorist Threat in the Post-September 11 Era', in Didier Bigo and Anastassia Tsoukala (eds), *Terror, Insecurity and Liberty: Illiberal Practices of Liberal Regimes after 9/11* (Abingdon: Routledge, 2008), pp. 49–99.

55 Raphael Bossong, *The Evolution of EU Counter-Terrorism: European Security Policy after 9/11* (Abingdon: Routledge, 2012).

56 There has been only a small number of studies in this area, although there is a growing literature on the effectiveness of EU counter-terrorism policy in particular. See, for example, Oldrich Bures, *EU Counterterrorism Policy: A Paper Tiger?* (Farnham: Ashgate, 2011); Sarah Leonard, 'Border controls as a dimension of the European Union's counter-terrorism policy: a critical assessment', *Intelligence and National Security*, 30:2–3 (2015), 306–332; Fiona de Londras and Josephine Doody, *The Impact, Legitimacy and Effectiveness of EU Counter-Terrorism* (Abingdon: Routledge, 2015); Cynthia Lum, Leslie W. Kennedy and Alison Sherley, 'Are counter-terrorism strategies effective? The results of the Campbell systematic review on counter-terrorism evaluation research', *Journal of Experimental Criminology*, 2:4 (2006), 489–516.

57 Leonard, 'Border controls'.

58 European Parliament, *EU Counter-Terrorism Policy: Main Achievements and Future Challenges*, 2010/2311(INI), Brussels, 14 December 2011.

59 Hayes and Jones, 'Report on How the EU Assesses the Impact', p. 4.

60 Laura J. Shepherd, *Gender, Violence and Security: Discourse as Practice* (London: Zed Books, 2008), p. 33.

61 European Commission, *Increasing the Capacity of the EU to Fight International Terrorism*, 18 September 2001, SEC (2001) 1429/3.

62 Council, *The European Union Counter-Terrorism Strategy*, pp. 6–16.

63 Wyn Rees, *Transatlantic Counter-Terrorism Cooperation: The New Imperative* (London and New York: Routledge, 2006).

64 Council of the European Union, 'EU–US Declaration on Combating Terrorism', press release, Dromoland Castle, 26 June 2004, 10760/04; Council of the European Union, *Toledo Joint Statement, as Adopted on 21 January 2010*, Brussels, 10 February 2010, 6261/10.

65 Richard Jackson, *Writing the War on Terrorism: Language, Politics and Counter-Terrorism* (Manchester: Manchester University Press, 2005).

Select bibliography

Key policy documents

Post-September 11 period

Council of the European Union, *Declaration by the European Union*, CL01-053EN, 12 September 2001.

Council of the European Union, *Joint Declaration by Heads of State and Government of the European Union, President of the European Parliament, President of the European Commission, High Representative for the Common Foreign and Security Policy*, CL01-054EN, 14 September 2001.

Council of the European Union, *Conclusions Adopted by the Council (Justice and Home Affairs)*, Brussels, 20 September 2001, SN3926/6/01 Rev 6.

Council of the European Union, *Conclusions and Plan of Action of the Extraordinary European Council Meeting on 21 September*, 2001, SN 140/01.

Council of the European Union, *EU Strategy against Proliferation of Weapons of Mass Destruction*, Brussels, 10 December 2003, 15708/03.

Council of the European Union, *A Secure Europe in a Better World: European Security Strategy*, Brussels, 12 December 2003.

'Council Framework Decision of 13 June 2002 on Combating Terrorism' (2002/475/JHA), *Official Journal*, L164, 22/06/2002.

'Council Framework Decision of 28 November 2008 Amending Framework Decision 2002/475/JHA on Combating Terrorism' (2008/919/JHA), *Official Journal*, L330/21, 09/12/2008.

European Commission, *Increasing the Capacity of the EU to Fight International Terrorism*, 18 September 2001, SEC (2001) 1429/3.

Post-Madrid period

Council of the European Union, *Declaration on Combating Terrorism*, Brussels, 25 March 2004, 7906/04.

Council of the European Union, *EU Action Plan on Combating Terrorism*, Brussels, June 2004, 10010/04.

Council of the European Union, *The Hague Programme: Strengthening Freedom, Security and Justice in the European Union*, Brussels, 13 December 2004, 16054/04.

Council of the European Union, *The Strategy for Combating Radicalisation and Recruitment to Terrorism*, 24 November 2005, 12781/1/05

Council of the European Union, *The European Union Counter-Terrorism Strategy*, Brussels, 30 November 2005, 14469/4/05.

Council of the European Union, *A Strategy for the External Dimension of JHA: Global Freedom, Security and Justice*, Brussels, 30 November 2005, 14366/3/05

Council of the European Union, *Revised EU Strategy for Combating Radicalisation and Recruitment to Terrorism*, Brussels, 14 November 2008, 15175/08.

Council of the European Union, *Report on the Implementation of the European Security Strategy: Providing Security in a Changing World*, Brussels, 11 December 2008, S407/08.

Council of the European Union, *The Stockholm Programme: An Open and Secure Europe Serving and Protecting Citizens*, Brussels, 2 December 2009, 17024/09.

Council of the European Union, *Draft Internal Security Strategy for the European Union: Towards a European Security Model*, Brussels, 8 March 2010, 7120/10.

European Commission, *Communication Concerning Terrorist Recruitment: Addressing the Factors Contributing to Violent Radicalisation*, Brussels, 21 September 2005, COM (2005) 313 final.

European Commission, *The EU Counter-Terrorism Policy: Main Achievements and Future Challenges*, Brussels, 20 July 2010, COM (2010) 386 final.

European Commission, *The EU Internal Security Strategy in Action: Five Steps towards a More Secure Europe*, Brussels, 22 November 2010, COM (2010) 673 final.

Post-Breivik period

Council of the European Union, *Preventing Lone Actor Terrorism: Food for Thought*, Brussels, 23 April 2012, 9090/12.

Council of the European Union, *Draft Council Conclusions Calling for an Update of the EU Strategy for Combating Radicalisation and Recruitment to Terrorism*, Brussels, 15 May 2013, 9447/13.

Council of the European Union, *Revised EU Strategy for Combating Radicalisation and Recruitment to Terrorism*, Brussels, 19 May 2014, 9956/14.

Council of the European Union, *Outline of the Counter-Terrorism Strategy for Syria and Iraq, with Particular Focus on Foreign Fighters*, Brussels, 16 January 2015, 5369/15.

Council of the European Union, *Council Conclusions on the EU Regional Strategy for Syria and Iraq as well as the ISIL/Da'esh Threat*, Brussels, 16 March 2015, 7267/15.

Books and articles

Amoore, Louise and de Goede, Marieke (eds), *Risk and the War on Terror* (Abingdon: Routledge, 2008).

Aradau, Claudia and van Munster, Rens, 'Governing terrorism through risk: taking precautions, (un)knowing the future', *European Journal of International Relations*, 13:1 (2007), 89–115.

Argomaniz, Javier, *The EU and Counter-Terrorism: Politics, Polity and Policies after 9/11* (Abingdon: Routledge, 2011).

Baker-Beall, Christopher, 'The discursive construction of EU counter-terrorism policy: writing the "migrant other", securitisation and control', *Journal of Contemporary European Research*, 'Special Issue: Security and Liberty in the European Union', 5:2 (2009), 188–206.

Baker-Beall, Christopher, 'Writing the Threat of Terrorism in Western Europe and the European Union: An Interpretive Analysis', in Mark Bevir, Ian Hall and Oliver Daddow (eds), *Interpreting Global Security* (Abingdon: Routledge, 2013).

Baker-Beall, Christopher, 'The evolution of the European Union's "fight against terrorism" discourse: constructing the terrorist "other"', *Cooperation and Conflict*, 49:2 (2014), 212–238.

Baker-Beall, Christopher, Heath-Kelly, Charlotte and Jarvis, Lee (eds), *Counter-Radicalisation: Critical Perspectives* (Abingdon: Routledge, 2015).

Bevir, Mark, Hall, Ian and Daddow, Oliver (eds), *Interpreting Global Security* (Abingdon: Routledge, 2013).

Bigo, Didier, 'Globalized (In)Security: The Field and the Ban-Opticon', in Didier Bigo and Anastassia Tsoukala (eds), *Terror, Insecurity and Liberty: Illiberal Practices of Liberal Regimes after 9/11* (Abingdon: Routledge, 2008).

Bigo, Didier and Tsoukala, Anastassia (eds), *Terror, Insecurity and Liberty: Illiberal Practices of Liberal Regimes after 9/11* (Abingdon: Routledge, 2008).

Bossong, Raphael, 'The Action Plan on Combating Terrorism', *Journal of Common Market Studies*, 46:1 (2008), 27–48.

Bossong, Raphael, *The Evolution of EU Counter-Terrorism: European Security Policy after 9/11* (Abingdon: Routledge, 2012).

Bretherton, Charlotte and Vogler, John, *The European Union as a Global Actor*, 2nd edn (London: Routledge, 2006).

Bures, Oldrich, 'EU counterterrorism policy: a paper tiger?', *Terrorism and Political Violence*, 18:1 (March 2006), 57–78.

Bures, Oldrich, *EU Counterterrorism Policy: A Paper Tiger?* (Farnham: Ashgate, 2011).

Campbell, David, *Writing Security: United States Foreign Policy and the Politics of Identity* (Manchester: Manchester University Press, 1992).

Coolsaet, Rik (ed.), *Jihadi Terrorism and the Radicalisation Challenge in Europe* (Aldershot: Ashgate, 2008).

Croft, Stuart, *Culture, Crisis and America's War on Terror* (New York: Cambridge University Press, 2006).

Croft, Stuart, *Securitizing Islam: Identity and the Search for Security* (Cambridge: Cambridge University Press, 2012).

Croft, Stuart and Moore, Cerwyn, 'The evolution of threat narratives in the age of terror: understanding terrorist threats in Britain', *International Affairs*, 8:4 (2010), 821–835.

de Goede, Marieke, 'European Security Culture: Preemption and Precaution in European Security', University of Amsterdam Inaugural Lecture (Vossiuspers UvA: Amsterdam University Press, 2011).

de Londras, Fiona and Doody, Josephine, *The Impact, Legitimacy and Effectiveness of EU Counter-Terrorism* (Abingdon: Routledge, 2015).

den Boer, Monica and Monar, Jörg, 'Keynote article: 11 September and the challenge of global terrorism to the EU as a security actor', *Journal of Common Market Studies*, 40:1 (2002), 11–28.

Doty, Roxanne Lynn, 'Foreign policy as social construction: a post-positivist analysis of US counterinsurgency policy in the Philippines', *International Studies Quarterly*, 37:3 (1993), 297–320.

Doty, Roxanne Lynn, *Imperial Encounters: The Politics of Representation in North–South Relations* (Minneapolis: University of Minnesota Press, 1996).

Durodié, Bill, 'Fear and terror in a post-political age', *Government and Opposition*, 42:3 (2007), 427–450.

Edwards, Geoffrey and Meyer, Christoph O., 'Introduction: charting a contested transformation', *Journal of Common Market Studies*, 46:1 (2008), 1–25.

Githens-Mazer, Jonathan and Lambert, Robert, 'Why conventional wisdom on radicalization fails: the persistence of a failed discourse', *International Affairs*, 86:4 (2010), 889–901.

Hansen, Lene, *Security as Practice: Discourse Analysis and the Bosnian War* (London and New York: Routledge, 2006).

Hassan, Oz, 'Constructing crises, (in)securitising terror: the punctuated evolution of EU counter-terror strategy', *European Security*, 19:3 (2010), 445–466.

Heath-Kelly, Charlotte, 'Counter-terrorism and the counterfactual: producing the "radicalisation" discourse and the UK PREVENT strategy', *British Journal of Politics & International Relations*, 15:3 (2013), 394–415.

Heath-Kelly, Charlotte, Baker-Beall, Christopher and Jarvis, Lee, 'Introduction', in Christopher Baker-Beall, Charlotte Heath-Kelly and Lee Jarvis (eds), *Counter-Radicalisation: Critical Perspectives* (Abingdon: Routledge, 2015).

Huysmans, Jef, *The Politics of Insecurity: Fear, Migration and Asylum in the EU* (London: Routledge, 2006).

Jackson, Richard, *Writing the War on Terrorism: Language, Politics and Counter-Terrorism* (Manchester: Manchester University Press, 2005).

Jackson, Richard, 'An analysis of EU counterterrorism policy discourse', *Cambridge Review of International Affairs*, 20:2 (2007), 233–247.

Jackson, Richard, Breen Smyth, Marie and Gunning, Jeroen (eds), *Critical Terrorism Studies: A New Research Agenda* (Abingdon: Routledge, 2009).

Jackson, Richard, Jarvis, Lee, Breen Smyth, Marie and Gunning, Jeroen, *Terrorism: A Critical Introduction* (Basingstoke: Palgrave Macmillan, 2011).

Jarvis, Lee, *Times of Terror: Discourse, Temporality and the War on Terror* (Basingstoke: Palgrave Macmillan, 2009).

Larsen, Henrik, *Analysing the Foreign Policy of Small States in the EU: The Case of Denmark* (Basingstoke: Palgrave, 2005).

Leonard, Sarah, 'Border controls as a dimension of the European Union's counterterrorism policy: a critical assessment', *Intelligence and National Security*, 30:2–3 (2015), 306–332.

Manners, Ian, 'Normative power Europe: a contradiction in terms?', *Journal of Common Market Studies*, 40 (2002), 235–258.

Manners, Ian J. and Whitman, Richard G., 'Towards identifying the international identity of the European Union: a framework for analysis of the EU's network of relationships', *Journal of European Integration*, 21:3 (1998), 231–249.

Manners, Ian J. and Whitman, Richard G., 'The "difference engine": constructing and representing the international identity of the European Union', *Journal of European Public Policy*, 10:3 (2003), 380–404.

Milliken, Jennifer, 'The study of discourse in International Relations: a critique of research and methods', *European Journal of International Relations*, 5:2 (1999), 225–254.

Monar, Jörg, 'Common threat and common response? The European Union's counter-terrorism strategy and its problems', *Government and Opposition*, 42:3 (2007), 292–313.

Moore, Cerwyn, *Contemporary Violence: Postmodern War in Kosovo and Chechnya* (Manchester: Manchester University Press, 2010).

Moore, Cerwyn, 'Introductory comments to Foreign Fighters Research: special mini-series', *Terrorism and Political Violence*, 27:3 (2015), 393–394.

Moore, Cerwyn and Farrands, Chris (eds), *International Relations and Philosophy: Interpretive Dialogues* (Abingdon: Routledge, 2010).

Moore, Cerwyn, and Tumelty, Paul, 'Foreign fighters and the case of Chechnya: a critical assessment', *Studies in Conflict & Terrorism*, 31:5 (2008), 412–433.

Neal, Andrew, 'Securitization and risk at the EU border: the origins of Frontex', *Journal of Common Market Studies*, 47:2 (2009), 333–356.

Neumann, Peter, 'The trouble with radicalization', *International Affairs*, 89:4 (2013), 873–893.

Rees, Wyn, *Transatlantic Counter-Terrorism Cooperation: The New Imperative* (London and New York: Routledge, 2006).

Shepherd, Laura, J., *Gender, Violence and Security: Discourse as Practice* (London: Zed Books, 2008).

Smith, Steve, 'The Contested Concept of Security', in Ken Booth (ed.), *Critical Security Studies and World Politics* (London: Lynne Rienner Publishers, 2005).

Spence, David (ed.), *The European Union and Terrorism* (London: John Harper Publishing, 2007).

Tsoukala, Anastassia, 'Democracy against security: the debates about counter-terrorism in the European Parliament, September 2001–June 2003', *Alternatives: Global, Local, Political*, 29:4 (2004), 417–439.

Wæver, Ole, 'Securitization and Desecuritization', in Ronnie D. Lipschutz (ed.), *On Security* (New York: Columbia University Press, 1995), pp. 46–86.

Zulaika, Joseba and Douglass, William A., *Terror and Taboo: The Follies, Fables, and Faces of Terrorism* (Abingdon: Routledge, 1996).

Zwolski, Kamil, 'The EU as an international security actor after Lisbon: finally a green light for a holistic approach?', *Cooperation and Conflict*, 47:1 (2012), 68–87.

Index